I Suffer, Therefore I Am

Engaging with Empathy in
Contemporary French Women's Writing

LEGENDA

LEGENDA is the Modern Humanities Research Association's book imprint for new research in the Humanities. Founded in 1995 by Malcolm Bowie and others within the University of Oxford, Legenda has always been a collaborative publishing enterprise, directly governed by scholars. The Modern Humanities Research Association (MHRA) joined this collaboration in 1998, became half-owner in 2004, in partnership with Maney Publishing and then Routledge, and has since 2016 been sole owner. Titles range from medieval texts to contemporary cinema and form a widely comparative view of the modern humanities, including works on Arabic, Catalan, English, French, German, Greek, Italian, Portuguese, Russian, Spanish, and Yiddish literature. Editorial boards and committees of more than 60 leading academic specialists work in collaboration with bodies such as the Society for French Studies, the British Comparative Literature Association and the Association of Hispanists of Great Britain & Ireland.

The MHRA encourages and promotes advanced study and research in the field of the modern humanities, especially modern European languages and literature, including English, and also cinema. It aims to break down the barriers between scholars working in different disciplines and to maintain the unity of humanistic scholarship. The Association fulfils this purpose through the publication of journals, bibliographies, monographs, critical editions, and the MHRA Style Guide, and by making grants in support of research. Membership is open to all who work in the Humanities, whether independent or in a University post, and the participation of younger colleagues entering the field is especially welcomed.

ALSO PUBLISHED BY THE ASSOCIATION

Critical Texts
Tudor and Stuart Translations • *New Translations* • *European Translations*
MHRA Library of Medieval Welsh Literature

MHRA Bibliographies
Publications of the Modern Humanities Research Association

The Annual Bibliography of English Language & Literature
Austrian Studies
Modern Language Review
Portuguese Studies
The Slavonic and East European Review
Working Papers in the Humanities
The Yearbook of English Studies

www.mhra.org.uk
www.legendabooks.com

RESEARCH MONOGRAPHS IN FRENCH STUDIES

The *Research Monographs in French Studies* (RMFS) form a separate series within the Legenda programme and are published in association with the Society for French Studies. Individual members of the Society are entitled to purchase all RMFS titles at a discount.

The series seeks to publish the best new work in all areas of the literature, thought, theory, culture, film and language of the French-speaking world. Its distinctiveness lies in the relative brevity of its publications (50,000–60,000 words). As innovation is a priority of the series, volumes should predominantly consist of new material, although, subject to appropriate modification, previously published research may form up to one third of the whole. Proposals may include critical editions as well as critical studies. They should be sent with one or two sample chapters for consideration to Professor Diana Knight, Department of French and Francophone Studies, University of Nottingham, University Park, Nottingham NG7 2RD.

❖

PUBLISHED IN THIS SERIES

www.rmfs.mhra.org.uk

I Suffer, Therefore I Am

Engaging with Empathy in Contemporary French Women's Writing

❖

KATHRYN ROBSON

LEGENDA

Research Monographs in French Studies 56
Modern Humanities Research Association
2019

Published by Legenda
an imprint of the Modern Humanities Research Association
Salisbury House, Station Road, Cambridge CB1 2LA

ISBN 978-1-78188-675-5 (HB)
ISBN 978-1-78188-676-2 (PB)

First published 2019
Paperback edition 2021

Copy-Editor: Charlotte Brown

CONTENTS

❖

For Rebecca and Charlotte, with love

ACKNOWLEDGEMENTS

❖

This book found its origins (and its title) in an article I wrote for *French Studies*, published in 2015 on psychic plagiarism and child death in Camille Laurens's *Philippe* and Marie Darrieussecq's *Tom est mort*. I have presented early versions of parts of Chapter Three in London and at Queens University, Belfast, and the resulting discussions helped me to nuance my ideas. Chapter One on eating disorders found its inspiration in a paper given in London in 2014, followed by a book chapter and a journal article. I am grateful for all comments and suggestions given in response to all of these.

I would like to thank the colleagues in Newcastle who discussed my ideas with me and offered support, particularly Máire Cross, Shirley Jordan, Sarah Leahy, Teresa Ludden and Beate Muller. Shirley also kindly read and offered useful comments on Chapter Four. Teresa's reading group in 2016-17 offered a fantastic opportunity for really fruitful engagement with theory in general and specifically with Judith Butler's work on framing, which allowed me to think through some of the theoretical ideas articulated in this book. I am particularly indebted to Nigel Harkness, who more or less told me – nicely, over lunch! – to write this book and without whose encouragement I probably wouldn't have.

My parents-in law, Derek and Glenyce Meacher, have helped me immensely by lending me books and correcting the trickiest translations into English (Chloé Delaume!). They also put me in touch with Corinne Arman, to whom I am immensely grateful for the beautiful image on the cover of this book. Victoria Best has been a constant long-distance support and source of wisdom. My parents, Gordon and Anne Robson, have been a total inspiration to me in coping with illness and disability without self-pity, as well as offering unstinting practical support in looking after my children. I am, as always, extremely grateful to my husband, Simon Meacher, and my daughters, Rebecca and Charlotte Meacher, for their admirable tolerance of my laptop and my (many…) books. I have largely written this book on the sofa in my living room amidst the chaos and noise of family life and a constant parade of visiting children, through whom (as through my students) I have learnt much about approaching other people's suffering. This book is dedicated to my daughters, who have taught me to recognize the possibilities and the limits of my own empathy and who challenge and stimulate me every day.

K.R., Newcastle, April 2019

INTRODUCTION

❖

Engaging with Empathy in Contemporary French Women's Writing

'Est-il interdit d'écrire fictivement la souffrance à la première personne?'
[Is it forbidden to write fiction about suffering in the first person?][1]

This book finds its roots (and its title) in Marie Darrieussecq's parodic assertion in a study of allegations of literary plagiarism that 'je souffre donc je suis' [I suffer therefore I am], theorizing a persona whose identity is determined by the articulation of pain.[2] *Rapport de police: accusations de plagiat et autres modes de surveillance de la fiction* [Police Report: Accusations of Plagiarism and Other Forms of Surveillance of Fiction] was written following Darrieussecq's bitter public conflict with fellow writer Camille Laurens, which began in 2007 when Laurens accused Darrieussecq of plagiarizing her memoir, *Philippe*, in the novel *Tom est mort* [Tom is Dead]. The former text recounts the still-birth of Laurens's son, whilst *Tom est mort* is a fictional first-person narrative from the perspective of a bereaved mother. Whilst the debate between Laurens and Darrieussecq was ostensibly over the latter's alleged plagiarism, the subtext was somewhat different: the question of whether particular types of suffering can or should be fictionalized (and written in the first person) by writers who have not experienced them personally. Laurens's article 'Marie Darrieussecq ou le syndrome du coucou' [Marie Darrieussecq or the Cuckoo Syndrome] interrogates the possibility of writing fiction about the death of a child: 'oui, je suis indignée qu'on fabrique un suspense avec la mort d'un enfant, qu'on fasse de la souffrance un exercice de style, qu'on emprunte des phrases écrites dans la douleur pour nourrir et vendre une fiction' [yes, I am outraged that suspense is created out of a child's death, that suffering is turned into a stylistic exercise, that phrases written in pain are borrowed to feed and sell fiction].[3] This raises multiple questions about the limits of the imagination and of representation: Laurens is suggesting that Darrieussecq could never imagine losing a child and that she has no right to turn this 'expérience limite' [limit experience] into a profit-making stylistic experiment.[4] Her concerns over fiction also potentially apply to autobiographical writing, which could equally stylize and profit from suffering. The ethical dilemmas raised by Laurens frame the analyses in this book. The key question is this: what is at stake in reading narratives of other people's pain?

In *Rapport de police*, Darrieussecq's mocking contention that 'je souffre donc je suis' highlights that autobiographies of suffering are typically authenticated through their apparent representation of a (real-life) suffering subject whose experience anchors the text and whose identity is confirmed through the narrativization of this experience. If, as Leigh Gilmore wrote in 2001, 'memoir has become *the* genre in the skittish period around the turn of the millennium',[5] its most prominent manifestation is now in the form of the commonly-termed 'misery memoir',[6] a 'surefire bestseller' that has won its own section on bookshop shelves.[7] The selling point of best-selling misery memoirs both in the United Kingdom (with its subcategory of 'tragic life story') and in France (where there is no singular equivalent title: *confessions intimes* might come closest), is the claim that the almost implausibly horrific stories that they recount are rooted in lived experience. The 'pacte autobiographique' [autobiographical pact][8] as labelled by Philippe Lejeune is particularly crucial, and equally precarious, in representations of trauma, given that 'something of a consensus has already developed that takes trauma as the unrepresentable to assert that trauma is beyond language in some crucial way'.[9] Suffering also, however, seems to invite narrativization, if the volume of texts published in recent years recounting emotional and physical pain are to be taken into account. This may be attributable to a form of 'scriptotherapy', according to which writing offers a means of healing through putting difficult experiences into words,[10] or a means of identity construction (as suffering subject) through narrative as sketched by Darrieussecq above, or indeed a testimony to experiences hitherto socially ignored.[11] Narratives of suffering are not, however, confined to the singular genre of the misery memoir; recent French women's autobiographical, autofictional, and fictional writing more widely also represents suffering, often in challenging ways that can help us to rethink our approach to stories of suffering. The increase in the visibility and popularity of narratives of suffering and in the academic interest they generate ('Other people's pain has become one of the core interests of literary and cultural studies') has gone hand in hand with a notable emphasis on the limits and possibilities of compassion and even more strikingly of empathy.[12] This study aims to explore how different responses to the recent proliferation of representations of 'other people's pain' are shaped by constraints around the ways in which suffering can be articulated and framed.

Many of the texts explored in this book could loosely be described as what Serge Doubrovsky labelled 'autofiction', a term which has been extensively interrogated, meaning autobiographical fiction, fictional autobiography, or something in between.[13] Shirley Jordan noted in 2013 that 'a distinct phase in women's self-narrative in French is under way; one that is remarkable for the extraordinarily difficult material it explores, for the sophisticated channels of self-apprehension it furrows, and for its fertile repositionings of the "I"'.[14] The use of the first person in fictional or semi-fictional texts — because it mimics the autobiographical form but also because it appears to carry a certain power — seems particularly problematic for Laurens: 'le *Je* prend ici toute sa puissance hypnotique, imprime à l'histoire un réalisme atroce que le pronom de troisième personne n'aurait pas' [the *I* takes on here all its hypnotic power, imprints on the story an atrocious realism that the third person pronoun would not allow].[15] Laurens's assumption about the impact of the use of the first person is fraught: as Suzanne Keen observes in her exploration of empathy and narrative, 'Contrasting first person with third person puts the question too broadly, with too many other variables, to reach a valid conclusion'.[16] Part of the innovation in recent French women's writing is precisely the interrogation of the possibility of representing suffering — be it one's own experience or that of others — which in turn leads to a general privileging of autofiction over straightforward autobiography, unsettling the possibility of establishing identity as a suffering subject of narrative.

In *Rapport de police*, Darrieussecq describes a 'certificat doloriste' [certificate of pain] through which the narrative of suffering both creates and confirms a suffering subject legitimized through the acknowledgement of lived experience.[17] The reader, in this model, is constrained by the imperative not to undermine the subject of suffering. In the French texts explored in this book, however, the subject of suffering is undone rather than confirmed through narrative, disorientating the reader. This is partly due to the ways in which these texts interrogate the boundary between truth and fiction and partly due to stylistic choices: frequent use of shifting narrative subject positions, gaps, points of confusion, for example. Narrative experimentation is, of course, endemic in contemporary French writing, yet in the context of accounts of suffering, this can be acutely difficult to navigate for the reader. Contrary to Darrieussecq's mocking assertion, narrating oneself as a suffering subject does not necessarily confer or shore up identity; it can, as we shall see, instead undermine the notion of stable subject positions in a context of suffering (translating into 'I suffer therefore I am *not*'). More, Darrieussecq's 'je souffre donc je suis' is not a statement to be taken in isolation (unlike its Cartesian source): in this context, identity is conferred not through the articulation of suffering, but through external affirmation of it. Put otherwise, 'I am' not because I suffer, but because other people recognize my suffering, and because my suffering prevents my story from being called into question; the self-validation is contingent upon external corroboration and approval. How then is a reader positioned in relation to the account of suffering?

If, as Darrieussecq suggests, the 'certificat doloriste' creates and confirms a suffering subject, it also compels the reader to adopt a specific position, which could, as Darrieussecq suggests, be restrictive, but could equally be comforting or even pleasurable. The booming sales of narratives recounting pain and trauma suggest that these offer tantalizing possibilities and vicarious pleasure for readers. Nancy K. Miller and Jason Tougaw highlight that 'Narratives of illness, sexual abuse, torture or the death of loved ones have come to rival the classic, heroic adventure as a test of limits that offers the reader the suspicious thrill of borrowed emotion'.[18] Yet reading texts that recount suffering may also be troubling: Sara Ahmed observes that witnessing suffering means 'being open to being affected by that which one cannot know or feel',[19] whilst Shine Choi writes that 'the ungraspability of the pain of Others is what defines the experience of the spectator who is touched by suffering'.[20] It would be impossible to predetermine the effects of reading on individuals: as Régine Detambel puts it, 'Peut-on penser que quelqu'un maîtrisera un jour l'effet d'un livre sur le lecteur? Doit-on ignorer que tout principe actif est à la fois remède et poison, et qu'un livre peut blesser effroyablement?' [Can we think that someone will one day control the effect of a book on its reader? Must we ignore that any chemical entity is both remedy and poison, and that a book can injure terribly?].[21] This book aims to explore not only how narratives of suffering seek to position the reader, but if and how the reader can resist or disrupt this positioning.

Empathy, Sympathy, Compassion: Entangled Definitions

As Amy Coplan writes, 'Over the past few decades, there has been a surge of interest in the concept of empathy, which has come to occupy a central role in countless debates taking place in both public and academic discourse'.[22] Empathy has been described as 'the grand theme of our time'[23] and 'the most valuable resource in our world',[24] possibly because it is commonly assumed to generate altruism. In current liberal discourses, for instance, 'empathy is both the emotional ingredient that binds us together as human subjects and communities and the affective panacea to a wide range of social, political and economic divisions and grievances'.[25] Although the assumption that empathy can resolve socio-political conflicts is evidently problematic, empathy is still frequently evoked as a means of engendering understanding and enabling emotive (and subsequently pragmatic) connections.[26] Carolyn Pedwell observes in an analysis of contemporary socio-political discourses ranging from philosophy (exemplified in the work of Roman Krznaric) to mainstream political manifestoes (citing amongst others Barack Obama): 'Empathy is everywhere and is viewed, by definition, as positive. Understood in shorthand as the ability to put oneself in the other's shoes, empathy is, according to these narratives, what we want to cultivate in ourselves and in others'.[27] If 'empathy, it would seem, has become a Euro-American political obsession',[28] its importance is reiterated in French discourses: Jacques Hochmann writes that 'l'empathie a été promue, depuis peu, bonne à tout faire du management, du marketing, de la médecine, du travail social et de l'éducation' [empathy has been appointed, in recent times, as the servant of management, marketing, medicine, social work, and education].[29] The prevalence of the concept of empathy across disciplinary boundaries is also noted by Megan Boler: 'Across the political and disciplinary spectrum, conservatives and liberals alike advocate variations of empathy as a solution to society's "ills"'.[30] Boler is certainly not alone, however, in interrogating the uncritical advocacy of empathy as agent of social transformation, as we shall see: critics have called into question its implicit gender-differentiation (empathy is often associated with the feminine) and its pro-social impact (or lack thereof) amongst other factors, not least the difficulty in defining empathy (and its connection with and difference from sympathy and compassion in particular).

According to Hochmann, the origins of what we now call 'empathy' lie in the German *Einfühlung*, which dates from 1873; the English term 'empathy' was first used in 1909, while the French *empathie* appears only from 1960 onwards.[31] The word is derived from the Greek *empatheia*, meaning 'affection or passion'.[32] Empathy is most commonly understood, as Keen postulates, as 'a vicarious, spontaneous sharing of affect' which 'can be provoked by witnessing another's emotional state, by hearing about another's condition, or even by reading', and is usually distinguished from sympathy or compassion as follows: in empathy, 'I feel what you feel', whereas in sympathy, 'I feel pity for your pain'.[33] In other words, empathy implies a sharing of affect or emotion, in contradistinction to sympathy or compassion which entail witnessing someone else's emotion, without necessarily experiencing it oneself. Martha Nussbaum's observation that 'empathy is an imaginative reconstruction of another person's experience, whether that experience is happy or sad, pleasant or painful or neutral, and whether the imaginer thinks the other person's situation good, bad, or indifferent', offers one distinction. In her model, compassion, sympathy, or pity are prompted by the assumption that the other is suffering or in pain whereas empathy is not necessarily generated by suffering and can also be elicited through more positive emotional states like relief or joy.[34]

Given, however, that suffering is the point of focus of this book, it is worth attempting to sketch out the similarities and differences between sympathy, pity, and compassion before looking more closely at empathy. Peter Goldie claims that 'there are various sorts of sympathy, such as pity, commiseration, concern and compassion', classifying pity and compassion as subcategories of sympathy.[35] Nussbaum suggests that '"pity" has recently come to have nuances of condescension and superiority to the sufferer', which sympathy does not.[36] Similarly, Marjorie Garber argues that compassion (its etymology meaning 'to suffer with') in its earliest uses meant 'both *suffering together with one another*, or "fellow feeling", and an emotion felt on behalf of another who suffers'. The latter usage came to dominate, with the result that 'compassion was felt not between equals but from a distance — in effect from high to low'.[37] This differentiates compassion from sympathy: 'Where *compassion* quickly tipped in the direction of inequality, charity, or patronage (the nonsufferer showing compassion to the sufferer), *sympathy* remained historically a condition of equality or affinity'.[38] Reading Hannah Arendt, meanwhile, Elizabeth V. Spelman observes the following distinction between compassion and pity:

> For Arendt there appear to be only two kinds of emotional responses to suffering, and neither has a place in public and political life. On the one hand, one might be so 'stricken' with the suffering of another that one suffers as the other does, bears the suffering of the other. Such sharing precludes or obviates the need for deliberation and discussion that are definitive of public life. On the other hand, one can feel for the suffering of another in a way that reflects and announces the distance between nonsufferer and sufferer. But this doesn't open up public space, because the nonsufferer doesn't allow the sufferer a particular face or a particular voice. So if in the first case there is not the variety of perspectives characteristic of public life because two potential subjects have been collapsed into one by the fact of cosuffering, in the second case there is not a variety of perspectives because one subject makes him or herself into a ventriloquist for the other. Arendt calls the first kind of situation 'compassion' and the second one 'pity'.[39]

For Arendt, both compassion (which appropriates the other's position) and pity (which denies the other a voice) silence the suffering other; it is not entirely clear where sympathy fits into this schema. Garber suggests that the word 'empathy' may have emerged when 'the strongest sense of *sympathy* began to decline or become merged with *compassion*'; strikingly, the meanings of 'sympathy' and 'compassion' have both changed their meanings over time.[40] Meghan Marie Hammond points out, for instance, that '"Sympathy" has, at one time or another, expressed nearly everything that we have come to associate with the younger concept of "empathy"',[41] whilst Stanley Olinick argues that 'empathy is becoming a "buzz" word, signifying what formerly was the domain of sympathy'.[42]

Distinctions between 'sympathy', 'compassion', and 'empathy' are, then, neither straightforward nor consistent. Firstly, the difference between empathy and sympathy is usually associated with distance between self and other: Hammond argues that 'sympathy depends on distance, on acknowledgment that the other is other',[43] whereas empathy is typically associated with bridging gaps. Howard Sklar observes that 'in contrast with empathy, sympathy requires greater distance between the individual who feels it and the individual to whom it is directed'.[44] Secondly, however, it is also argued that empathy precedes and can generate sympathy: Keen notes that 'empathy is thought to be a close precursor to its semantic close relation, sympathy'.[45] Goldie contends that empathy or 'understanding another's suffering or distress, whether or not through an imaginative process, is not sufficient for ethical motivation: an ethical outlook towards the world, of which sympathy is one sort, is also necessary'.[46] This does not of course mean that empathy necessarily produces sympathy or compassion. Nussbaum asserts that 'empathy does not suffice for compassion', because 'people may have considerable empathetic understanding of someone for whose suffering they refuse compassion'.[47] Tania Singer and Olga M. Klimecki propose that 'an empathic response to suffering can result in two kinds of reactions: empathic distress, which is also referred to as personal distress; and compassion, which is also referred to as empathic concern or sympathy' and which is more likely to promote a prosocial response.[48] In this formulation, sympathy and compassion are positive, whereas empathy is ambivalent — connected either with distress or with compassion, which, confusingly, here take on properties that elsewhere are associated with empathy. It is, then, difficult to maintain clear distinctions between definitions of sympathy, empathy, and compassion, terms which have often been used interchangeably and have a complex history in French and in English.[49]

It is, however, empathy, rather than sympathy or compassion, that has received an enormous amount of attention in the past few decades, appearing in the popular press, political campaigns, and in the study of a wide range of topics':[50] given 'today's empathy craze',[51] 'whatever empathy is, it's important'.[52] Defining empathy remains tricky: 'There are probably nearly as many definitions of empathy as people working on the topic'.[53] In Coplan's words, 'empathy is a complex imaginative process in which an observer simulates another person's situated psychological states while maintaining clear self-other differentiation', sharing another person's perspective, without appropriating his or her position.[54] Elsewhere, Coplan differentiates between self-oriented empathy ('pseudo-empathy')[55] and other-oriented empathy, which she labels 'genuine empathy'.[56] 'Self-oriented perspective taking' involves 'an attempt to adopt a target individual's perspective by imagining how we ourselves would think, feel, and desire if we were in the target individual's position'. In other words, we do not imagine how they feel, but how we would feel if we were in their position, so that we do not actually take their perspective, but project our own onto them. By contrast, 'other-oriented perspective taking', in which 'a person represents the other's situation from the other person's point of view and attempts to simulate the target individual's experiences as though she were the target individual', does not mean imagining oneself in the other person's position, but imagining how the other person must feel *as other* and recognizing the other person's differing background, experiences, and belief systems.[57] Although this 'other-oriented empathy' is evidently what is usually meant when we refer to empathy, it is particularly difficult, if not, arguably, impossible, particularly where the other person's circumstances are very different, to imagine how they might feel without making appropriative assumptions. It is noteworthy that Coplan 'ends up saying very little about how empathy proper is to be understood', as Christian Miller points out.[58]

The contrast between 'pseudo-empathy' and 'genuine empathy' is mirrored in the implicit distinctions drawn between what Clare Hemmings defines as 'bad empathy, which would somehow imagine that you *can* take the other's position as your own and therefore speak for them in some way', and 'good empathy', which 'would mean that you can recognize and witness the other's subjectivity in ways that [...] don't simply draw on your own set of interests but still foreground a kind of affective relationship that ties you to another'.[59] There is a risk in assuming that '"good" empathy will always be appreciated', as the other might reject or feel threatened by the terms of engagement. Moreover, the empathizing subject can never know whether the empathetic position has captured the other's perspective at all (and making the judgement as to whether said empathy is 'good' or 'bad', 'genuine' or 'pseudo', is itself possibly appropriative).[60] Moreover, even if ('good') empathy were possible, this does not necessarily mean that it promotes prosocial responses: as Boler notes, 'While empathy may inspire action in particular lived contexts [...] I am not convinced that empathy leads to anything close to justice, to any shift in existing power relations'.[61]

One of the risks of assuming the possibility of empathy is that 'liberal claims to "know" or represent the experiences of others through empathy often involve forms of projection and appropriation on the part of "privileged" subjects which can reify existing social hierarchies and silence those at the margins'. This means that 'the act of "choosing" to extend empathy or compassion can in itself be a way to assert power'.[62] Studies have also highlighted a tendency to empathize with people most similar to ourselves, with the potential outcome that 'empathy is biased, pushing us in the direction of parochialism and racism',[63] 'exclusion and ethnocentrism'.[64] Even where empathy can be mobilized, for example, to promote cross-cultural feminist solidarity, the dynamics underpinning it are fraught, as Breda Gray observes: 'For example, the assumed logics of empathy constitute some women as in need of inclusion or support and others as potentially empathic, cosmopolitan and inclusive citizen-subjects, or enlightened feminists'.[65] This should not, however, totally discourage attempts to be empathetic (rather than to 'extend empathy', a phrase which is already politically loaded) if these are mindful of the intrinsic risks inherent in empathy. Pedwell proposes an alternative: 'rather than assuming that empathy is a "good" thing and searching desperately (if futilely) for ways to create it', she suggests exploring:

> Those circumstances in which empathy reaches its limit point, is ignored or rejected by its intended recipient(s), has antithetical consequences to those anticipated, or simply makes no sense (or difference) in the midst of given social conditions and political hierarchies.[66]

In other words, rather than attempting to determine whether empathy has succeeded or failed, the key is to analyze its limits and the power structures that underpin these. This also means interrogating the position from which subjects seek to empathize, with others, and — as I will discuss in Chapter 3 on representations of maternal filicide — exploring whether empathy may mask other underlying anxieties and fears and hide less socially visible subjects of suffering.

Framing Approaches to Suffering

Lauren Berlant observes that even where compassion (which she defines similarly to empathy) with some subjects of suffering is possible, it is only through the dismissal of others:

> What if it turns out that compassion and coldness are not opposite at all but are two sides of a bargain that the subjects of modernity have struck with structural inequality? Normatively, the bargain would go like this: the experience of pain is pre-ideological, the universal sign of membership in humanity, and so we are obligated to be responsible to it; but since some pain is more compelling than some other pain, we must make judgments about which cases deserve attention.[67]

The question here is not only on what basis we make such judgements (can we operate an emotive equivalent of the sort of token system whereby the supermarket shopper votes to divert charity funds to one of three pre-selected charities?), but how critically we apply our judgements (in the supermarket example, we choose rapidly, without questioning whether such a choice is simple and fair). This is in a context in which privilege is already taken for granted (the shopper who can afford to buy groceries in Waitrose, for instance, choosing which charity to support whilst weighed down by shopping bags and privilege) and the supermarket's charity support is both important and yet insufficient. Clearly there is a difference between empathizing with someone else's suffering and paying to alleviate it (the funds are finite; the feelings may also be limited, but in a different way), but in practice empathy, like money, cannot be extended without limits.

In *The Threshold of the Visible World*, Kaja Silverman recounts how walking past crowds of homeless people induces in her an 'irrational panic', which she initially interprets 'in strictly economic terms — as the imperative to give but the impossibility of doing so to everyone who asks'. She subsequently recognizes that the anxiety is not only financial but specular: she avoids looking at the homeless people, because 'I feel myself being asked to [...] locate myself within bodies that would, quite simply, be ruinous of my middle-class self', as though this encounter requires of her an identification that, were it possible, would destroy her.[68] It is unclear who is asking her for this identification, or whether this is an imperative she places upon herself; either way, her response is to look away, as empathy with them (although she does not use this word) would undo her sense of self. Silverman's analysis of identification here is also a useful model for empathy:

> It has occurred to me that I find it difficult but not impossible to identify with the structural position of homelessness, since I imagine that in such a situation I would still coincide with that corporeal fiction which I call 'me'. But the homeless bodies on Telegraph Avenue dispel this comforting fiction; they show me that if homeless, I would precisely no longer be 'myself'.[69]

Whilst on an abstract level she imagines she can identify (or empathize) with homelessness, looking at these homeless people places a burden upon her to which she cannot respond. By not looking, she seeks to evade the reality of the other and to protect herself, not only from the threat of identification (or empathy), but also from having her protective self-fictions shattered. Silverman acknowledges her own failure to see the homeless people as subjects through repeated use of the phrase 'homeless bodies' (also 'calloused', 'grimy' bodies), whilst her clarification that 'in our culture, homeless bodies signify the unraveling of the bodily ego' emphasizes that the homeless are seen only as objects in relation to more dominant subject positions.[70] The risk for Silverman lies in looking at the homeless people, whether or not they look back, and to this extent, her encounter with them is purely specular, an encounter with a threat to her own identity rather than an encounter with the other. Audrey Jaffe suggests that Silverman's story tracks 'the tendency to ward off actual bodies in the sympathetic encounter, replacing them with cultural fictions and self-protection'; 'the difference between looking and not looking' is collapsed here as Silverman's gaze actually conceals or turns away from the bodies, shielding her through protective fictions.[71] Thus 'looking at' the other is just as self-reflexive as not looking; there can be no uncompromised ethical position in relation to the scene of someone else's suffering.

One way of approaching the question of how we see, or fail to see, other people's pain is through Judith Butler's work on framing. In *Precarious Life: The Powers of Mourning and Violence*, Butler argues that some subjects are deemed to have lives worth living and mourning, whilst others are culturally negated. She draws examples from dominant Western media representations of deaths on 9/11 in the United States, for instance, which are memorialized and commemorated, whereas deaths in Iraq or Afghanistan, for example, are not. Butler asks: 'Who counts as human? Whose lives count as lives? And, finally, *What makes for a grievable life?'*.[72] Her point that some lives are deemed more worthy than others offers an alternative perspective on suffering as well as death. Ann Cvetkovich's 2003 study, *An Archive of Feelings*, for example, is motivated by the question, '"Whose feelings count?" in thinking about whose trauma gets recognized in the national public sphere'.[73] The representations of personal pain discussed in this book are constructed within a wider socio-political context within which some suffering is more visible than others and some subjects of suffering are more acknowledged than others. In contemporary French women's writing, for example, certain topics dominate (eating disorders; bereavement) whilst others remain strikingly under-represented (hunger, homelessness, for instance). This may be because writing remains largely inaccessible to those in extreme poverty, but it is also to do with the ways in which subjects of suffering are culturally coded or 'framed', to use Butler's term, more widely. In a critical account of Western responses to killing and violence, Butler observes that 'the frames through which we apprehend, or, indeed, fail to apprehend the lives of others as lost or injured (lose-able or injurable) are politically saturated'. The emphasis here on the frames of representation, the prisms through which subjects are apprehended and recognized (or not recognized as such), is particularly germane to the analysis of literary depictions of suffering.[74] It is striking that there is no privileged space outside the frames that shape how we see others, their 'precarious lives', and their suffering; academic discourse itself is also necessarily implicated within — both constructed by and contributing to — the frames.[75] The frame is not fixed, but is repeatedly reiterated, with the effect that it also shifts and possibly ruptures: 'The frame that seeks to contain, convey, and determine what is seen [...] depends upon the conditions of reproducibility in order to succeed', which in turn 'entails a constant breaking from context', so that 'the "frame" does not quite contain what it conveys, but breaks apart'.[76] The emphasis on a lack of containment and the possibility of overspill is suggestive: whilst we cannot escape the frame, we can track its points of rupture. Butler's notion of the frame helps to shape how we understand what is at stake in reading narratives of suffering (as well as how reading itself, as we shall see, overspills its own frames). I will now look more closely at empathy and reading, beginning with studies of empathy and reading, their conclusions and their limitations, and moving on to explore different models of reading texts that recount suffering, including notions of bearing witness, empathic unsettlement, and sentimental spectatorship, before setting up an alternative model of approaching narratives of suffering.

Reading, Ethics, and Empathy

Much has been written in recent years on the relation between empathy and reading: from Suzanne Keen's *Empathy and the Novel*, which explores how different forms of fiction and of narrative elicit reader responses that might facilitate or prohibit empathy, to scientific analyses of the effects of reading on emotional intelligence or awareness.[77] The notion that reading (fiction) offers a means of developing empathy has been reiterated in the media in the United Kingdom, foregrounded by the organization of 'World Empathy Day' on 13 June and its focus on libraries, and reading, as spaces in which empathy can be fostered.[78] The conclusions reached by different studies vary strikingly. Keen suggests that 'fiction does disarm readers of some of the protective layers of cautious reasoning that may inhibit empathy in the real world',[79] so that fiction is more likely than non-fiction to induce empathy. She also criticizes 'the commonplace that first person fiction more readily evokes feeling responsiveness than the whole variety of third person narrative situations', emphasizing the relevance of genre, setting, time-frames, use of (reported) monologue, and other narrative devices.[80] Research on empathy and reading focuses on the impact of transportation (becoming engrossed in the plot to the extent of possibly losing sight of its fictionality), usually seen as conducive to empathy: P. Matthijs Bal and Martijn Veltkamp note that 'transportation into fictional narratives influence empathy over time; a lack of transportation is related to lower empathy, while a high level of transportation might be related to higher empathy'.[81] Their research relies, however, on comparison between the reading of fiction (part of a Sherlock Holmes novel; a short story) and non-fiction in the form of newspaper articles. Autobiography and autofiction sit uncomfortably here, neither one nor the other, possibly inviting transportation, equally arguably precluding it if, following Keen's argument, the knowledge that the events described are based on lived experience triggers the reader to self-protect. Transportation may also, of course, foreclose empathy, as the reader identifies with the characters rather than empathizing with them (thereby forgetting his or her own distance from the text); identification is certainly not synonymous with empathy.

Scientists David Comer Kidd and Emanuele Castano, in a study of the effects of reading literary fiction, offer a very different take on reading and empathy (which they define as a product of 'theory of mind', or 'TOM'). They claim that 'literary fiction, which we consider to be both writerly and polyphonic, uniquely engages the psychological processes needed to gain access to characters' subjective experiences', because it subverts rather than conforms to our prejudices and expectations. In this way, they suggest, 'readers of literary fiction must draw on more flexible interpretive resources to infer the feelings and thoughts of characters'.[82] It is not the content as such that matters, but the act of reading itself: 'we propose that by prompting readers to take an active writerly role to form representations of characters' subjective states, literary fiction recruits TOM [theory of mind]' and thereby promotes potential empathy.[83] Here, then, empathy is associated not with transportation in reading (which implies passivity or consumption) but with a more active model of reading, which also evokes Roland Barthes's distinction between 'lisible' [readable] and 'scriptible' [writable] texts. Whilst Kidd and Castano assume that 'literary fiction' (which is not clearly defined beyond being labelled as 'polyphonic', but which implies a problematic contrast with 'non-literary fiction') is 'scriptible', clearly in practice it is not easy to define literary fiction. Also 'literary fiction' is not necessarily 'scriptible', whilst popular fiction might be, depending on the individual text and the reader (the emphasis on the reader here is also useful given that empathy in reading necessarily also depends upon the reader's experience and position: one does not read in a vacuum). The emphasis here on the reader as active agent rather than passive recipient or spectator is, however, useful, and underpins the discussions of empathy and reading in this book, although I do not look empirically at reader responses to texts, focusing rather on the way in which texts position their reader.[84]

Theories of empathy in reading are typically bound up in assumptions about authorial intention: as Keen observes, 'Most theories of narrative empathy assume that empathy can be transacted accurately from author to reader by way of a literary text'. By contrast, this study approaches empathy not as a function of authorial intention, but as a potential outcome of textual inscriptions of suffering, that resists control either on the part of the author or of the reader.[85] As this brief overview of studies of empathy and reading shows, there is no clear critical consensus on the relation between reading and empathy, nor on the most productive types of text, or modes of reading, to promote empathy, but perhaps what does emerge most clearly is that empathy cannot be assumed. The championing of empathy as unequivocally positive and transformative is already troubling; the relation between reading and empathy is also fraught, not least because it cannot easily be defined and measured. My aim here is not to gauge the extent to which specific texts may or may not induce empathy in different readers, but to explore instead the structures of narratives of suffering and the ways in which reading is inscribed within and projected by the text. This means analyzing texts that recount different forms of trauma, violence, or illness (and clearly these are not synonymous) in order to explore what is at stake in reading narratives of other people's suffering.

Compassion and Spectatorship in Reading

There are a number of risks to empathizing with — or presuming to empathize with — suffering subjects in texts. Berlant's compelling critique of compassion may help to unpick some of the issues at stake in empathy as well as compassion:

> This is a peculiarly modern topic, because members of mass society witness suffering not just in concretely local spaces but in the elsewhere brought home and made intimate by sensationalist media, where documentary realness about the pain of strangers is increasingly at the center of both fictional and nonfictional events. The Freudian notion of *Schadenfreude*, the pleasure one takes in the pain of another, only begins to tell the unfinished story of the modern incitement to feel compassionately — even whilst being entertained.[86]

For Berlant, compassion (and empathy, whilst different from compassion, carries similar risks) incorporates voyeurism and pity and is inextricably part of a spectacle within which other people's pain appears to be brought closer. The illusion of feeling proximity to and intimacy with that pain (supported by recent technologies, but equally possible in the context of reading) within a frame of entertainment is particularly fraught. In an article entitled 'Poor Eliza', Berlant highlights the political risks of assuming empathetic identification:

> Here is a hypothesis: when sentimentality meets politics, it uses personal stories to tell of structural effects, but in so doing it risks thwarting its very attempt to

perform rhetorically a scene of pain that must be soothed politically. Because the ideology of true feeling cannot admit the nonuniversality of pain, its cases become all jumbled together and the ethical imperative to ward social transformation is replaced by a civic-minded but passive ideal of empathy. The political as a place of acts oriented toward publicness becomes replaced by a world of private thoughts, leanings, and gestures.[87]

Berlant is effectively arguing that if a scene of suffering moves its spectator to tears, this does not necessarily lead the spectator to act on the political injustices invoked, but instead restores the spectator to the private emotional sphere, wherein he/she is indulging his or her own emotional catharsis (assuming that he/she can understand and identify with a projected universal pain), rather than acting to change the wider structural injustice. Here, empathy and compassion are depoliticized by privileging private/individual feelings that work to erase or cover up injustices. Reading about other people's suffering is very different from being physically confronted with it, as in the case of Silverman recounted above; where Silverman actively turns away (to avoid her bodily identity being dissolved), reading about others' pain is potentially less threatening. Kathleen Woodward summarizes Berlant's argument as follows:

> The narrative affords the pleasure of consuming the feeling of vicarious suffering — and its putative moral precipitate, the feeling of self-satisfaction that we wish to do the right thing and hence are virtuous. But the experience of being moved by these sentimental scenes of suffering, whose ostensible purpose it is to awaken us to redress injustice, works instead to return us to a private world far removed from the public sphere. Hence, in a crippling contradiction, Berlant concludes, the result of such empathetic identification is not the impulse to action but rather a 'passive' posture. Fundamentally, therefore, the sentimental narrative is deliciously consumable and cruelly ineffective.[88]

The suggestion here is that reading narratives of suffering, far from eliciting prosocial responses, is ultimately solipsistic, as the reader — whilst assuming empathy with the subject in pain — privileges his or her own personal feelings so that passivity prevents a more politicized response. Two issues emerge: firstly, that the tendency to react emotionally impedes rather than triggers proactive reactions; and secondly, that there is something uncomfortable about the 'delicious' 'self-satisfaction' implied in the encounter with the 'deliciously consumable' text, which induces a different sort of discomfort than that described by Silverman above. I would like to pause here to think through what it means to be uncomfortable, which will be key to my readings in this book.

Reading Suffering: Uncomfortable Witnesses

If texts recounting suffering invite empathy, they also potentially involve voyeuristic contemplation of someone else's pain or a fraught attempt to understand. Interpreting texts of suffering is necessarily contradictory:

> When cultural work engages with other people's trauma, it does so with a double emphasis on contradictory terms: the impossibility of fully grasping the traumatic moment and translating it into language and the necessity to transmit knowledge of these traumas.[89]

This emphasis on transmission is concomitant with an insistence on testimony or the imperative to bear witness, outlined by Shoshana Felman and Dori Laub in *Testimony: Crises of Witnessing in History and Culture*. The notion of bearing witness addresses the apparent impossibility of passing on a story that defies narrativization, as the witness, in Felman and Laub's model, does not receive and repeat a coherent story, but becomes engaged in an exchange shaped around what cannot be recounted. The witness is invoked as ethical agent, as it is through the dialogue with the witness that the survivor can begin to externalize his or her story. The reader is called upon to respond constructively, rather than — like the nit-picking historians in Laub's example of an Auschwitz survivor describing an uprising — insisting upon inaccuracies of tiny detail and thereby detracting from the more crucial message at stake.[90] The problem of framing the encounter between narrative and reader, as if between survivor and listener, within this ethical model is that, as Susannah Radstone observes, 'criticism and debate can easily appear callous, or even unethical, in a context where an audience is being asked to bear witness to unspeakable sufferings'.[91] The reader/listener risks being effectively silenced by the fear of undermining the narrative of suffering, not only by openly casting into doubt its veracity, but even by debating its terms of reference; this is of course also part of the effect of Darrieussecq's notion of the 'certificat doloriste'. Whilst Darrieussecq derides the constraints that this places on the reader, it would be inappropriate to disregard ethical questions entirely, even if we refuse to be completely limited (or fixed) by the narrative of suffering.

Butler's discussion of framing prompts us to track the limits of the frames that shape our readings and to detect our own blind spots as readers, trying to see both what narratives themselves conceal or fail to articulate, and what we as readers do not see, as well as the ways in which the frames themselves potentially shift and break. Martin Modlinger and Philipp Sonntag argue that 'the responsibility of the witness is not to *become* the victim, to partake of the victim's pain; rather [...] it is to regard the other's pain as something alien, unfathomable, and as an outrage which should be stopped'.[92] The reader-as-witness is, however, always already too late to stop the particular outrage being recounted, even if the point is to militate against future atrocities that find origins or reflections in this one. Being outraged/shocked/horrified is, however, possibly productive, in the sense that it invokes critical distance and perhaps generates proactive reactions (although it could equally induce a sense of powerlessness or of individual helplessness inspired by the assumption that nothing can be changed). The words 'alien', 'unfathomable', here seem to contraindicate the possibility of empathy with someone else's pain, unless that empathy can be rooted in acknowledgement that the other's suffering is incomprehensible, other, inaccessible. Yet perhaps empathy can productively emerge from being outraged by a pain that one can recognize (as other) but cannot understand; that is, from (acknowledgement of) affective dissonance, rather than consonance, with the other.

The possibility of reading through affective dissonance is taken up by Boler and Hemmings. In a critique of models of empathetic identification, Boler notes that 'passive empathy absolves the reader through the denial of power relations' and the presumed annihilation of difference between self and other, proposing instead 'testimonial reading' that 'recognizes its own limits, obstacles, ignorances and zones of numbness'.[93] She roots an alternative notion of 'testimonial reading' in Felman and Laub's model of testimony and in an insistence on self-reflexive interrogation, within which empathy relies upon a recognition of the limits of our understanding of (and access to) the other's feelings. Hemmings cautions against a wholesale commendation of bearing witness, observing that 'witnessing has a whiff of innocence about it, one that locates its subject outside rather than caught up in the conditions that make intersubjective recognition impossible in the first place', yet Boler's understanding of 'testimonial reading' foregrounds the reader-witness's complicity within socio-political hierarchies.[94] Both Hemmings and Boler advocate acknowledgement of affective dissonance or distance between self and other in models of empathy, shifting from identification, which attempts to erase the gap between self and other ('empathetic identification requires the other's difference in order to consume it as sameness')[95] to a recognition of difference and distance ('the discomfort of distance' as Hemmings puts it).[96] Part of this entails acknowledging one's own complicity within the hierarchical structures that empathy might be perceived to break through but potentially rather reinforces. If 'empathy is usually only given to those perceived to be in need, those with less power or resources', then empathy is itself a hierarchical relation that may shore up the inequalities that it appears to resolve, unless it can include recognition of these irreducible differences.[97] Sara Ahmed points out that 'the investment in the figure of the suffering other gives the Western subject the pleasures of being charitable', by reinforcing the empowerment of the self-consciously empathic subject who whilst extending charity to the other is nonetheless also reaffirming the distance and difference between them.[98]

Dominick LaCapra, warning against the risks of assuming identification with others who are suffering, proposes 'empathic unsettlement' (as opposed to a more straightforward notion of empathy), which would articulate and allow for the disruptive effects of the encounter with other people's pain. In empathetic unsettlement, he suggests, 'one puts oneself in the other's position while recognizing the difference of that position and hence not taking the other's place'. He notes that:

> Empathic unsettlement also raises in pointed form the problem of how to address traumatic events involving victimization, including the problem of composing narratives that neither confuse one's own voice or position with the victim's nor seek facile uplift, harmonization, or closure but allow the unsettlement that they address to affect the narrative's own movement in terms of both acting out and working through.[99]

The rejection of 'closure' or resolution, on the one hand, is countered by the refusal of simplistic identification on the other; the subject who witnesses someone else's pain, in LaCapra's model, must simultaneously accept unsettlement and attempt to work through it. The point here is that empathic unsettlement can never be planned, controlled, or fixed; the key, LaCapra suggests, is self-reflexive awareness of the dynamics that underpin the encounter with other people's pain, which resonates with Hemmings's insistence on the 'discomfort of distance' outlined above.

As Woodward argues, 'In a culture dominated by the media, much of our emotional experience, once understood in terms of a psychology of depth and interiority, has been reduced to intensities or sensations'.[100] Engaging with other people's pain must go beyond the fleeting intensity of emotion (offering coins to a homeless beggar, on the one hand, or feeling revulsion and turning away from less palatable suffering, on the other) to allow for empathic unsettlement. The question of how as readers we accept and indeed tolerate empathic unsettlement generated by the encounter with the text is necessarily complex and fraught. Jill Bennett advocates an 'empathy grounded not in affinity (*feeling for* another insofar as we can imagine *being* that other), but on a *feeling for* another that entails an encounter with something irreducible and different, often inaccessible'.[101] Whilst these two possibilities are clearly different — the first rooted in an assumption of understanding and the latter in alterity — both emphasize '*feeling*', which is unsurprising as a basis for empathy but also potentially ephemeral rather than 'grounded'. What is key here is the notion of the 'encounter' with an 'inaccessible' text: the reader is called upon to recognize the fragility and unreliability of 'feeling' and to interrogate the emotive responses engendered by texts that may often seem all too accessible (as I argue in Chapter 4), yet whose alterity must not be denied.

Engendering Empathy: Suffering and Women's Writing

This book examines contemporary French women's writing, not to suggest that women are more likely to write about suffering, nor indeed to show empathy, but to highlight that both experiences of suffering and notions of empathy, as well as the types of story that are culturally permissible to tell, are gender-inflected. Trauma and suffering have featured very heavily in French women's writing since 1990; whilst many of the experiences depicted are not exclusive to women, they are lived differently by male and female subjects.[102] Eating disorders, for example, whilst more common in women, also affect men; nonetheless, they are 'markedly gendered illnesses' which are culturally framed very differently for men than for women.[103] Another persistent theme in recent French writing is the loss of children: whilst this might arguably be seen to place mother and father in parallel positions of grief, the maternal and paternal roles are shaped by gendered cultural expectation and the resulting narratives may differ significantly. This is not of course to argue that all mothers experience the loss of their children in the same way, or use the same words to recount it, nor indeed that other background factors (ethnicity, class, and so on) do not also inflect experiences and narratives of suffering. One aim of this book is to explore disparities between different narratives and different subjects of suffering and the extent to which some subjects of suffering displace others. Yet it is significant that suffering is such a key theme in contemporary French women's writing, and discourses on empathy are also gender-inflected, bound up in associations around differences between men and women.

The feminist writer Andrea Lobb criticizes the 'persistent sex stereotyping of empathy', which she calls 'empathism'.[104] She cites the developmental psychologist Simon Baron-Cohen's assumption that 'the female brain is, (in general) an empathizing brain [...] hard-wired for this kind of natural, effortless empathizing' whereas the male brain is (most commonly) a 'systematizing brain' which finds empathy more difficult.[105] Lobb warns against the risks of assuming that women are intrinsically more capable of empathy than men without recognizing the effects of gendered socialization and expectation that might compel (or enable) women to adopt more empathetic perspectives. Whilst we tend to conceive of an empathizing subject being autonomous (and often in a position of power and privilege),[106] Lobb suggests that empathy may also develop out of necessity from a position of powerlessness. Disempowered subjects, she notes, may orient outwards to more dominant groups: 'Empathic "other-orientation", when conducted from a position of persistent powerlessness, rather than one of empowered agency, may be a long way from the vision of empathy as the harbinger of social and ethical reparation or justice'.[107] Even where women are not visibly disempowered, they are tacitly disadvantaged by the expectation that they show empathy. If 'instances of male empathy stand in a supplemental relation to (dominant) definitions of masculinity (and paternity), whereas female empathy figures more as an essential component of definitions of femininity (and, a fortiori, of maternity)', this can affect workplace expectations, as female empathy is expected, yet not noticed unless it is absent, whereas male empathy will be more recognized and perhaps more valued (or possibly denigrated).[108] In other words, the association between empathy and the feminine, whilst prevalent, requires careful negotiation and interrogation, through attention to the conditions that make empathy either expected on the one hand or difficult and prized on the other. This is of course also bound up in the types of story that are available to tell about suffering which are also implicitly gendered (yet which are also inevitably inflected by other social differences too, so clearly an over-rigid demarcation of gender difference would be unhelpful). This may also apply to gender differences in reading, which is not to suggest that female readers are more likely to empathize, nor that there might be a specifically gendered mode of reading. The point is more about whether there might be alternative ways of reading invited by contemporary French women's writing that could open up empathy more productively. One productive way of considering the depiction of suffering in women's writing and its effect on the reader is to look at how it both tends to privilege the other (to be 'other-orientated', to borrow Coplan's terminology), but also interrogates the very possibility of a genuine encounter with alterity ('irreducible and different, often inaccessible', to return to Bennett's formulation).

To explore this further, I turn briefly to an early text by Hélène Cixous, best known for her theorization of an *écriture féminine*, a writing that aims to break down rigid social, gendered, and literary categories through a reconfiguration of the relation between mind and body. In *Vivre l'orange/To Live the Orange*, a bi-lingual text, the narrator contemplates an orange, in painstaking detail, through a close reading of the Brazilian writer Clarice Lispector. The poetic reflection on the layers of the orange is interrupted within the text by a telephone call from a friend urging Cixous to join a protest against violence in Iran. Cixous's reply (that she is too busy looking at an orange) is self-consciously provocative, seeming to set up a sharp distinction between political engagement (outwardly directed, showing concern for others) and reading (focusing on minutiae, solipsistic). Cixous's emphasis on contemplating the orange is both self-mocking (her meditation is represented as self-indulgent and introspective, coupled with repeated assertions that she has 'lost' time that by implication could have usefully been spent otherwise) and yet also other-orientated, because the orange constitutes a means of access to the 'other' (in the form of Lispector's writing). Cixous asks:

> (A quelles conditions, une femme pourrait-elle dire, sans mourir de honte, —
> ce que je n'arrive à écrire ce lundi qu'après trois jours d'une terreur suffocante:
> 'l'amour de l'orange aussi est politique' — à quel prix?)

> (Under what conditions, could a woman say without dying of shame, — what
> I am able to write this Monday only after three days of a suffocating terror –:
> 'the love of an orange is political too' — at what cost?)[109]

This question, formulated within parentheses as though somewhat secondary, is never fully answered in *Vivre l'orange*, which politicizes the act of reading (and of writing) as a means of opening up to the other, yet also notes its limits through the references to women suffering in Iran, as well as to the feminist demonstration in Paris in support of suffering Iranian women (that Cixous does not attend because she is reading). On the one hand, 'in order to think about the materiality of the other (the women in Iran) one has to think responsively'. On the other hand, what that might mean is to ignore a context in which one knows that another suffers (and one does not work to alleviate this) or, equally, to respond to one call of alterity whilst disregarding another; the ethical issues underpinning these decisions are complex.[110] Part of what emerges from this text is the difficulty of connecting reading/writing with activism/direct action; also pressing is Cixous's insistence on the need to read as a means of opening up to alterity in ways that might ultimately allow for political action. Yet whilst many critics have convincingly celebrated Cixous's open-ended generosity as a writer (to her reader), her analysis of Lispector's text may also be seen as appropriative. Rosemary Arrojo notes that 'it is Cixous who has had the upper hand, it is Cixous who gets to keep a "proper", authorial name and who has had the (also academic) power to create authority and to write it her own way'.[111] This suggests that whilst Cixous describes her own reading as an engagement with alterity, a means of approaching someone else's pain, it may also be appropriative, not only because Cixous starts from a position of privilege (she is the better known of the two, for one) but also because any attempt to read someone else's story is also necessarily to rewrite it in some way. Arrojo's criticism of Cixous comes close to suggesting that Cixous's reading of Lispector — like her non-attendance of the demonstration for Iranian women — reflects her failure to engage with the experience and suffering of the other. Yet Cixous's awareness in *Vivre l'orange* of others' suffering and of the limits of her own attempts to relate to it is striking, even from the title, which evokes life, but the life of an orange, rather than a violated woman; this text highlights its own limits. Cixous attempts to approach the other differently, examining in painstaking detail Lispector's textual representation of 'the living proximity of the wor(l)d via ear, touch, smell, taste';[112] it is the intimacy of the reading encounter as practised by Cixous juxtaposed with her awareness of wider political tortures that inaugurates her response to alterity.[113] Herein, perhaps, lies the challenge: not (only) how to read in the knowledge that reading both distracts from and makes visible other people's suffering, but also to reflect differently on one's own position in relation to that suffering. This involves a reconsideration of the ethics of reading suffering. How can the reader engage with the suffering recounted without presuming to understand (and imposing an interpretation upon it) or without voyeurism or prurient curiosity? This takes us back to the notion of 'being uncomfortable', which underscores my reading of Cixous's text (it is extremely uncomfortable to read that she is too busy contemplating an orange to participate in action against violence), and which frames my readings of empathy in this study.

Discomfort and Indigestion: Engaging with Empathy in Christine Angot

To begin to explore what it means to read narratives of suffering with discomfort, I turn to the controversial writer, Christine Angot, whose autofiction frequently returns both to her experience of childhood incest and to questions of reading. Angot's texts avoid the expected narrative of individual trauma: whilst her childhood incestuous relations with her father are a recurrent theme throughout her writing, she repeatedly frames incest within wider socio-political structures rather than as a story of her personal pain, asserting that 'je ne lave pas MON linge sale. Mais le drap social' [I am not washing MY dirty linen. But the social sheet].[114] The implicitly gendered (laundry being typically associated with women) notion of 'dirty linen' suggests something personal and private being rendered visible in public, with connotations of inappropriate and even shameful revelation (such as incest). Angot reframes dirty linen/incest (individual, private, hidden) in terms of a 'social sheet', part of a wider social cover (or cover-up). Jordan argues that in Angot's work, 'Incest is refigured, the emphasis shifted from a personal experience that conditions one woman's life to a textual strategy and master narrative that conditions something far broader'.[115] Angot's writing reshapes the personal story of suffering and is therefore worth pausing over; this alternative narrative of suffering — framed in and shaped by wider social discourses — positions the reader somewhat differently from the sentimental spectacles theorized by Berlant.

Many of Angot's texts return to the theme of incest, including *Un amour impossible* [An Impossible Love] (2015), which recounts the liaison between Rachel and Pierre (the former a health service worker, the latter from a military background), from the perspective of their daughter Christine. The 'amour impossible' of the title could refer to the relationship between Rachel and Pierre (he rejects her as socially inferior) or between Pierre and Christine (the taboo of incest, following a number of years in which he refused to acknowledge her), or, indeed, the difficult relationship established between Rachel and her daughter, against a backdrop of paternal abandonment and later abuse. Incest here is recounted tangentially and minimally. This is presumably not, however, a mark of the impossibility of articulating trauma (given that in Angot's earlier texts, the narrating character ' "Christine" speaks her abuse freely, repeatedly and in vivid detail'), but a deliberate narrative strategy to decentre the subject of suffering.[116] The revelation of incest is made by Christine's friend Marc, who tells Rachel that 'il la sodomise depuis des années' [he has been sodomizing her for years].[117] After learning of her daughter's abuse, the mother reacts somatically with a fallopian tube infection and fever that result in her hospitalization that same night. The narrative focuses on the mother's pain, which is experienced physically as a bodily infection (located in her reproductive organs, figuring not her daughter's suffering, but her own difficulty in hearing about the abuse that she as mother failed to prevent or even acknowledge). Whilst the mother retrospectively describes her infection as protective (because her hospitalization meant Christine could not visit her father that particular weekend as planned), the daughter counters this with the insistence that 't'as pas porté plainte, t'as rien dit, t'as rien fait' [you haven't complained, you've said nothing, you've done nothing].[118]

On the one hand, then, the mother's somatic response is highly inadequate: whilst it may indicate empathy (literally performing the daughter's suffering in her place), it elicits no action, not even a verbal acknowledgement. On the other hand, Christine situates her mother's lack of action within a specific context: 'C'est pas l'histoire d'une petite bonne femme, aveuglée et qui perd confiance' [It's not the story of a little woman, blinded and losing confidence]; 'Quelqu'un comme toi devait rester dans la voie sans issue. A l'intérieur du tunnel, là où on voit rien justement' [Someone like you should stay in the dead-end. Inside the tunnel, where you can't see anything].[119] The personal story of incest is thus located within and defined by wider socio-political structures which allow the father to dominate, which 'blind' the mother (imagery of non-seeing and blindness recur in this part of the text) and violate the child. Berlant's notion of 'the passive ideal of empathy' is displaced here, as the focus is on the ambivalent figure of the mother, who does not see, and whose lack of foresight fails to protect her child, yet who is also depicted as a victim of socio-economic structures.

The mother's seeming passivity in failing to notice her daughter's abuse is one inadequate response to Christine's suffering. The brief sentence, spoken by someone else, stating that Christine was sodomized by her father also impacts upon the reader who, given any familiarity with Angot's earlier texts, would not be surprised. The reader is left relieved that details are being spared and frustrated by unanswered questions (did he 'just' sodomize her, or was that formulation chosen to stand in for other sexual abuses too? When did it begin? And above all, how does she feel?). There is no space for empathy in this text, but equally the displacement of individual suffering is jarring. When Rachel tells her daughter that she felt powerless to help her, Christine's casual 'C'est pas grave, maman' [It doesn't matter, mum] is unconvincing; whilst Christine claims to understand her mother's position and thus not to blame her, the off-hand dismissal of sexual violation by her father is very uncomfortable to read.[120] This is particularly so as playing down the impact and violence of her father's abuse seems to be the condition of possibility for her relationship with her mother.

Angot states in an interview that 'Mon ambition c'est d'etre ingérable; que les gens m'avalent et qu'en meme temps ils ne puissent pas me digérer' [My ambition is to be indigestible; for people to swallow me but at the same time be unable to digest me].[121] Where Berlant refers to narratives of suffering as 'deliciously consumable', Angot's self-representation is also described in terms of eating, but the food here is indigestible rather than delicious. This metaphor is interesting in relation to empathy more generally, which inevitably risks, as Boler writes, establishing 'a binary power relationship of self/other that threatens to consume and annihilate the very differences that permit empathy'.[122] This can be understood more specifically in the context of reading narratives of suffering: the figure of the 'indigestible' text (or subject of suffering, like Angot's self-construction) constitutes a useful approach to understanding how texts of suffering position the reader, inviting (compelling?) the reader to swallow, but also impeding digestion. Angot's model does not deny the risks of attempting to consume the other or the text — on the contrary, her texts emphasize the pervasiveness of consumer culture, and as Ruth Cruickshank notes, 'Angot often foregrounds the co-implication of the reader *qua* consumer' — but indigestion arguably renders the reader too uncomfortable to consume the text fully.[123] The uncomfortable reader is not in an analogous position to the suffering subject within the text (indeed, part of the discomfort lies in recognition of the gap between reader and text), but discomfort (or indigestion) could offer a means of rethinking how we approach narratives of other people's suffering, as we shall see in the chapters that follow. This indigestion relates to the tension between personal or personal pain caused by others and wider social structures that enable and frame that suffering; the reader is compelled to negotiate between recognizing individual guilt, suffering, and responsibility and acknowledging the socio-political and gendered constraints that shape these.

Reading with Discomfort (and Empathy)

Chapter 1 explores a range of memoirs and novels (including autobiographical texts by Delphine de Vigan and Amélie Nothomb) that recount eating disorders to show that these narratives stage a performative relation with the reader rooted in both proximity and distance or alienation. These texts, I argue, seek not (only) to construct a (coherent) subject of suffering whose pain is validated by an external agent (the reader), but also shift the ways in which textual engagement with the subject of anorexia can work. The narratives of anorexia discussed here do not invite, or demand, empathy from their reader. Instead, they disrupt the relation between the reader and the subject of anorexia by shifting their focus from emotions (and from the body) to the shifting and fractured relation between self and other to show that narrative and identity cannot find origins or authentication in the assumption or performance of suffering.

In Chapter 2, I explore how autobiographical accounts of the loss of a child (typically defined as a limit-experience, beyond understanding or empathy) by Camille Laurens, Laure Adler, and Sophie Daull seek to describe the death of a child in and through the recognition that no prospective reader can 'know how they feel'. Their texts evoke and simultaneously undermine the distinction between fantasy and reality, dream and waking, the frames of which blur and overlap. Drawing on psychoanalytic theories around traumatic loss, specifically Cathy Caruth's readings of Sigmund Freud and Jacques Derrida, I argue that knowledge and understanding are displaced here as the bereaved narrators themselves struggle to 'know how they feel' other than through dream/fantasy and, crucially, through citation (other people's words). This in turn poses a challenge to readers to recognize the extent to which the encounter with the subject of suffering within the text is mediated in and through other people's words.

Chapter 3 discusses why (feminist) readers and critics have surprisingly easily claimed to empathize with contemporary literary (fictional) representations of infanticidal mothers who might more usually seem to be beyond compassion. This empathy is, I argue, founded through denial of the conditions of its own possibility and through an assumption of shared subject positions that shore up the reader's pre-existing ideals of maternity in particular. My readings of Marguerite Duras, Véronique Olmi, Mazarine Pingeot, and Laurence Tardieu draw instead on what Hemmings has called 'the discomfort of distance': in these texts, this means exploring what empathy might mask and looking critically at, rather than seeking to bridge, gaps or establish cohesion.

In Chapter 4 I turn to Judith Butler's *Giving an Account of Oneself* to consider what is at stake in the attempt to both narrate and account for oneself in autofictional texts by Chloé Delaume and Delphine de Vigan. These texts do not demand or elicit empathy but do interrogate the basis of an ethical relation between self and other rooted in injury and violence. I advocate a shift away from empathy defined as putting oneself in someone else's shoes, to conceive of empathy instead in terms of mutual woundedness and dispossession that recognizes a responsibility to the other founded in a lack (of cohesion or completeness) through which one can begin to approach the suffering of the other. This forms the basis for my concluding chapter, which suggests that we rethink empathy in terms of what does not fit neatly, or comfortably, in narrative or in reading. Rather than seeking to become more comfortable, I propose that engaging with empathy in reading means taking discomfort — and also taking responsibility for one's own discomfort, and the structures that underlie this — as a basis for approaching narratives of other people's suffering.

Notes to the Introduction

1. Marie Darrieussecq, *Rapport de police: accusations de plagiat et autres modes de surveillance de la fiction* (Paris: P.O.L., 2010), p. 298. Unless otherwise stated, all English translations are my own.
2. Ibid., p. 21.
3. Camille Laurens, 'Marie Darrieussecq ou le syndrome du coucou', *La Revue Littéraire*, 32 (Autumn 2007), 1–14 (p. 2).

4. Ibid., p. 8.

5. Leigh Gilmore, *The Limits of Autobiography: Trauma and Testimony* (London: Cornell University Press, 2001), p. 1.

6. Anne Rothe, *Popular Trauma Culture: Selling the Pain of Others in the Mass Media* (New Brunswick, NJ: Rutgers University Press, 2011). p. 88.

7. Tim Adams, 'Feel the Pain', <http://www.guardian.co.uk/books/2006/jan/29/biography.features> [accessed 7 March 2019].

8. Philippe Lejeune, *Le Pacte autobiographique* (Paris: Du Seuil, 1975).

9. Gilmore, *The Limits of Autobiography*, p. 6.

10. Louise DeSalvo, *Writing as a Way of Healing: How Telling Our Stories Transforms our Lives* (London: The Women's Press, 1999).

11. See Shoshana Felman and Dori Laub, *Testimony: Crises of Witnessing in Literature, Psychoanalysis and History* (New York: Routledge, 1992).

12. Martin Modlinger and Philipp Sonntag, 'Introduction: Other People's Pain — Narratives of Trauma and the Question of Ethics', in *Other People's Pain: Narratives of Trauma and the Question of Ethics*, ed. by Martin Modlinger and Philipp Sonntag (Oxford: Peter Lang, 2011), pp. 1–18 (p. 1).

13. See Serge Doubrovsky, *Fils* (Paris: Galilée, 1977). There are too many critical studies of autofiction to list all here, but key works in French include: Marie Darrieussecq, 'L'Autofiction: un genre pas sérieux', *Poétique*, 107 (1996), 369–80; Vincent Colonna, *Autofictions et autres mythomanies littéraires* (Auch: Tristram, 2004); Philippe Gasparini, *Est-il je? Roman autobiographique et autofiction* (Paris: Du Seuil, 2004); Yves Baudelle, 'Autofiction et roman autobiographique: incidents de frontière', in *Vies en récit: formes littéraires et médiatiques de la biographie et de l'autobiographie*, ed. by Robert Dion and others (Quebec: Éditions Nota bene, 2007), pp. 43–70; Philippe Vilain, *L'Autofiction en théorie; suivi de deux entretiens avec Philippe Sollers et Philippe Lejeune* (Paris: Éditions de la Transparence, 2009).

14. Shirley Jordan, 'Autofiction in the Feminine', *French Studies*, 67.1 (2013), 76–84 (p. 77).

15. Laurens, 'Le Syndrome du coucou', p. 10.

16. Suzanne Keen, 'A Theory of Narrative Empathy', *Narrative*, 14 (2006), 207–36 (p. 216).

17. Darrieussecq, *Rapport de police*, p. 17.

18. Nancy K. Miller and Jason Tougaw, 'Introduction: Extremities', in *Extremities: Trauma, Testimony, and Community*, ed. by Nancy K. Miller and Jason Tougaw (Urbana: University of Illinois Press, 2002), pp. 1–24 (p. 2).

19. Sara Ahmed, *The Cultural Politics of Emotion* (New York: Routledge, 2012), p. 30.

20. Shine Choi, *Re-Imagining North Korea in International Politics: Problems and Alternatives* (New York: Routledge, 2014), p. 101.

21. Régine Detambel, *Les Livres prennent soin de nous* (Arles: Actes Sud, 2015), p. 28.

22. Amy Coplan, 'Will the Real Empathy Please Stand Up? A Case for a Narrow Conceptualisation', *Southern Journal of Philosophy*, 49 (2011), 40–65 (p. 41).

23. Frans de Waal, *The Age of Empathy: Lessons for a Kinder Society* (New York: Crown Publishing Group, 2009), p. xi.

24. Simon Baron-Cohen, *The Science of Evil: On Empathy and the Origins of Cruelty* (New York: Basic Books, 2011), p. 157.

25. Carolyn Pedwell, 'Affect at the Margins: Alternative Empathies in *A Small Place*', *Space and Society*, 8 (2013), 18–26 (p. 18).

26. In 2015 the Empathy Museum opened in London, with the following mission statement: 'Launched in 2015, the Empathy Museum is dedicated to helping us look at the world through other people's eyes. Through a series of participatory arts projects with a focus on storytelling and dialogue, it explores how empathy can not only transform our personal relationships, but also help tackle global challenges such as prejudice, conflict and inequality'. A recent interactive installation at the museum, entitled 'A Mile in My Shoes', invites visitors to walk a mile in someone else's shoes while listening to their life story, to 'take the visitor on an empathetic as well as a physical journey', <http://www.empathymuseum.com/#ourmission> [accessed 7 March 2019]. The UK organization EmpathyLab promotes the development of empathy in

children: 'In today's divided world, the need for more empathy has never been more urgent', <http://www.empathylab.uk/what-we-do> [accessed 7 March 2019].

27. Carolyn Pedwell, *Affective Relations: The Transnational Politics of Empathy* (London: Palgrave Macmillan, 2014), pp. ix–x.

28. Ibid., p. ix.

29. Jacques Hochmann, *Une histoire de l'empathie* (Paris: Odile Jacob, 2012), p. 11.

30. Megan Boler, 'The Risks of Empathy: Interrogating Multiculturalism's Gaze', *Cultural Studies*, 11.2 (1997), 253–73 (p. 254).

31. Hochmann, *Une histoire de l'empathie*, p. 13.

32. Robert Plutchik, 'Evolutionary Bases of Empathy', in *Empathy and its Development*, ed. by Nancy Eisenberg and Janet Strayer (Cambridge: Cambridge University Press, 1987), 38–46 (p. 38).

33. Keen, 'A Theory of Narrative Empathy', p. 208.

34. Martha Nussbaum, *Upheavals of Thought: The Intelligence of Emotions* (Cambridge: Cambridge University Press, 2001), p. 302.

35. Peter Goldie, *The Emotions: A Philosophical Exploration* (Oxford: Clarendon Press, 2000), p. 213, n. 8.

36. Nussbaum, *Upheavals of Thought*, p. 301.

37. Marjorie Garber, 'Compassion', in *Compassion: The Culture and Politics of an Emotion*, ed. by Lauren Berlant (New York & London: Routledge, 2004), pp. 15–27 (p. 20).

38. Ibid., p. 23.

39. Elizabeth V. Spelman, *Fruits of Sorrow: Framing our Attention to Suffering* (Boston: Beacon Press, 1998), p. 67.

40. Garber, 'Compassion', p. 24.

41. Meghan Marie Hammond, *Empathy and the Psychology of Literary Modernism* (Edinburgh: Edinburgh University Press, 2014), p. 6.

42. Stanley Olinick, 'A Critique of Empathy and Sympathy', in *Empathy*, ed. by Joseph Lichtenberg, Melvin Bornstein and Donald Silver (Hilisdale, NJ: Erlbaum, 1984), pp. 137–66 (p. 137).

43. Hammond, *Empathy and the Psychology of Literary Modernism*, p. 4.

44. Howard Sklar, *The Art of Sympathy in Fiction: Forms of Ethical and Emotional Persuasion* (Amsterdam: John Benjamins, 2013), p. 26.

45. Keen, 'A Theory of Narrative Empathy', p. 208.

46. Goldie, *The Emotions*, p. 213.

47. Nussbaum, *Upheavals of Thought*, p. 329.

48. Tania Singer and Olga M. Klimecki, 'Empathy and Compassion', *Current Biology*, 24.18 (22 September 2014), R875–78 (p. R875).

49. See Katherine Ibbett, 'Pity, Compassion, Commiseration: Theories of Theatrical Relatedness', *Seventeenth-century French Studies*, 30.2 (2008), 196–208 (p. 201). As Lauren Wispé writes, 'The concepts of sympathy and empathy are frequently confused, and both have been variously and vaguely defined' ('The Distinction Between Sympathy and Empathy: To Call Forth a Concept, a Word is Needed', *Journal of Personality and Social Psychology*, 50.2 (2008), 314–21 (p. 318)).

50. Amy Coplan, 'Understanding Empathy: Its Features and Effects', in *Empathy: Philosophical and Psychological Perspectives*, ed. by Amy Coplan and Peter Goldie (Oxford: Oxford University Press, 2011), pp. 3–18 (p. 3).

51. Steven Pinker, *The Better Angels of Our Nature: Why Violence has Declined* (New York: Viking, 2011), p. 576.

52. Coplan, 'Understanding Empathy', p. 4.

53. Frédérique de Vignemont and Tania Singer, 'The Empathic Brain: How, When and Why?', *Trends in Cognitive Science*, 10.10 (2006), 435–41 (p. 435).

54. Coplan, 'Understanding Empathy', p. 5.

55. Coplan, 'Will the Real Empathy Please Stand Up?', p. 56.

56. Ibid., p. 58.

57. Ibid., p. 55.

58. Christian Miller, 'Defining Empathy: Thoughts on Coplan's Approach', *The Southern Journal of Philosophy*, 49 (2011), 66–72 (p. 71).

59. Yasmin Gunaratnam, 'Interview with Clare Hemmings: Why Do Stories Matter?', podcast, <http://www.case-stories.org/clare-hemmingsnew-page/> [accessed 7 March 2019].
60. Clare Hemmings, 'Affective Solidarity: Feminist Reflexivity and Political Transformation', *Feminist Theory*, 13.2 (2012), 147–61 (p. 152).
61. Boler, 'The Risks of Empathy', p. 255.
62. Pedwell, 'Affect at the Margins', p. 19.
63. Paul Bloom, 'Empathy and its Discontents', *Trends in Cognitive Sciences*, 21.1 (2017), 24–31 (p. 25).
64. Anne Whitehead, 'Writing with Care: Kazuo Ishiguro's *Never Let Me Go*', *Contemporary Literature*, 52.1 (Spring 2011), 54–83 (p. 57).
65. Breda Gray, 'Empathy, Emotion and Feminist Solidarities', in *Sexed Sentiments: Interdisciplinary Perspectives on Gender and Emotion*, ed. by Willemijn Ruberg and Kristine Steenbergh (Amsterdam: Rodopi, 2011), pp. 207–32 (p. 208).
66. Pedwell, 'Affect at the Margins', p. 25.
67. Lauren Berlant, 'Introduction: Compassion (and Withholding)', in *Compassion: The Culture and Politics of an Emotion* (New York & London: Routledge, 2004), pp. 1–13 (pp. 10–11).
68. Kaja Silverman, *The Threshold of the Visible World* (London: Routledge, 1996), p. 26.
69. Ibid.
70. Ibid., pp. 26, 57.
71. Audrey Jaffe, *Scenes of Sympathy: Identity and Representation in Victorian Fiction* (Ithaca, NY: Cornell University Press, 2000), p. 7.
72. Judith Butler, *Precarious Life: The Powers of Mourning and Violence* (New York: Verso, 2004), p. 20.
73. Ann Cvetkovich, *An Archive of Feelings: Trauma, Sexuality, and Lesbian Public Cultures* (Durham, NC: Duke University Press, 2003), p. 278.
74. Judith Butler, *Frames of War: When is Life Grievable?* ((London: Verso, 2009), p. 1.
75. As Susannah Radstone writes, 'Trauma theory has no greater claim to ethical purity than any other critical practice' ('Trauma Studies: Contexts, Politics, Ethics', *Paragraph*, 30.1 (2007), 9–29 (p. 25)); John Mowitt, meanwhile, argues that the so-called 'ethical turn' in academia (which tends to subscribe to a belief in the universality of pain) evidenced in trauma studies masks a shift away from socio-political criticism (because it assumes that we can all understand other people's pain) ('Trauma Envy', *Trauma and its Cultural Aftereffects*, special issue of *Cultural Critique*, 46 (Autumn, 2000), 272–97).
76. Butler, *Frames of War*, p. 10.
77. Suzanne Keen, *Empathy and the Novel* (Oxford: Oxford University Press, 2007); David Comer Kidd and Emanuele Castano, 'Reading Literary Fiction Improves Theory of Mind', *Science*, 342.6156 (18 October 2013), 377–80.
78. See Miranda McKearney and Sarah Mears, 'Lost for Words? How Reading Can Teach Children Empathy', *Guardian*, 13 May 2015; Kate Parker, 'How Reading Can Boost Empathy', *Times Educational Supplement*, 12 June 2018, <https://www.tes.com/news/how-reading-can-boost-empathy> [accessed 7 March 2019].
79. Keen, 'A Theory of Narrative Empathy', p. 213.
80. Ibid., p. 215.
81. P. Matthijs Bal and Martijn Veltkamp, 'How Does Fiction Reading Influence Empathy? An Experimental Investigation on the Role of Emotional Transportation', *PLos One*, 8.1 (January 2013), 1–11 (pp. 10–11).
82. Kidd and Castano, 'Reading Literary Fiction Improves Theory of Mind', p. 378.
83. Ibid., p. 380.
84. Interestingly, Keen includes readers' comments on their experiences of reading in *Empathy and the Novel* but does not define her approach as empirical (p. 65).
85. Keen, 'A Theory of Narrative Empathy', p. 221.
86. Berlant, 'Introduction: Compassion (and Withholding)', p. 5.
87. Lauren Berlant, 'Poor Eliza', *American Literature*, 70.3 (1998), 635–68 (p. 641).
88. Kathleen Woodward, 'Calculating Compassion', in *Compassion*, ed. by Lauren Berlant (New York & London: Routledge, 2004), pp. 59–86 (p. 71).

89. Modlinger and Sonntag 'Introduction: Other People's Pain', p. 4.
90. Felman and Laub, *Testimony*, p. 59.
91. Radstone, 'Trauma Studies', p. 22.
92. Modlinger and Sonntag, 'Introduction: Other People's Pain', p. 30.
93. Boler, 'The Risks of Empathy', pp. 261, 266.
94. Hemmings, 'Affective Solidarity', p. 153.
95. Boler, 'The Risks of Empathy', p. 258.
96. Gunaratnam, 'Interview with Clare Hemmings'.
97. Hemmings, 'Affective Solidarity', p. 153.
98. Ahmed, *The Cultural Politics of Emotion*, p. 162.
99. Dominick LaCapra, *Writing History, Writing Trauma* (Baltimore, MD: Johns Hopkins University Press, 2000), p. 78.
100. Woodward, 'Calculating Compassion', p. 61.
101. Jill Bennett, *Empathic Vision: Affect, Trauma and Contemporary Art* (Stanford, CA: Stanford University Press, 2005), p. 10.
102. Gill Rye and Michael Worton, 'Introduction', in *Women's Writing in Contemporary France: New Writers, New Literatures in the 1990s*, ed. by Gill Rye and Michael Worton (Manchester: Manchester University Press, 2003), pp. 1–26 (p. 16).
103. Lucille Cairns, 'Bodily Dis-ease in Contemporary French Women's Writing: Two Case Studies', *French Studies*, 69.4 (2015), 494–508 (p. 494).
104. Andrea Lobb, 'The Agony and the Empathy: The Ambivalence of Empathy in Feminist Psychology', *Feminism & Psychology*, 23.4 (2013), 426–41 (p. 429).
105. Simon Baron-Cohen, *The Essential Difference: Male and Female Brains and the Truth About Autism* (New York: Basic Books, 2003), pp. 28, 61.
106. Hemmings, 'Affective Solidarity', p. 153.
107. Lobb, 'The Agony and the Empathy', p. 433.
108. Ibid., p. 435.
109. Hélène Cixous, *Vivre l'orange/To Live the Orange* (Paris: Des femmes, 1979), pp. 27, 26.
110. Abigail Bray, *Hélène Cixous: Writing and Sexual Difference* (London: Palgrave Macmillan, 2004), p. 122.
111. Rosemary Arrojo, 'Interpretation as Possessive Love: Hélène Cixous, Clarice Lispector, and the Ambivalence of Fidelity', in *Postcolonial Translation: Theory and Practice*, ed. by Susan Bassnett and Harish Trivedi (London: Routledge, 1999), pp. 141–61 (p. 155).
112. Verena Andermatt Conley, *Hélène Cixous: Writing the Feminine* (Lincoln & London: University of Nebraska Press, 1984), p. 101.
113. I draw this term from Emma Wilson, *Sexuality and the Reading Encounter: Identity and Desire in Proust, Duras, Tournier, and Cixous* (Oxford: Clarendon Press, 1996).
114. Christine Angot, *Quitter la ville* (Paris: Stock, 2000), pp. 161–62.
115. Shirley Jordan, 'Reconfiguring the Public and the Private: Intimacy, Exposure and Vulnerability in Christine Angot's *Rendez-vous*', *French Cultural Studies*, 18.2 (2007), 201–18 (p. 214).
116. Ibid., p. 213.
117. Christine Angot, *Un amour impossible* (Paris: Flammarion, 2015), p. 156.
118. Ibid., p. 212.
119. Ibid., p. 203.
120. Ibid., p. 212.
121. Christine Angot, in *Libération*, 29 June 1999, cited in Ruth Cruickshank, *Fin de millénaire French Fiction: The Aesthetics of Crisis* (Oxford: Oxford University Press, 2009), p. 208.
122. Boler, 'The Risks of Empathy', p. 258.
123. Cruickshank, *Fin de millénaire French Fiction*, p. 199.

❖

CHAPTER 1

The Subject of Anorexia: Reading Beyond the Performance of Suffering

Self-starvation is above all a performance. Like Hamlet's mouse-trap, it is staged to trick the conscience of its viewers, forcing them to recognize that they are implicated in the spectacle that they behold [...]. Even though the anorectic body seems to represent a radical negation of the other, it still depends upon the other as spectator in order to be read as representative of anything at all. Thus its emaciation, which seems to indicate a violent rebuff, also bespeaks a strange adventure in seduction.[1]

If anorexia nervosa is often described as a 'spectacle', a performance intended to be seen, critical readings of narratives of eating disorders focus more on the performative acts themselves than on the ways in which they imbricate their spectator.[2] Frank Senninger notes that 'l'anorexie est une vengeance, une rebellion qui se retourne contre soi' [anorexia is a revenge, a rebellion that turns back against the self] as 'plutôt que d'exprimer contre l'autre sa colère' [instead of expressing anger towards the other], the anorexic turns the aggression into a battle 'contre la nourriture' [against food]; the refusal of food thus constitutes both a refusal and a displacement of the other.[3] The implication here is that the anorexic performance both ensnares (in Isabelle Meuret's words, 'you cannot really starve without obliging the other to intervene') and simultaneously negates its viewer, so that its 'seductive' (to borrow Maud Ellmann's term) spectacle is necessarily underwritten by violence.[4] This is compounded as the performance also positions the anorexic subject as 'other' (even abject) and object of the viewer's gaze, as this chapter will show. There are several issues to be explored further here, not least the depiction of anorexia as a displaced performance of conflict or of suffering, articulated through the body rather than in language, which recalls Sigmund Freud's accounts of hysterics enacting unspoken pain through bodily symptoms or acts. In other words, the anorexic performance depends precisely on its spectator's attempts to look beyond the body to imagine psychological trauma or anxiety. Yet the metaphor of Hamlet's mouse-trap may also be taken further in relation to the performance of anorexia. The play-within-a-play commissioned by Hamlet presents a possible enactment of his father's death, intended to trap his uncle Claudius, positioned as spectator, into revealing (through his emotional response to watching the play) that he murdered his brother. Hamlet's test depends upon Claudius being unable to conceal his guilt as a spectator watching a representation of his own violence. Claudius is therefore drawn into the play that he initially believed himself to be watching; more, he is being judged on his reaction to the performance. Is Ellmann implying that the anorexic performance is also somehow scripted to facilitate a particular response from its (unknowing) spectator? Are the spectator's responses effectively pre-scripted (or at least aimed at eliciting particular responses), or do the performances make space for alternative interpretations?

These questions are particularly apt in relation to narratives of anorexia, which reframe the anorexic performance in writing, typically through recounting it in the first person and in the past tense from a self-confessed position of 'recovery'. The performance of anorexia is mediated through writing and, most often, is narrated as an experience in the past; the reader does not directly witness the anorexic performance or see the underweight body. Yet narratives of eating disorders may also be read as performing anorexia in and through writing. Meuret divides texts that recount eating disorders into three categories. In the first category, which she labels 'renunciation/disincarnation', the narrator/protagonist is 'still in the throes of anorexia' and the narrative itself is typically 'opaque, schizophrenic, fragmented', featuring 'an abundant use of different pronouns and impersonal sentences', and consequently 'impenetrable and confusing for the reader'. Texts that belong to the second category, that she names 'enunciation/incarnation', 'gather testimonies written by women mostly in their recovery process' and 'typically use the pronoun "I", a sign that they have regained their subjectivities': these texts are more intelligible and feature a more coherent narrative subject. Finally the third category of texts, labelled 'denunciation/reincarnation', invoke 'a certain distance' from anorexia and 'resort to third person pronouns, as if to keep the pathology at bay'.[5] Most of the narratives of anorexia selected by Meuret belong to this third category, possibly due to the difficulties inherent in trying to recount anorexia without some (psychological and narrative) distance; as Meuret observes elsewhere, this distance is crucial to being able to identify anorexic thought and behaviour patterns.[6] The distinctions between Meuret's three categories are, however, difficult to sustain: to take the example of Geneviève Brisac's *Petite*, for instance, the narrative voice shifts perpetually between the first and third person, disrupting the narrative subject portrayed, and could therefore arguably belong to more than one of the categories established by Meuret.[7] Rather than attempt to classify narratives of anorexia within this schema, this chapter explores the various ways in which texts recounting eating disorders seek to engage with the reader. In Meuret's schema, only the first category of texts poses difficulties of interpretation, which implies that the majority of narratives of anorexia are legible and coherent, but this does not, of course, mean that they are transparent reflections of lived experience. This chapter explores French narratives of anorexia as alternative performances that should be considered in terms of their engagement with a projected spectator, in this case the reader.

The mousetrap analogy above is particularly relevant, yet while Ellmann's model involves the spectator (reader) being ensnared and thereby disempowered, I chart the dynamics within the reading encounter somewhat differently. The reader is not necessarily trapped within power structures set up by the narrative, but can occupy a different position, through a voyeuristic gaze upon the anorexic body, for example, or an envious gaze (the underweight body is not only source of horror, but also envy, as the anorexic exhibits a socially-desired willpower to refuse food). This chapter explores the ways in which narratives recounting eating disorders — autobiographical, autofictional, and fictional — seek not only to construct a coherent subject of suffering whose pain is validated by an external agent (the reader), but also to interrogate the position of the reader as spectator. That is, as this chapter will show, these narratives of eating disorders foreclose the possibility of empathy and shift textual engagement with the subject of anorexia in order to privilege a mode of reading that goes beyond the notions of performance and spectatorship outlined above.

Eating Disorders and the Language of the Body

Eating disorders, including anorexia nervosa, bulimia nervosa, and binge-eating disorder, are commonplace in France: approximately 2,500 new cases are diagnosed annually, whilst anorexia mainly affects adolescents (5 to 13 per cent of teenagers are affected by it, compared to 1 per cent of the total population); around 95 per cent of known cases in France are female.[8] Lucille Cairns observes a 'relatively slow appearance of anorexia on the scene of French women's writing', as most of the texts featuring anorexia in French have been published since 1990 and even more strikingly in the twenty-first century, whereas anglophone narratives of anorexia began to proliferate in the 1980s; this mirrors 'what appears to be a lower incidence of anorexia among young females (the demographic most affected) in France compared to global incidences'.[9] Despite the slightly lower statistics on anorexia in France in comparison with other European countries, the recurrence of anorexia and to a lesser extent other eating disorders such as bulimia or binge-eating disorder within contemporary French women's writing highlights that eating disorders are far from uncommon in France. The prevalence of various forms of eating disorders, particularly amongst women, is reflected in the recurrence of anorexia as a theme in contemporary French women's writing: as Amaleena Damlé notes, 'the anorexic, a ghostly figure characterized by a conflict between presence and absence, has in particular haunted the texts of women writing in French in recent years'.[10] Some examples include Brisac's *Petite*, Nancy Huston's *Dolce agonia* [Sweet Agony] and *Lignes de faille* [Fault-lines], Corinne Solliec's *Le Petit Corps* [The Little Body], Amélie Nothomb's *Robert des noms propres* [The Book of Proper Names], and Delphine de Vigan's *Jours sans faim* [Days Without Hunger] (first published under the pseudonym Lou Delvig), as well as a plethora of memoirs and testimonies mainly written by women and mostly recounting anorexia nervosa experienced (and recovered from) during adolescence.[11] Here one might include Marta Aleksandra Balinska's *Retour à la vie: quinze ans d'anorexie* [Return to Life: Fifteen Years of Anorexia], Emilie Durand's *Ma folie ordinaire: allers et retours à l'hôpital Sainte-Anne* [My Ordinary Madness: Return Trips to the St Anne Hospital], Mathilde

Monaque's *Trouble-tête: journal intime d'une depression* [Muddled Mind: Intimate Diary of a Depression], Justine and Marie-Thérèse Cuny's *Ce matin j'ai décidé d'arrêter de manger* [This Morning I Decided to Stop Eating], and Alice Bairoch's *Voyage en anorexie* [Journey into Anorexia], as well as Janine Teisson's *L'Enfant plume* [The Feather Child] (also autobiographical, but written from a mother's perspective on her daughter's anorexia); this list is by no means exhaustive.[12] In the majority of these texts, anorexia is narrated in the past tense from the perspective of recovery, which in turn is implicitly associated with reintegration into dominant social and linguistic structures. In Damlé's words:

> Literary texts that deal with anorexia, whether testimonial or fictional, tend to read (or to be read) as fairly straightforward recovery narratives, insofar as they might not only relate a transition from a pathological body to a 'healthy' one, but also rescue the subject from the maladies of her depleted corporeal existence and reinsert her into language. Writing about anorexia, then, becomes the verbalisation of a trauma that has thus far been corporeally communicated and the body is now reconciled and restituted into words.[13]

Narratives recounting eating disorders typically fit into (or are understood in terms of) wider cultural assumptions about the relation between the 'pathological body' (the anorexic body, which articulates a suffering that cannot be verbally expressed) and the 'healthy body'. The latter is restored through narrative integration both of the anorexia itself and its projected causes and origins, so that anorexia can be understood as part of a coherent life story. In other words, anorexia is implicitly related to hysteria while the anorexic performance (both the rejection of food and the display of the underweight body) tends to be read as an intrinsically hysterical spectacle, staged by the 'pathological' body and both pointing to and covering up a trauma that resists articulation.

Following Freud's work on hysteria, 'the association between anorexia nervosa and hysteria developed as the dominant means of explaining food refusal in women' (in the words of Julie Hepworth), as manifested in the writing of Ernest Charles Lasègue and William Withey Gull.[14] The association between hysteria and anorexia has lingered in recent accounts of anorexia: Elisabeth Young-Bruehl argues, for instance, that 'anorexia is [...] a form of hysteria [...] a means of avoiding sexuality or transferring sexual fantasies into other modes'.[15] Hannah Decker observes: 'Hysteria is no longer a common occurrence in the late twentieth-century urban West. But in its place there is a largely female disease whose manifestations correspond to a new feminine ideal: the illness of anorexia nervosa'. The consequence of this is that 'one hundred years apart, hysteria and anorexia — two emotional illnesses expressed physically — represent futile and self-damaging exercises in power by women who feel powerless'.[16] In both cases, the assumption that a straightforward causal link may be traced between 'emotional illness' (be it individual suffering or conflict with others) and bodily performance (in the case of anorexia, the refusal to eat in a socially sanctioned manner and the insistence on maintaining body mass index below a medically defined accepted level) is problematic. The causes of anorexia are surprisingly difficult to pin down in a context in which interpretations of eating disorders have proliferated and diverged: Abigail Bray, for instance, suggests that 'eating disorders are constituted by an "epidemic of signification"' generating multiplying discourses and explanations.[17] To conceive of anorexia as a form of hysteria is to imply that the refusal to eat both marks and points to an intelligible psychological suffering that can ultimately be detected and articulated as the anorexic subject recovers, in other words, that the performance of anorexia can be 'read' coherently. The French narratives discussed in this chapter, however, typically reject singular or straightforward explanations for eating disorders, as well as, for the most part, avoiding representing the anorexic body (or bodily spectacle) as legible either for the anorexic subject or for the reader. Part of the issue here is to avoid spectacularizing the (culturally over-exposed) anorexic body more than it has been already and thus to prevent the power dynamics charted in Ellmann's mousetrap analogy above, within which the reader may be both entrapped and empowered in different ways. This chapter unpicks the ways in which modern French texts renegotiate the relation between the subject of suffering and the reader beyond paradigms of performance and spectatorship (as suggested in the opening quotation). This allows us to rethink the position of the reader in relation to narratives of eating disorders and to the suffering anorexic subject (and body) in particular. I begin with memoirs, before moving on to fictional and autofictional texts, which enable us to rethink the questions at stake here more productively.

The Reader and the Abject Anorexic Body in Memoirs

Whilst most memoirs avoid over-emphasizing the anorexic body, they typically refer to it as repulsive and almost inhuman, a spectre of death. In *Trouble-tête*, Monaque — recounting her adolescent experience of depression and anorexia — likens her image in the hospital bathroom mirror to 'un fantôme' [a ghost], a 'squelette vivant' [a living skeleton], embodiment 'de vie autant que de mort' [of life as much as of death] (*Trouble-tête*, pp. 30–31), which repels others: 'Entre mes pensées d'outre-tombe et mon apparence de squelette, je fais peur aux gens qui me voient. Ils m'évitent, soit par un sourire gêné, soit par un regard traumatisé' [Between my thoughts from beyond the grave and my skeletal appearance, I scare the people who see me. They avoid me, either with an embarrassed smile, or with a traumatized look] (p. 49). In *Ma folie ordinaire*, which traces repeated episodes of anorexia, binge-eating, self-harm, and suicide attempts, Durand recalls someone looking at her hand during her period of hospitalization for anorexia and exclaiming, 'Ta main! Ta main, on dirait celle qu'un squelette!' [Your hand. Your hand, it looks like a skeleton's hand!] (p. 31), whilst in *Ce matin j'ai décidé d'arrêter de manger*, Justine's mother describes her as a 'squelette ambulant' [walking skeleton] (p. 63), and Bairoch in *Voyage en anorexie* describes herself as 'l'espèce de fantôme qui se reflète dans le miroir' [the kind of ghost reflected in the mirror] (p. 97). The recurring images of skeletons highlight the wider cultural insistence on representing the anorexic body as abject and liminal, between life and death, terrifying yet fascinating.[18] Debra Ferreday suggests that the fantasized anorexic 'walking skeleton' of the contemporary Western imagination is 'at once utterly Other, abject, and yet utterly desirable' in its invocation of an over-invested idealization of whiteness and thinness that simultaneously inspires repulsion and — because the slender (and white) body represents a cultural ideal for women — envy.[19] In the context of narratives of anorexia, then, the positioning of the reader in relation to the imagined anorexic body is potentially contradictory, caught between disgust, adulation, envy, and incomprehension. This is exemplified in Isabelle Caro's memoir, *La Petite Fille qui ne voulait pas grossir*, which is strikingly unusual as an anorexia memoir in its inclusion of a sequence of photographs of Caro's extremely underweight body during her period of anorexia.

La Petite Fille qui ne voulait pas grossir hit the headlines mostly thanks to Caro's celebrity as the nude figure of the photographer Oliviero Toscani's much-publicized 'Nolita' campaign in 2006 to show up the damaging effects of anorexia (and of the fashion industry's body requirements). The 'Nolita' publicity was controversial, not least because the images of Caro's naked body inspired envy and emulation, as evidenced by the admissions on pro-ana forums of a desire to look like Caro, as well as revulsion.[20] Referring to the naked shots of Caro, Susie Orbach insists that 'we are not yet inured to the horror they portray. We can still see them', implicitly distinguishing between the 'we' who are horrified by the photographs of Caro and the anorexic viewers who are inspired by them.[21] In other words, 'we', like Orbach, assume that we can see the distinction between conventional fashion images of thin bodies (that 'we' might admire/desire to emulate) and the photographs of Caro featured in the Nolita campaign (showing a body that has in Orbach's view clearly surpassed an imagined shared socially acceptable limit of thinness). Yet as Ferreday observes, the anorexic body in the Nolita campaign is insufficient in itself as evidence of the destructive effects of anorexia; it is framed by the slogan 'No Anorexia', as indeed by awareness of Toscani's previous controversial image of a dying victim of AIDS, so that the image of Caro's emaciated body is inevitably culturally overlaid by images of illness and death.[22] In other words, we are only 'not inured' to the horror of the image thanks to the way in which the image is mediated; the image is in itself insufficient and 'we' cannot necessarily see as clearly as Orbach implies. Similarly, *La Petite Fille qui ne voulait pas grossir* features a photograph of Caro weighing 25 kg (at which point she was hospitalized in a semi-coma due to abnormally low potassium levels), glossed by the statement that 'Cette image est très dure, je le sais' [This image is very difficult, I know], acknowledging how difficult it is both for Caro herself and the reader to look at this self-described 'squelette' [skeleton], yet the caption simultaneously implicitly underscores the need for words to frame and give context to the image.[23] In the first three paragraphs of the memoir's prologue, Caro comments on the naked Nolita photograph that is posited as point of origin for her memoir as though the body in question belonged to somebody else ('La femme semble vivante mais on imagine aisément quelle morte elle fera' [The woman seems alive but you can easily imagine her dead, p. 11), as well as reiterating disgust at her 'corps cadavérique' [corpse-like body] with its 'peau [...] distendue et flasque' [distended and flabby skin] (p. 12). She both highlights the horror of her own underweight body and distances herself from it, whilst inviting the reader to occupy a shared perspective (of repulsion). Ferreday asks:

> How is it possible to speak of the anorexic as subject when s/he is doubly silenced: first by being positioned as the object of a gaze (and a gaze, at that, which is oriented to the act of turning away) and, second, through a mental health discourse that positions her words as the mere ramblings of hysteria?[24]

In Caro's text, the anorexic constructs herself as subject in writing precisely through conceiving of her anorexic self as somehow 'other' (and aligning herself with the reader), as she recounts her years of anorexia as though describing someone else's experience and body.

The separation between Caro and the 'petite fille' whom she describes as another person (*La Petite Fille*, p. 11) is, however, less stable than it initially seems. She admits that she is at the time of writing torn between the urge to eat to stay alive and the desire to starve herself to avoid gaining weight (p. 275), still trapped in seemingly absurd rituals that govern her eating habits, and still — even in the photographs of Caro included at the time of writing, which feature her smiling and bearing slogans that assert her lust for life — visibly fitting the profile of what Ferreday calls 'the really skinny one'.[25] As well as her memoir, Caro wrote a blog, entitled *L'Anorexie ou la faim de vivre: faire le pas vers la guérison* [Anorexia or the Hunger for Life: Taking the Step Towards Recovery], and appeared on television in the United Kingdom in the programme *Supersize vs Superskinny* as well as in various documentaries on French and Italian television channels to denounce the celebration of skeletal bodies in fashion. Within this context, however, Caro's own voice was subdued, as she could speak only in the guise of 'almost the embodiment of ana' to insist on the frailty of her body and blame her eating disorder on the requirements of an over-exacting fashion industry.[26] Her words in interviews were effectively pre-scripted for her but what mattered above all was the repeated projection of her emaciated body as figure of abjection and repulsion.[27] To describe her experience of anorexia, then, Caro needs to construct her past anorexic body as 'other', to reiterate her revulsion towards it through constructing a shared position with the reader contemplating images of her anorexic body. The emphasis in this text on that body (and the foregrounding of its appearance through the photographs), however, highlights the extent to which Caro could never quite distance herself sufficiently from 'la petite fille qui ne voulait pas grossir' upon whose identity her celebrity was anchored.[28]

Caro's memoir explicitly aims to construct a different way of looking at the anorexic subject: 'Avec cet ouvrage, je ne compte pas apporter de solution [...] mais j'espère que mon récit contribuera à changer le regard porté sur l'anorexie' [With this book, I don't expect to provide a solution [...] but I hope that my story will contribute to changing the way anorexia is regarded] (p. 274). Yet the emphasis on changing 'le regard' is problematic not least because her text continues to rely upon visual models that root anorexia in the (underweight) body, seen from outside. For the reader, the tension lies precisely in the invitation to contemplate the subject of anorexia differently, countered by the difficulty in 'seeing' Caro other than as the emaciated body that is relentlessly represented. The text makes an appeal to the reader to engage differently with the subject of anorexia, yet it forecloses the possibilities of mobilizing engagement through the photographs that limit the subject to images of the body and thereby engender repulsion and fascination, repeating the mechanisms the underpin the conflictual engagement between performance and spectator in the model from Ellmann with which this chapter began.

One way in which texts can, to borrow Caro's phrase, 'changer le regard porté sur l'anorexie', is by moving away from such tropes of looking in relation to over-exposed images of skeletal bodies that reduce the anorexic subject to abject 'other' and force — or enable — the reader to occupy the position of voyeur (be it envious, repulsed, empowered, or weakened). If we move from Caro's memoir to other French autobiographical narratives of anorexia, it is clear that most insistently shift emphasis away from the body to highlight the limits of vision. As Monaque states, the anorexic subject (as opposed to her over-exposed body) is never really visible as such: 'Je n'avais pas de consistence, ma présence n'apportait rien: ils ne me voyaient pas' [I had no consistency, my presence provided nothing: they didn't see me] (*Trouble-tête*, p. 162). This is echoed by Durand, who describes her body as she recovers from a period of being severely underweight due to anorexia/bulimia as 'un corps visible, c'est-a-dire un corps que l'on regarde normalement, un corps existentiel, une présence' [a visible body, that is a body that people look at normally, an existential body, a presence] (*Ma folie*, p. 41), which suggests that the anorexic body is not visible, or deemed to be present. Yet these texts do not track subjects seeking presence and visibility (and by extension identity) through gaining weight: part of the pathology underpinning the rejection of food seems to be a desire to be invisible. Monaque writes that that during her self-starvation, 'pour les gens de l'extérieur, ceux pour qui je me privais, je disparaissais lentement' [for people outside, people I was depriving myself for, I was disappearing slowly] (*Trouble-tête*, p. 105). She perceives herself as 'un poids pour eux' [a weight on them] that she must alleviate, ideally through losing her body altogether (pp. 52–53). She projects her anxiety about burdening others onto her body; losing weight becomes paradoxically both a means of attracting others (p. 105) and of escaping from their 'regard' (p. 54). Ellmann's reference to 'seduction' is reformulated here as the desire to be seen, yet also to be invisible; underlying this is an implicit recognition of anorexia as a performance that both foregrounds and seeks to hide the body in which it is enacted. Where Caro's memoir effectively prevents the reader from engaging with anorexia beyond looking at the anorexic body, other narratives of anorexia seek to invite the reader to engage with the subject of suffering by highlighting the extent to which the seemingly highly visible and legible markers of anorexia (as figured in the fantasized anorexic body) mask invisible and inaudible subjects seeking and yet also evading presence in the eyes of others. Gaining weight, here, means both becoming an existential presence and yet also losing an identity rooted in the desire to be absent and unseen. Meuret's schema of disincarnation/renunciation, followed by incarnation/enunciation, is complicated as recovery is bound up in visibility, rather than with the reconstruction of (corporeal) identity. For the reader, then, this raises questions as to how we can 'look at' the subject of anorexia as represented in writing without simplistically seeking to 'see through' the (narrative representation of the) anorexic body to the subject whose suffering it performs. One way forward is to take seriously the claim elucidated in the memoirs analyzed here that the anorexic subject is somehow invisible and inaudible, and to explore it further; to do so, I now turn to Marie Darrieussecq's short story, 'Encore là' [Still There].

Disincarnation and Invisibility: 'Encore là'?

The relation between anorexia, disincarnation, and invisibility is taken further in Darrieussecq's fictional 'Encore là', which opens the multi-authored volume *Naissances*, a collection of short stories by contemporary women writers in French about childbirth and motherhood more generally.[29] This story, a first-person narrative from the perspective of a woman who missed her daughter's birth (due to being anaesthetized for an emergency C-section) and subsequently developed post-natal depression and anorexia, is somewhat surprising (even tangential) in a collection explicitly devoted to birth narratives.[30] Whilst the representation of anorexia here appears superficial (the narrator is at least initially more concerned about fitting into her pre-pregnancy jeans than about taking care of her children), this story traces precisely the 'renunciation' and 'disincarnation' that Meuret attributes to the first category of texts about eating disorders. The narrator gives up life as well as food (becoming too weak to move out of bed, replaced as maternal figure by the hired nanny) and her body shrinks to the point of disappearing altogether: by the end of the story, her children and nanny cannot see her. From the opening line ('lorsque j'ai accouché, on m'a endormie [when I gave birth, they put me to sleep], 'Encore là', p. 11), wherein her agency is removed from her ('*on* m'a endormie'), the story traces her dissolution as subject, as she struggles to recognize her daughter, to make contact with others (her telephone stops working; she is too weak to do the school run), and eventually speaks without being seen or heard ('Personne ne m'entendait. Je parlais, pourtant' [Nobody could hear me. I was speaking, however], p. 29). The disintegration of the narrative subject is figured through the disjointed, incoherent narrative, as well as through the narrator's inability to grasp what is happening around her (it is not even clear whether her telephone problems are technical or imagined) highlighted by the recurring references to the unceasing rain that smears her windows and restricts her view.

If the renunciation and disincarnation traced in 'Encore là' initially appear to be gradual processes that culminate in the dissolution of the subject at the end of the story, in fact the narrative begins with her loss of subjectivity (missing her daughter's birth) and ends when the subject is not disintegrated (or at least not more so than at the beginning), but invisible and inaudible. The narrator is still speaking at the end of the story, which closes with her insistence that 'je continuais à parler' [I continued to speak] ('Encore là', p. 29); the point is that nobody else can see or hear her as the reader, like her family, struggles to understand her thought processes. Part of the problem is that she keeps interrupting herself with seemingly irrelevant narrative detours, one example of which stems from her husband's job as a railway engineer who works at night, replacing worn-out Eurostar tracks.

The narrator notes that the trains can run smoothly every day only through the unseen work to undo and then reconstruct the tracks every night, which points to a vulnerability underpinning the rail connection between France and England. This is compounded by her references to the bodies of fleeing migrants, found crushed in the tunnel (p. 22); these damaged bodies, unseen by train travellers but uncovered by the engineers, mark the violent underside of the seemingly smooth connection between the two countries. The narrator's limited awareness of the socio-political conditions that might lead migrants to risk their lives trying to get through the tunnel may be seen to mirror her lack of understanding of her self-starvation, which she repeatedly links to the desire to be thin. The reader can identify other triggers, such as her loneliness (her husband works long hours and suffers from insomnia; no friends are mentioned; the telephone seems to be broken), the trauma of the emergency C-section, and missing her daughter's birth, and so on. This story invites us to consider that the narrative here is the equivalent of the record of trains crossing the tunnel; what we cannot see are the damaged subjects that lie beneath the trains or indeed behind the story of childbirth and anorexia. The reader's vision, like that of the narrator, is limited, so that when the narrator asserts that she is 'encore là', the reader is called upon to recognize that while we never really see or hear her (in a sense she is missing from her own story as from her daughter's birth, even if she is the narrator of it), nonetheless she is present and still trying to make herself understood. The point is not to try to look through the story to see the bodies that lie underneath (which would mean assuming that we can see them independently of the discourses that construct them), nor to try to explain or render intelligible the suffering that they denote, but to register the limits of our own vision faced with the revelation of suffering bodies.

The question of how to hear and respond to the inaudible first-person plea from the anorexic subject remains open — or impossible to answer — in this story, because the reader, like the narrator's family, can never read or understand the words that the (by now invisible) narrator is speaking from her bed at the end of her story. Thus the relation between the reader and the subject of anorexia here is ultimately one of detachment, not seduction or entrapment as suggested in the opening quotation from Ellmann; indeed, any engagement with the subject of anorexia here is limited. Part of the reason that this text fails to engage the reader with the subject of anorexia lies in the narrator's own entrapment within her condition (she stops leaving the house and later her bed and cannot communicate). The possibility of renegotiating the relation between text and reader depends precisely on the possibility of articulating the experience of anorexia from beyond the phase of self-starvation, which is in turn bound up in the process of recovery, impossible within the critical phase of illness in which Darrieussecq's narrator remains caught. Yet the reader's alienation from the text is also related to the narrator's perpetual narrative detours, which make it difficult to establish even what the main subject of the story is meant to be. Disincarnation, here, is bound up not so much in the disintegration of the body as in the failure or inability to communicate, or, at least, these are inextricably connected in this text. The reader, made aware that the narrator is trying to articulate words that cannot be understood, registers both the appeal, and his or her own inability to engage further.

'Encore là' goes beyond Caro's memoir in highlighting the limits of the reader's vision, understanding, and engagement; it shows the complex structures underpinning the relation between anorexia, (loss of) identity, and recognition as a subject — or a presence, to borrow Durand's term, which is particularly apt here — in society. Reading this text compels the reader to acknowledge his or her own complicity with the disintegration of the anorexic subject, whose inability to speak is bound up in and possibly generated by other people's inability to hear. There is no quick-fix solution, because the narrator's words are difficult to follow, confused, disorientating; the point is not to render them intelligible, but to understand that part of the narrator's struggle to express herself is caused by the inability of others to listen. Furthermore, her suffering cannot be conceived of in discrete terms as belonging entirely to the individual subject, because its prolongation (and potential alleviation) are caught up in relations with others, including the reader. My analysis of Darrieussecq's short text thus raises the question of how as readers we can approach the subject of anorexia without silencing the anorexic subject whose identity is described as under erasure, a question I address through analysis of an extended autofictional account of anorexia and recovery, Vigan's *Jours sans faim*.

Jours sans faim: Anorexic Identity Under Erasure

Vigan's *Jours sans faim*, which was first published in 2001 under the pseudonym of Lou Delvig, narrates a teenage girl's experience of life-threatening anorexia and her treatment in hospital. This text, labelled 'roman' [novel] on its cover, both finds its origins in and fictionalizes Vigan's own experience as an adolescent hospitalized with an eating disorder.[31] Vigan writes that: 'Quinze ans après, on ne raconte pas son passé, on le réinvente [...]. Si j'avais juste voulu témoigner, je n'aurais pas utilisé la troisième personne. Je l'aurais écrit sur un mode compassionnel, piège que je voulais absolument éviter' [Fifteen years later, one doesn't recount one's past, one reinvents it [...]. If I had just wanted to testify, I wouldn't have used the third person. I would have written it in a compassionate style, a trap that I totally wanted to avoid].[32] The compassion 'trap' evoked here resonates with Darrieussecq's notion of the 'certificat doloriste' that, if invoked, implicitly defines and confines both the text and its reception. Vigan's implication here that the third person narrative circumvents a compassion or empathy trap that a first-person narrative (particularly one that constitutes a form of testimony) might be unable to avoid needs further consideration, not least because it is not clear whether it is the writer, or the reader, who is potentially ensnared by the trap. In any case this is complicated here as the original version of *Jours sans faim* published under the pseudonym Lou Delvig in 2001 is written mainly in the third person but shifts in the short final chapter to use the first person to give the perspective of the protagonist, Laure, some years later, now a mother, recounting playing games with her children. When *Jours sans faim* was re-released in 2009, by a different publishing house and under Vigan's real name, however, this closing chapter written in the first person was not included. In email correspondence with me, Vigan explained that she omitted the final chapter because it seemed to work to fix the text into the form of a testimony:

> Lors de l'édition première de *Jours sans faim* je m'étais interrogée sur la nécessité de cette dernière page qui sortait le roman de la fiction ou de l'exercice littéraire. A l'époque, mon éditeur, qui pensait que le roman se vendrait mieux s'il se donnait à lire comme un témoignage, m'avait encouragée à la laisser. Quelques années plus tard, lorsqu'un autre éditeur m'a proposé de publier *Jours sans faim* en poche et sous mon vrai nom, j'ai relu le texte pour le corriger.
> Cette dernière page m'a semblé inutile. Et maladroite. J'ai pensé que le livre n'avait pas besoin de ça pour exister. Il m'a semblé que sa dimension autobiographique était évidente mais que pour autant j'avais le droit de revendiquer une part de fiction, et un travail littéraire sur la forme. Et que cette dernière page venait un peu contredire le reste de la démarche.[33]

> [When the first edition of *Jours sans faim* came out I questioned myself on the need for this final page which took the novel away from fiction or literary exercise. At the time, my publisher, who thought that the novel would sell better if it read like a testimony, had encouraged me to leave it in. Several years later, when another publisher offered to publish a paperback edition of *Jours sans faim* under my real name, I reread the text to correct it.
> This final page seemed to me to be useless. And clumsy. I thought that the book didn't need it to exist. I felt that the autobiographical dimension was evident but that I still had the right to claim a part to be fiction, and a literary work on form. And that this last page contradicted to some extent the rest of the approach.]

The last chapter of *Jours sans faim* therefore initially appears to constitute a compromise between Vigan's wish not to write a testimony and the publisher's counter-insistence on the text as a form of testimony. Yet the abrupt shift from Laure's release from hospital at the end of the penultimate chapter to her current position as a mother (showing her to be fertile and capable of reproduction, which anorexia would typically impede) offers no indication that the adult Laure is looking back to her period of anorexia. Nathalie Morello notes that in this chapter:

> Thematic oppositions contribute to emphasising distance: amenorrhea against fertility; hospital bed against home bed; silence against laughter; devastating inability to speak against rejoicing in inarticulacy as she shouts 'gââââââââ' with her children; the pain previously wasted on desperately attempting to control the environment against the joy of taking pleasure in chaotic play.[34]

This extremely brief final chapter, with its change of narrative voice, contrasts rather than connects Laure's current life with her previous period as an anorexic. This means that the reader in turn is not able to identify with Laure, looking back on past suffering, and instead registers the disconnection between the adolescent leaving hospital and the mother playing with her children, which in turn disrupts the 'compassion trap' and destabilizes the relation between reader and text. This is reinforced by the structure of the text as a whole, constructed around disconnected vignettes detailing episodes of Laure's recuperation, rather than through a coherent linear narrative beginning with the onset of anorexia and culminating in recovery. The reader is further disorientated by the inclusion of multiple voices, mostly of fellow hospital patients or nurses, whose comments Laure records without always clarifying who is speaking, and which read like streams-of-consciousness, not fully integrated into a narrative context. *Jours sans faim*, rather than offering the reader identification and empathy with its anorexic protagonist, instead traces the dissolution of borders between self and other, inside and outside, in order to set up an alternative model of reading that cannot fix and gaze upon the anorexic subject.

In this text, Laure's anorexic performance is self-confessedly primarily aimed at her parents ('Elle voulait leur faire mal, les blesser dans leur chair' [She wanted to hurt them, to wound them in their flesh], *Jours*, p. 21).[35] Her mother has made suicide attempts (p. 98), is depressively silent, and negligent (offering frozen fruit in place of meals (p. 71), drinking to excess and wetting herself, p. 76), whilst her father, who has gained custody of the children, verbally abuses his daughters, hurling at them 'des mots comme des ordures. Des mots périmés, avariés, qu'on ne digère pas' [words like rubbish. Expired, rotting words, that can't be digested] (p. 46), force-feeding them red meat that makes Laure nauseous, leaving her feeling assaulted by indigestible food and words. Their ambivalence to her anorexia ('elle y laissera sa peau sans qu'ils accusent réception' [she will leave them her skin without them acknowledging receipt], p. 21) both motivates and nullifies her anorexia as expression of pain. Shortly before Laure's hospitalization, her mother tells her she should go into hospital or she will die, 'comme elle aurait dit alors tant-pis passe-moi le sel' [as she would have said, oh well pass me the salt] (p. 77), with apparent total indifference and detachment. When Laure tries to explain her feelings of isolation and alienation, her mother retorts that Laure — who is loved by her family — has no right to such feelings, as she has not gone through what she herself experienced when she was sectioned and lost her job, home, and custody of her children. The mother insists that 'tu n'as pas le droit de parler comme ça Laure' [you don't have the right to talk like that Laure], a response Laure describes as hurting her 'comme une énorme gifle' [like a huge slap] (p. 110–11). Her mother is clearly ill (presumably with bipolar disorder, as recounted in Vigan's later text, *Rien ne s'oppose à la nuit*) and incapable of articulating emotion (and perhaps of feeling empathy at all), whilst her father brings her typical junk food snacks to eat in hospital as though completely oblivious to her eating disorder. Laure's rejection of food therefore self-consciously constitutes an appeal to her parents that is met with anger or indifference.

By contrast, Laure's emaciated figure appalls everyone else who sees it, either inciting judgement (if they see her weight as a vanity project) or pity (if they imagine that she is seriously ill with cancer, for example): 'A voix haute les insultes, à voix basse la compassion' [In a loud voice, insults; in a low voice, compassion] (*Jours*, p. 43). Both insults and compassion work as forms of self-distancing: other passengers stand up and move away, for example, when she boards a metro train ('on s'écartait pour la laisser s'asseoir' [people moved away to let her sit down], p. 43), implicitly distancing themselves from her either out of kindness (because she looks too fragile to stand) or out of fear of her alien appearance (p. 9). Outside her familial relationships, then, Laure's anorexic spectacle is successful in attracting attention, but only to alienate its spectator, who cannot see beyond the emaciated figure: as in the case of Caro, the anorexic subject is 'seen' only through the dangerously underweight body. Here however, this is shown to be a performance of alienation within which the subject constructs an identity rooted in self-erasure ('Elle ne voulait pas mourir, juste disparaître. S'effacer. Se dissoudre' [She didn't want to die, just to disappear. Fade away. Dissolve], p. 44) rather than in the (over-) visibility of the anorexic body. She does not perform to be seen, as such, even by her parents (whom she seeks to wound), and the narrative shifts away from visual paradigms as it does not dwell on her appearance or her weight, focusing instead on her bodily responses to self-starvation (her perpetual feeling of cold; the pain when sitting due to lack of flesh on her buttocks, for instance) and the simultaneous construction of the anorexic subject and dissolution of her embodied identity.

In refusing to eat, Laure acknowledges, 'elle a vidé ce corps de sa vie' [she has emptied her life out of this body] (*Jours*, p. 16) as a way to 'détruire son corps pour ne plus rien percevoir du dehors' [destroy her body in order to sense nothing from outside] (p. 20); anorexia works to reinforce — and indeed to set up — boundaries that separate inside from outside ('le jeûne comme [...] une forteresse' [fasting as a fortress]), rendering her 'plus forte, inaccessible' [stronger, inaccessible] (p. 93), creating the illusion that she can control her own bodily and psychic borders. Anorexia seems, at least initially, to allow her to construct and police herself as individual, bounded subject. Laure admits that 'elle s'accroche à cette maladie comme à la seule façon d'exister' [she clings to this illness as if it is the only way to exist] (p. 116), that is, she defines herself in and through the self-destruction of anorexia. The implication here is that the threat to her is from without, so that by refusing to eat or to assimilate her father's abuse, for instance, she can both protect herself and construct an identity rooted in the refusal of food. Anorexia is described as having originated from outside her ('C'était quelque chose en dehors d'elle qu'elle ne savait pas nommer' [It was something outside herself that she could not name]) while later, it is stated that 'le froid est entré en elle' [the cold entered into her] (p. 9) and she consents to medical treatment only when she realizes that 'le froid était parvenu jusqu'au bout des membres' [the cold had reached the tips of her limbs] (p. 13), that is, once the defensive boundaries set up by refusing food have been shown to give way to the cold. At the same time, however, her self-starvation creates a 'trou noir [...] dans le ventre [...] qui l'aspire de l'intérieur' [black hole [...] in the stomach [...] that sucks her up from inside] (p. 20) so that she is eroded from within as well as without, 'bouffée de l'intérieur à force de ne rien bouffer' [stuffed from inside through not eating anything] (p. 15). In other words, anorexia both originates in, and itself creates, an artificial division between inside and outside (of the body and subject) that ultimately cannot be sustained but upon which Laure as anorexic subject pins identity.

Laure's self-representation as anorexic to some extent fits Darrieussecq's formulation ('je souffre donc je suis... et certainement pas un(e) autre' [I suffer therefore I am... and certainly not another]) yet here the construction of the self is also contingent on the dissolution of the self. The second part of Darrieussecq's phrasing here ('et pas un(e) autre') is also crucial, because it implies a (possibly unwitting) self-distancing from the other: in Laure's case, anorexia allows her distance from her parents (both through the rejection of family mealtimes and later, literally, through her hospitalization — and, strikingly, her sister Louise wishes she could be in hospital rather than with her parents, *Jours*, p. 76); but also from the self her parents have forced her to be (the model pupil, daughter, and older sister who can succeed despite her background, p. 78). If anorexia may be understood as rigid over-compliance with social and familial (gendered) expectations (the ultimate expression of self-control), it allows Laure both to enact the model identity forced upon her and to evade it through self-erasure (i.e. through disappearing from her own projected role). In other words, part of the expression of suffering of anorexia is a distancing both from others and from the (fantasized) self: it is not — as we might assume particularly following the habitual analogy between anorexia and hysteria — a straightforwardly legible (or even a difficult to read) performance of an originary trauma or pain. Laure's attempt to both perform and evade her own projected identity thus suggests an alternative wording of Darrieussecq's statement: 'Je souffre donc je ne suis pas...' [I suffer therefore I am not] or perhaps more accurately, 'Je souffre donc je suis (pas) (une autre)' [I suffer therefore I am (not) (another)]. The implication here is that anorexia should not (exclusively) be read as the enactment or performance of suffering, but as an attempt at self-definition that is rooted in self-erasure and alienation. The reader is not invited to interpret *Jours sans faim* as charting a linear narrative of suffering, illness, and recovery, nor is anorexia depicted as simply a symptom of Laure's difficult childhood and adolescence but is part of her attempt to construct (and evade) identity, setting up the subject in and through its own dissolution. This in turn avoids the 'compassion trap', notably because the anorexic subject constructed under erasure cannot be fixed as object of compassion or empathy, but also because the relation between self and other here is both evoked and called into question. This complex re-inscription of the relation between anorexia, narrative, and identity is taken further in Nothomb's *Biographie de la faim*, to which I now turn.[36]

Biographie de la faim: Writing Inside-Out

Nothomb's adolescent anorexia is well-documented[37] and the theme of anorexia recurs through her work in, for example, the novel *Robert des noms propres*, which I discuss elsewhere, as well as in *Biographie de la faim*.[38] The latter text, like most of Nothomb's work, is self-consciously loosely related to episodes in her own life, but resists the label of autobiography, not least because this is a 'biography' (i.e. a written life-story) of 'hunger', rather than of a human subject (although Nothomb also self-confessedly recounts episodes from her own life). The text opens with a description of a population living in a climate with abundant vegetation who have never known hunger, because their appetites have always been sated. This example of a lack of hunger seems a curious point of departure in a story of hunger, until we register that this is the point, that is that hunger necessarily finds its origins in lack. Hunger is not here exclusively connected to food (Nothomb asserts that it means 'ce manque effroyable de l'être entier, ce vide tenaillant' [this appalling lack of the whole being, this gnawing emptiness]) but is a form of desire (*Biographie*, p. 20) that extends beyond the biological imperative to eat and manifests itself through repeated quests for more (food, love, possessions, and so on) that ultimately cannot be satisfied. As a child, Nothomb claims, she was constantly (excessively) hungry for sugar, but the extra food that she was offered (mainly protein) simply exacerbated her hunger. Following her mother, Nothomb defines her hunger as a 'bonne maladie' [good illness] (p. 25), evoking Freud's model of hysterical bodily symptoms performing unspoken anxiety:

> Plus tard, j'appris l'étymologie du mot 'maladie'. C'était 'mal à dire'. *Le malade était celui qui avait du mal à dire quelque chose. Son corps le disait à sa place sous la forme d'une maladie. Idée fascinante qui supposait que si l'on réussissait à dire, on ne souffrirait plus.*
> Si la faim était une bonne maladie, quelle était la bonne chose à dire qui m'en guérirait?' (*Biographie de la faim*, p. 26)

> [Later I learnt the etymology of the word 'malady'. It was 'hard to say'. *The invalid was the one who found it hard to say something. His/her body said it instead in the form of an illness. Fascinating idea which implied that if you succeeded in saying it, you wouldn't suffer any longer.*
> If hunger was a good illness, what was the good thing to say that would cure me of it?]

By implication here, hunger stands in for 'something' that resists articulation, hence the presumed possibility of a 'talking cure' that could put the suffering into words and alleviate it. This model is predictably deployed in discourses on anorexia that attribute eating disorders to prior experiences that have not been fully assimilated; it is evoked in *Jours sans faim* as Laure is described as literally unable to digest her father's verbal abuse (*Jours*, p. 67). There are hints of this in *Biographie de la faim*, too, in Nothomb's self-confessed disgust at her developing body emerging at the age of thirteen (*Biographie*, p. 162), which may be linked back to her account of having been sexually assaulted by a group of young men in the sea on holiday (pp. 151–52). Furthermore, in *Biographie* Nothomb's recovery from anorexia is associated with her beginning to write (suggesting a form of narrative recovery) as writing replaces self-starvation. *Biographie* also, however, subverts the model according to which eating disorders (as well as alcoholism and potomania, both of which the narrator recounts having experienced) may be understood as manifestations of earlier trauma or psychological struggles which can be resolved through narrative articulation. In this text, the origins of disordered eating are located not in tangible earlier experiences, but in hunger itself, as we shall see.

Nothomb's insatiable hunger (particularly for sugar) is charted as part of her identity ('La faim, c'est moi' [Hunger, it's me], *Biographie*, p. 19). Here hunger is not a reflection or symptom of an emotion that resists articulation, nor can it be explained by recourse to previous experiences, as it begins from her earliest years (p. 21); instead, hunger is described as part of herself (or synonymous with herself).

Her later anorexia is associated not only with her fear of bodily maturity, but also with her attempt to erase hunger: 'la faim fut lente à mourir' [hunger was slow to die]; 'la faim disparut' [hunger disappeared] (p. 166). It is not that there is 'quelque chose' that she cannot say (or that could be said) that prompts her self-starvation, but that she wishes to overcome her own desire (need) to eat. The title of this book implies that hunger has its own life story (with origins and endings), yet the very notion of a tangible origin — even one that resists articulation — is refused by the structure of *Biographie*, which begins with another culture's lack of hunger, moving on to illustrate her individual and insatiable hunger (which also originates in lack, albeit very differently) and then her attempts to resolve it (which include anorexia).[39] If the point of departure of this text is hunger, this marks not a clear origin, but an origin of lack, or perhaps a lack of origin; hunger also does not have a biography as such, unless this too may be understood to be structured around both lack and displacement. The effect of this is to prevent the reader from interpreting *Biographie de la faim* as a veiled autobiography of Nothomb herself. Although she states that 'je ne suis pas extérieure au sujet qui m'occupe' [I am not outside the subject that occupies me] (p. 19), this insistence that she is not 'outside' her subject does not mean that she is somehow 'inside it' (as though the narrative of hunger contains or reveals her identity, that is, as though she can recount herself through describing hunger). The shift in focus from Nothomb herself to hunger works to highlight the extent to which eating (or not-eating) cannot merely be understood as a legible performative response to particular experiences, feelings, or socio-cultural contexts, nor can the reader presume to be able to decode Nothomb's narrative (which seems somewhat inside-out) to decipher its origins.

Nothomb describes how, after her period of anorexia, she took up writing, resolving not to allow anyone else to read her work, prompting her sister Juliette's retort that 'Je ne suis pas quelqu'un d'autre' [I am not someone else]. Juliette interprets Nothomb's adolescent story featuring a giant, apocalyptic egg as 'autobiographique' [autobiographical] (*Biographie*, p. 180): this extraordinary interpretation not only reminds us that all writing (however unlikely) may inevitably be read as autobiographical, but also that autobiographical writing does not necessarily follow the typical expected structure of a life story recounted retrospectively in the first person and that the relation between writing and life is in any case difficult to pin down. The account of Juliette's reading of the egg story is also crucial in other ways, firstly because the egg in question exploded. Geneviève de Clerck writes that 'l'autographie nothombienne, par l'image [...] de l'oeuf et de l'omelette, revendique le vide comme nécessaire à l'écriture du Moi' [Nothombian writing, through the image of the egg and the omelette, claims the void as necessary to the writing of the Self], so that 'c'est par un anéantissement subjectif que peut se réaliser la construction de soi, par et dans l'écriture' [it is through a subjective destruction that the construction of the self can be realized, in and through writing]. The (shattered) egg becomes a figure for Nothomb's self-annihilation and the omelette that it produces is a motif for her self-reconstruction through writing.[40] Whilst this echoes Nothomb's description of her coming to writing after anorexia (wherein her body had been 'décomposé' [decomposed] and the attempt to write 'constitua une sorte de tissu qui devint mon corps' [constituted a sort of fabric that became my body], p. 179), the assumed correlation between Nothomb and the egg oversimplifies the positioning of the subject in the text by positing an origin (in the form of the egg) that can then be shattered and reconstituted. In *Biographie*, by contrast, the subject (hunger) is intangible and without origins, linked to the egg through the trope of metamorphosis (the egg turns into an omelette, but one 'qui évoluerait dans le vide cosmique jusqu'à la fin du temps' [which would evolve in the cosmic void until the end of time], p. 181) rather than through a linear trajectory of destruction and reconstruction. *Biographie de la faim* does not construct an identity rooted in lack; instead, it charts a subject in metamorphosis, whose identity is mediated not through what she chooses to eat (or to not eat) but through her hunger. Juliette's reading also crucially depends upon her self-positioning as not 'someone else', erasing the difference between Amélie the writer and Juliette the reader (which mirrors the repeated doubling of the two sisters throughout *Biographie*: the writing of this text is also contingent to this doubling of identity). The reader inscribed within the text is one who explicitly refuses the position of 'quelqu'un d'autre' [someone else], which echoes and subverts Darrieussecq's formulation that 'je souffre donc je suis... et certainement pas un(e) autre'. Here, it is the reader who states 'je ne suis pas une autre', as a precondition of assuming the position of ideal reader; it is also the reader — not the writer — who first labels the story of the egg as autobiographical.

This is not, of course, to argue that the reader of *Biographie de la faim* is placed in an analogous position to Juliette, that is, as Nothomb's twin or double, allowing for no difference (or distance) between authorial subject, text, and reader. The point here is that the dynamic outlined by Darrieussecq as underpinning the first-person narrative of suffering should be understood primarily in relational terms. This does not mean that the reader can both consolidate the constructed identity and by extension shore up his or her own (as a subject with compassion) through a mutual conferral of identity in relation to the narrative of suffering. Instead, *Biographie de la faim* works not to create or to consolidate identity through proximity, but to disrupt it through the repeated evocation of a lack of origins and endings. The final words in this text are spoken not by Nothomb herself, but by her childhood nanny, Nishio-san, during a telephone call after she has lost her house and all her money (kept in her house, rather than in a bank account) after an earthquake. Nishio-san rejects Nothomb's suggestion that she should open a bank account ('Qu'est-ce que ça fait? Je suis en vie' [What's the point of that? I am alive] (p. 190), privileging her survival over money. *Biographie de la faim* begins with the description of a population without hunger (sharply contrasted with Nothomb as the embodiment of hunger) and ends with her nanny (again, embodying radically different priorities from Nothomb). This shows the extent to which this text, if it may be seen as autobiographical, roots its autobiography in displacement and difference, which, in turn, leaves the reader disorientated and distanced (rather than either a passive spectator or registering empathy).

Conclusion: Beyond Spectacle

This chapter began, following Ellmann, by describing anorexia as a performance that both ensnares and rebuffs its spectator; the discussion of Caro's memoir, in particular, highlights the extent to which narrative representations of eating disorders also risk reproducing a visual dynamic within which the reader only 'sees' the anorexic body, which renders the anorexic subject invisible and inaudible. My reading of Darrieussecq's short story 'Encore là' emphasizes the need for alternative models of engagement with the subject of anorexia: part of this involves a renegotiation of the relation between self and other (beyond the paradigm of spectacle and spectator) in terms of representations of eating disorders. *Jours sans faim*, meanwhile, avoids inviting compassion or empathy by foregrounding anorexia not as an expression of suffering, but as a performance of identity in dissolution. It is striking that the final phone call recounted in Nothomb's *Biographie de la faim* follows the trauma of an earthquake in Japan, during which Nothomb's childhood nanny lost her home and all of her possessions. This text ends not with Nothomb's own suffering, but with that of someone else, whilst the conversation transcribed between Nothomb and Nishio-san focuses on money, rather than feelings. Whilst Nothomb's concern is evident in her repeated attempts to speak to her old nanny on the telephone, the emphasis here is less on her compassion for Nishio-san than on the cultural gulf separating them. Thus this text ends with the distance and difference between self and other, even as it highlights their interdependence (through the deployment of the voice of the other as the last word in the text). The choice to end the text with this final exchange shows that if Nothomb cannot root identity in her own suffering, nor can she construct an identity through compassion for (or even in relation to) that of someone else.

To return to Darrieussecq's mocking formulation, 'Je souffre donc je suis', in these texts suffering is not an origin or basis, let alone one from which identity can be clearly constructed; furthermore, the reader is not called upon to authenticate the 'certificat doloriste' through acknowledging the suffering recounted, because that suffering is surprisingly difficult to locate and pin down. These narratives of anorexia do not invite, or demand, empathy from their reader, nor do they allow the reader to establish identity in and through the connection with the subject of anorexia in the text. Instead, they disrupt the relation between the reader and the subject of anorexia by shifting their focus from emotions and the body to the relation between self and other, to show that narrative and identity cannot find origins or authentication in the assumption (or performance) of suffering. In this way, then, the relation between reader and the subject of anorexia is complicated, shifting away from the paradigms of performance and spectatorship evoked by Ellmann at the beginning of this chapter and opening up a more dynamic and troubled relation between the reader and the narrative of someone else's pain, which I will explore further in the context of narratives of the loss of a child in Chapter 2.

Notes to Chapter 1

1. Maud Ellmann, *The Hunger Artists: Starving, Writing and Imprisonment* (Cambridge, MA: Harvard University Press, 1993), p. 17.
2. See Carole Spitzack, 'The Spectacle of Anorexia Nervosa', *Text and Performance Quarterly* 13.1 (1993), 1–20, and Megan Warin, *Abject Relations: Everyday Worlds of Anorexia,* Cambridge Studies in Medical Anthropology (New Brunswick, NJ: Rutgers University Press, 2010), p. 9.
3. Franck Senninger, *L'Anorexie: le miroir intérieur brisé* (Paris: Jouvence, 2004), pp. 20, 23.
4. Isabelle Meuret, 'Writing Size Zero: Figuring Anorexia in Contemporary World Literatures', in *Social Studies of Health, Illness and Disease: Perspectives from the Social Sciences and Humanities,* ed. by Peter Twohig and Vera Kalitzkus (Amsterdam: Rodopi, 2008), pp. 75–93 (p. 76).
5. Meuret, 'Writing Size Zero', p. 82.
6. Isabelle Meuret, *Writing Size Zero: Figuring Anorexia in Contemporary World Literatures* (Brussels: European Interuniversity Press, 2007), pp. 187–88.
7. Isabelle Caro's *La Petite Fille qui ne voulait pas grossir* does not fit into any of Meuret's categories. Whilst it includes elements of 'enunciation' and 'denunciation' (elucidating critiques of the fashion industry as well as of Caro's family upbringing), these are never fully articulated without recourse to images of the anorexic body, whilst the distance set up between narrator and anorexic 'petite fille' also fails, as I will show in my discussion of this text later in this chapter.
8. Senninger, *L'Anorexie*, p. 8.
9. Cairns, 'Bodily Dis-ease in Contemporary French Women's Writing', p. 495.
10. Amaleena Damlé, 'The Becoming of Anorexia and Text in Amélie Nothomb's *Robert des noms propres* and Delphine de Vigan's *Jours sans faim*', in *Women's Writing in Twenty-first Century France: Life as Literature,* ed. by Amaleena Damlé and Gill Rye (Cardiff: University of Wales Press, 2013), pp. 113–26 (p. 113).
11. Nancy Huston, *Dolce agonia* (Arles: Actes Sud, 2002) and *Lignes de faille* (Arles: Actes Sud, 2012); Corinne Solliec, *Le Petit Corps* (Paris: Gallimard, 2006); Amélie Nothomb, *Robert des noms propres* (Paris: Albin Michel, 2002); Lou Delvig, *Jours sans faim* (Paris: Grasset, 2001). As Damlé notes, 'The prevalence of anorexia as a literary theme is of course a stark reflection of reality, as anorexia has become the (gendered) turn-of-the-millennium epidemic to rival nineteenth-century hysteria' ('The Becoming of Anorexia and Text', p. 114). It is perhaps unsurprising, given that eating disorders are disproportionately common amongst teenagers, that anorexia is a key theme in fiction aimed at adolescents, see for instance Marie Bertin and Roselyne Bertin, *Journal sans faim* (Paris: Rageot, 2004).
12. Marta Aleksandra Balinska's *Retour à la vie: quinze ans d'anorexie* (Paris: Odile Jacob, 2003); Emilie Durand, *Ma folie ordinaire: Allers et retours à l'hôpital Sainte-Anne* (Paris: Les Empêcheurs de penser en rond, 2006); Mathilde Monaque, *Trouble-tête: journal intime d'une dépression* (Paris: les Arènes, 2006); Justine and Marie-Thérèse Cuny, *Ce matin j'ai décidé d'arrêter de manger* (Paris: Oh!, 2007); Alice Bairoch, *Voyage en anorexie* (Paris: Presses du Belvédère, 2007); Janine Teisson, *l'Enfant Plume* (Paris: NiL, 1997). See Cairns, 'Bodily Dis-ease in Contemporary French Women's Writing' for a more extensive list of contemporary French women writers whose texts touch on anorexia or related eating disorders.
13. Damlé, 'The Becoming of Anorexia and Text', pp. 152–53.
14. Julie Hepworth, *The Social Construction of Anorexia Nervosa* (London: Sage, 1999), p. 38; Ernest Charles Lasègue, 'De l'anorexie hystérique', *Archives générales de médecine,* 21 (April 1873), 385–403; William Withey Gull, 'Anorexia Nervosa (Apepsia Hysterica, Anorexia Hysterica)', *Transactions of the Clinical Society of the London,* 7 (1874), 22–28. It should be pointed out that Gull also interrogated the assumed connection between anorexia and hysteria (see Joan Jacobs Brumberg, *Fasting Girls: The History of Anorexia Nervosa* (Cambridge, MA: Harvard University Press, 1988), p. 149), and that anorexia has certainly not been analyzed exclusively in relation to models of hysteria, even within psychoanalytic theorizations.
15. Elisabeth Young-Bruehl, *Subject to Biography: Psychoanalysis, Feminism, and Writing Women's Lives* (Cambridge, MA: Harvard University Press, 1998), p. 210.
16. Hannah Decker, *Freud, Dora and Vienna 1900* (New York: Free Press, 1991), pp. 207, 208.

17. Abigail Bray, 'The Anorexic Woman: Reading Disorders', *Cultural Studies*, 10.3 (October 1996), 413–29 (p. 413).

18. See Kathryn Robson, 'Voicing Abjection: Narratives of Anorexia in Contemporary French Women's (Life-)Writing', *L'Esprit créateur*, 56.2 (Summer 2016), 108–20.

19. Debra Ferreday, 'Haunted Bodies', *Borderlands e-Journal* 10.2 (2011), 1–21 (p. 19), <http://www.borderlands.net.au/vol10no2_2011/ferreday_bodies.pdf> [accessed 24 February 2019]. Ferreday's article offers an intelligent and convincing account of the cultural connections between anorexia and abjection.

20. Caro insisted that the campaign spoke for itself but, according to Mark Anspach, 'Alas, the message was not clear at all [...] A "pro-ana" site ran her photo with the caption "Die young, stay pretty"' ('Why Did Isabelle Caro Die?', 24 March 2011, <https://journaldumauss.net/spip.php?page=imprimer&id_article=790> [accessed 7 March 2019]).

21. Susie Orbach, 'Size Matters', *Guardian*, 27 September 2007, cited in Ferreday, 'Haunted Bodies', p. 10.

22. See Ferreday, 'Haunted Bodies', p. 3.

23. Isabelle Caro, *La Petite Fille qui ne voulait pas grossir* (Paris: Poche, 2010), p. 11.

24. Debra Ferreday, 'Anorexia and Abjection: A Review Essay', *Body and Society*, 18.2 (2012), 139–55 (p. 142).

25. Ferreday, 'Haunted Bodies', p. 12.

26. Ibid., p. 11.

27. Caro herself, in an interview with Jessica Simpson for the latter's MTV series, *The Price of Beauty*, insisted explicitly that the fashion industry was not responsible for her eating disorder, but this statement was edited out of the subtitles, to allow the programme to maintain the anti-fashion message of the original campaign, regardless of Caro's own perspective. See Ferreday, 'Haunted Bodies', p. 14.

28. Her death at the age of twenty-eight in 2010 — due to respiratory problems related to long-term anorexia — is perhaps unsurprising given that she never clearly 'recovered' fully (even if full recovery is itself not necessarily possible).

29. Marie Darrieussecq, 'Encore là', in *Naissances: récits*, ed. by Isabelle Lortholary (Paris: Iconoclaste, 2005), pp. 11–29.

30. Colette Trout reads this story as 'une métaphore de la disparition [...] de la femme lorsqu'elle devient mère' [a metaphor for the disappearance of the woman when she becomes a mother] (*Marie Darrieussecq: ou voir le monde à neuf* (Leiden: Brill, 2016), p. 104), the mother diminishing as the daughter gains weight through her mother's milk.

31. In Vigan's later novel, *Rien ne s'oppose à la nuit* [Nothing Holds Back the Night], the narrator writes that '*Jours sans faim* est un roman en partie autobiographique' but 'aucun des personnages secondaires n'a vraiment existé, le roman comporte une part de fiction' (Delphine de Vigan, *Rien ne s'oppose à la nuit* (Paris: J. C. Lattès, 2011), p. 331).

32. Cited in Lucille Cairns, 'Dissidences charnelles: The Female Body in Revolt', in *The Flesh in the Text*, ed. by James Baldwin, James Fowler, and Shane Weller (Oxford: Peter Lang, 2007), pp. 205–25 (p. 206).

33. Delphine de Vigan, email to Kathryn Robson, 25 December 2016.

34. Nathalie Morello, 'Anorexia, Anger, Agency: Investigating Quests for Self in Three Contemporary Narratives in French', in *Starvation, Food Obsession and Identity*, ed. by Petra M. Bagley, Francesca Calamita and Kathryn Robson (Oxford: Peter Lang, 2017), pp. 121–41 (p. 130).

35. All page references for *Jours sans faim* refer to Delphine de Vigan, *Jours sans faim* (Paris: J'ai lu, 2009).

36. Amélie Nothomb, *Biographie de la faim* (Paris: Poche, 2006), first published by Albin Michel in 2004.

37. Amélie Nothomb: 'A l'âge de 13 ans, j'ai commencé une anorexie. Je n'ai pas avalé un seul aliment pendant deux ans' [Aged 13, I became anorexic. I didn't eat a single nutrient for two years] ('Amélie Nothomb: la stupéfiante', interview with Valerie Trierweiler in *Paris Match*, 12 August, 2012), <http://www.parismatch.com/Culture/Livres/Amelie-Nothomb-La-stupefiante-157133> [accessed 7 March 2019].

38. *Kathryn Robson, 'Reading the Anorexic Body: Eating Disorders in Contemporary French Women's Fiction', : Eating Disorders in Contemporary Women's Writing*, ed. by Petra M. Bagley, Francesca Calamita, and Kathryn Robson (Oxford: Peter Lang, 2017), pp. 257–76.

39. Erika Fülöp points out that for Nothomb, 'Far from being a lack or a negative tension, hunger — the desire to write — is a positive energy associated with jouissance' ('Amélie's Horse: Writing as Jouissance in Nothomb', in *Cherchez la femme: Women and Values in the Francophone World*, ed. by Erika Fülöp and Adrienne Angelo (Newcastle upon Tyne: Cambridge Scholars Publishing, 2011), pp. 209–24 (p. 219)). However, this positive energy still relates to, rather than replaces, lack, in *Biographie de la faim*.

40. Geneviève de Clerck, 'Le Dialogue hypermoderne d'Amélie Nothomb ou la poétique d'un sabotage heureux' (PhD thesis, University of Louisiana at Lafayette, 2006), p. 48.

CHAPTER 2

❖

You Don't Know How I Feel: Narrating the Death of a Child

Peu importe l'âge auquel meurt un enfant: si le passé est court, demain est sans limites. Nous portons le deuil le plus noir, celui du possible.

[The age at which a child dies is irrelevant: if the past is short, tomorrow is limitless. We carry the darkest grief, that of the possible.][1]

The loss of a child is deemed to be particularly difficult to verbalize and to understand: Celia Hindmarch insists that 'the death of a child is different from other bereavements',[2] whilst Emma Wilson describes it as 'a limit subject, a subject which reaches or exceeds the bounds of representation and normal, narrative resolution'.[3] This chapter explores how this seemingly unthinkable and unnarratable loss ('le deuil le plus noir', to borrow Camille Laurens's expression above) can be articulated and read, through analysis of contemporary French autobiographical texts written from the perspective of bereaved mothers. In these texts, the possibility of empathy is clearly rejected from the start: the texts highlight the impossibility of understanding or imagining how a bereaved parent might feel. Nonetheless, the question of how narratives of child death approach this 'limit subject' and position the reader remains urgent. I read these French texts alongside the trauma theorist and literary critic Cathy Caruth's 2013 monograph, *Literature in the Ashes of History*, which opens with the example of a mother whose teenage son was killed in Atlanta: that is, with a mother's response to the death of her child. My focus here is on reading as an 'encounter' — taking Caruth's word — and more precisely on how an encounter with a text that recounts the death of a child, in the first person, may be negotiated.

Numerous memoirs have been published by mothers following the death of their child(ren) in the last couple of decades in France, including Laurens's *Philippe*, Laure Adler's *À ce soir* [Until This Evening], Aline Schulman's *Paloma*, Anne-Marie Revol's *Nos étoiles ont filé* [Our Stars Have Gone], and Sophie Daull's *Camille, mon envolée* [Camille, My Fledgling], amongst others.[4] In Hélène Cixous's autofictional text *Le Jour où je n'étais pas là* [The Day I Wasn't There] the narrator (whose life-story mirrors Cixous's own) evokes the death of her young son, who died in Algeria while his mother was away working in France.[5] There have also been novels fictionalizing the death of a child: Laurence Tardieu's *Puisque rien ne dure* [Since Nothing Lasts], for instance, recounts both parents' perspectives on living after their child's unexplained disappearance, whilst Anne Godard's *L'Inconsolable* [The Inconsolable] depicts a mother's ambivalent grief following her teenage son's suicide, and Marie Darrieussecq's novel *Bref séjour chez les vivants* [A Brief Stay with the Living] narrates life after a boy's death by drowning from the points of view of various family members.[6] Darrieussecq later published the controversial novel *Tom est mort* [Tom is Dead], a fictional representation of maternal grief after her young son's accidental death which hit the headlines when Laurens accused Darrieussecq of plagiarizing her own memoir *Philippe* in *Tom est mort*. The subsequent fall-out, played out in the media (their shared publisher at P.O.L. publicly siding with Darrieussecq), raised the questions that I addressed in the Introduction about the ethics of writing fiction about traumatic experiences — particularly the loss of a child — in the first person.[7] I have explored debates around the ethics of writers imaginatively projecting themselves into the position of grieving parents in an article on 'psychic plagiarism' in *Philippe* and *Tom est mort* and in the Introduction to this book.[8] This chapter focuses instead on autobiographical texts, which, when recounting the death of a child tend to set up a division between 'us' and 'them', between those who have lived through it and those who have not (and therefore, the texts reiterate, cannot possibly understand). Whilst this may well be true of many experiences, not only traumatic ones, part of what is striking in Laurens's attack on Darrieussecq is her conviction that losing a child is somehow radically different from any other life experience and cannot be imagined, or compared, in any way.

In a study of contemporary French autobiographical accounts of the death of a child, including *Philippe,* Gill Rye writes:

> For the parents, the experience of losing a child is a 'limit experience', an irreparable loss. All too fearfully imaginable before its occurrence, such a loss nonetheless proves unimaginable even in the face of its stark and tragic reality. In the wider sociocultural sphere, the death of a child is so shocking — and, one might add, given its coverage in the popular media, so compelling — because it is felt to be a reversal of the natural order of things.[9]

The death of a child on the one hand represents an 'ultimate horror' as an imagined potential threat, yet on the other hand it paradoxically cannot be imagined; what is particularly difficult, perhaps, is imagining being a parent who has survived the death of a child.[10] This is highlighted in the actress Sophie Daull's 2015 text *Camille, mon envolée*, which may be read as taking the form of an extended letter to her daughter Camille, following her death, at the age of sixteen, from an infection:

> Tu sais, les gens sont terriblement gênés quand ils questionnent notre santé mentale. Ils ont des formules qui bégayent d'euphémismes maladroits. Ils disent: 'le drame', 'la tragédie', le 'grand malheur qui vous est arrivé' [...]. Alors, de la même manière que je leur ai demandé de prononcer ton nom de temps en temps, je leur dis de simplifier, d'appeler les choses par leur nom, de dire: 'La mort de Camille' [...]. Ce Grand Malheur s'appelle la Mort de Camille. Point barre. (*Camille*, p. 176)

[You know, people are terribly embarrassed when they question our mental health. They follow a formula of stammering awkward euphemisms. They say 'the drama', 'the tragedy', 'the great misfortune which happened to you' [...]. So, in the same way that I have asked them to pronounce your name from time to time, I tell them to simplify, to call things by their name, to say 'Camille's death' [...]. The Great Misfortune is called Camille's Death. Full stop.]

Whereas Laurens, in her memoir *Philippe*, describes other people's reactions to the death of her son as unthinking and cruel, as we shall see, Daull's (well-meaning) friends are depicted as struggling to know how to refer to Camille's death and even to acknowledge her by name. Daull's response is to ask them to name Camille and her death explicitly, in place of clumsy and dramatic euphemisms. If, as Paul Rosenblatt argues, 'there is little community empathy for bereaved parents', this is not necessarily because others are selfish or careless, but it may be because it is already widely assumed — amongst, and beyond, grieving parents — that understanding, and therefore empathy, are intrinsically impossible.[11] The point in Daull's text is that whilst others seek to show that they recognize how unthinkable Camille's death was by using language that emphasizes its horror, the words that they use to underscore the horror ultimately erase the reality of her life and death. The difficulty of empathy here is bound up in a linguistic dilemma: how to refer to the loss of a child without, on the one hand, recourse to dramatic imagery that intrinsically detracts from the reality of the loss and, on the other, the risk of minimizing its impact by banalizing it in everyday language that fails to acknowledge the incommensurate loss. The encounter between the bereaved parent and others is, then, rooted in the inadequacy of words, for both parties, to express the inexplicability and yet also the specificity of the loss.

It is worth pausing here over the word 'encounter', which I borrow from Caruth; while this word was also used frequently in her earliest writings on trauma, it is notably repeated twenty-one times in 'Parting Words: Trauma, Silence and Survival', the opening chapter of *Literature in the Ashes of History*.[12] The *OED* defines an 'encounter' (with an object or a person) as unexpected (and often difficult), the origins of the word suggest 'a meeting between adversaries' and this association of conflict resonates with the account of other people's responses to the death of Laurens's son Philippe, as I will argue later. Caruth uses the word 'encounter' repeatedly to refer to Freud's (literal) meetings with both his grandson (whom he observes playing the fort/da game), and the war veterans in 'Beyond the Pleasure Principle' (*Literature*, pp. 3–4, 15); to what she calls 'my encounter with a real child in Atlanta' (p. 5), and, most frequently, to the 'encounter with death' that in her theorization structures the experience of trauma (pp. 3, 5–7). The 'real child' in question, Greg, is a friend of a boy called Khalil who was murdered; Khalil's mother, Bernadette, set up a support group, entitled 'Kids Alive and Loved', to enable children who have witnessed violence to voice their feelings. Some of Bernadette's interviews with surviving children, including that with Greg, are recorded on video-tape for the Kids Alive and Loved Oral History Archive; the acronym (KAL) bears her son's initials and thereby commemorates him. In her response to an earlier version of Caruth's 'Parting Words', Peggy Phelan notes that 'the movement between the real child in Atlanta and the psychoanalytic child in Freud's text is a curious one for those of us who encounter both children (only?) in acts of reading'. This is not least because what Phelan refers to as 'the psychoanalytic child' is in fact Freud's own grandson, whilst Caruth does not apparently meet the 'real child', Greg, in person, but sees him only in the videotaped interview in the KAL Oral History Archive.[13] In other words, there is no direct, unmediated encounter between Caruth and either child, and Caruth's insistence on analyzing 'how Freud's text and the language of the real child shed light on each other' (*Literature*, p. 5) sets up a division that her own writing undermines by turning both Freud's grandson and the 'real child' Greg into characters encountered only within her own text. Phelan also suggests that 'the phrase "a real child in Atlanta" functions, perhaps, as a way for Caruth to register the reality of her own trauma, the pull toward death exerted by the death of her mother, to whom she dedicates her essay'; the 'real child' would, in this reading, be Caruth herself, following the loss of her mother.[14] In both Caruth's and Phelan's interpretations, then, there is slippage in the notion of the 'encounter' and of the 'real child': the possibility of identifying a 'real child' via layers of mediation (firstly through the videotaped interview and secondly through Caruth's theorization of it) is problematic. The 'real' here is encountered only through shifting levels of textual representation, even if Caruth does not herself acknowledge this. Moreover, in Phelan's reading of 'Parting Words', as, indeed in Shoshana Felman's response to an early (oral) version of this chapter, Caruth herself effectively shifts from reader (of Freud's text and of the archived interview) to bereaved child, or, possibly, occupies both positions simultaneously.[15] Caruth's text thus implicitly highlights the impossibility of sustaining a fixed position in relation to (or distance from) narratives of traumatic loss, or of an 'us/them' position, as her theorization of other people's trauma somehow repeatedly ends up re-inscribing her own personal loss through her various mediated encounters with other bereaved or suffering subjects.[16]

In the context of autobiographical writing recounting the death of a child, the key 'encounter' is clearly with the reader. In her study of recent French autobiographies of child death, Rye raises crucial questions about the positioning of the reader:

> Texts like these — dealing with tragic loss and overwhelming grief — are thus particularly challenging to the reader — for what is our place here? How or where are we situated in or by the text? Where can we place ourselves in relation to it? The critical reader of such texts faces a particular dilemma. To what extent is it unacceptably invasive to take a critical position on personal accounts of loss?[17]

The questions raised here chime with Darrieussecq's criticism in *Rapport de police* that I discussed in the Introduction, concerning the 'certificat doloriste' that impedes critical analysis by compelling the reader to confirm the identity of the suffering narrating subject. Rye's underlying assumption, however, that the reader can somehow assume a fixed position and perspective in relation to the text, requires further interrogation. As I showed in the Introduction, reading texts that recount suffering is potentially destabilizing; this is particularly true in the case of narratives dealing with the death of a child, precisely because it is repeatedly figured as incommensurable and unthinkable. The shifting (and frequently adversarial) encounter with the reader is part of the very structure of the texts discussed in this chapter (as in Caruth's text), as we shall see, and is caught up in the overlapping frames of fantasy through which the 'reality' of the loss of a child is negotiated without ever being properly assimilated.

Judith Butler's notion of the frames that render subjects 'grievable' or 'ungrievable', explored in the Introduction to this book, is played out slightly differently, and more literally, in the French autobiographical narratives of the death of a child analyzed in this chapter. These all implicitly call attention to their own framing — epigraphs, citations, intertext — as well as the ways in which their own narrative frames end up dependent upon frames of fantasy, as we shall see. I begin by looking at Laurens's *Encore et jamais* [Again and Never], which is not, ostensibly, about the death of her son Philippe; nonetheless, Philippe, and the memoir in which she recounted his life and death, are invoked in *Encore et jamais* through self-conscious use of repetition and citation. This leads me to explore the epigraphs and inscriptions that structure and frame the first-person narratives of the death of a child in three French autobiographical texts: Laurens's *Philippe*, Daull's *Camille mon envolée*, and the journalist Adler's *À ce soir*, written seventeen years after the death of Adler's young son Rémi. These texts associate inscription and framing with the notion of the trace, which is also integral to Caruth's readings of Wilhelm Jensen, Sigmund Freud, and Jacques Derrida in *Literature in the Ashes of History*. Caruth traces repeated figures of burning which are, in turn, associated with dream and with a reconfiguration of the relation between fantasy and so-called reality, and an interrogation of the limits of knowledge, not only of other people's suffering, but also, crucially, of one's own. Ultimately, then, the French texts I look at in this chapter, along with Caruth's *Literature in the Ashes of History*, reframe the encounter between text and reader, shifting it away from the standard paradigms of (failed) knowledge and empathy ('You cannot know how I feel...'). Instead, they highlight the extent to which this encounter is shaped by overlapping and sometimes competing fantasies through which a different relation, a shifting relation rooted in the unknown and in fantasy/dream, can be negotiated.

Inscribing the Death of a Child

In *Encore et jamais*, Laurens writes that 'j'ai eu un fils, je l'ai appelé Philippe. Après sa mort, j'ai écrit un livre, je l'ai appelé Philippe. Ce n'est pas la même chose, non' [I had a son, I called him Philippe. After his death, I wrote a book, I called it Philippe. It isn't the same thing, no] but nonetheless 'ce récit répète ou balbutie des syllabes qui ne sont pas étrangères au corps de Philippe' [this story repeats or stammers syllables which are not alien to Philippe's body].[18] Here she both refutes and claims a parallel between child and text — the latter somehow seems to mimic her son's body, through repeating, or stammering, syllables (not entire words, but disconnected segments of words that cannot be integrated coherently into complete words). The stuttering repetition, Laurens suggests, evokes the following quotation from Emmanuel Hocquard: 'L'élégie n'est pas dans les mots de la plainte. Elle est dans la répétition des mots de la langue. Elle est cette répétition' [The elegy isn't in the words of the lamentation. It is in the repetition of the words spoken. It is this repetition] (*Encore*, p. 164). In other words, the expression of grief is bound up in repetition of words, of citation, rather than in the intrinsic meaning of the selected words themselves; it is precisely through this repetition that her writing can begin to give voice to her loss. Repetition — which is also, in a way, citation — is figured in the eponymous title of the memoir recounting her son's death and birth, so that 'chaque fois qu'on me parle de mon livre j'entends le prénom de mon fils. Philippe n'est pas un titre, c'est un nom' [Every time someone talks to me about my book I hear the first name of my son. Philippe isn't a title, it's a name] (p. 164). By giving her book the name of her son, by repeating his name, she thereby inscribes his loss in such a way that any reference to her book also serves to recall her child. Elsewhere in *Encore et jamais*, she relates the fort/da game recounted by Freud in 'Beyond the Pleasure Principle' to the reading of poetry, observing that, when reading a poem, the repetition (of rhyme, alliteration, and assonance) leads to a kind of relief akin to that experienced when the mother returns in Freud's account of the child's game.[19] This implies that narratives of loss, like poems, may end up deploying an aesthetic or literary return that becomes comfortingly familiar, so that by implication the repeated re-inscription of Philippe in Laurens's writing could end up reassuring rather than destabilizing,[20] as the reader comes to expect to see his name.[21] This readerly anticipation is undermined in *Encore et jamais*, as the narrator opens one chapter with the provocative assertion (addressed to a two-way mirror that figures the reading encounter in terms of reflection): 'Non, tu te trompes, la page centrale de ce livre n'est pas la mort de Philippe, non' [No, you're wrong, the central page of this book isn't the death of Philippe, no] (p. 108). Thus the narrator undercuts the reader's expectation as to Philippe's central position within this text by both evoking his death at that mid-point and denying its status; in so doing, she both gives his death central position and, simultaneously, places this position under erasure, just as she both aligns text and child and disconnects them, as discussed above. This notion of narrating the death of a child whilst simultaneously denying the possibility of such a narrative destabilizes the reader, who is left unable to locate Philippe, or indeed *Philippe*, as Laurens deliberately uses the non-italicized word to represent both the title of her book and the name of her son, subsuming the former into the latter. In this way, Laurens's *Encore et jamais* returns to her earlier work to interrogate it, placing the relation between text and child under erasure, but also reframing it through calling into question the title, which is already a repetition and a citation, both an evocation of her traumatic loss but also troublingly over-familiar. The implication here — that narratives of the death of a child are articulated through and framed by inscription or quotation that both reiterate and somehow erase the trauma — is worth exploring further in texts that focus more explicitly on the loss of a child: Laurens's *Philippe*, Adler's *À ce soir*, and Daull's *Camille, mon envolée*.

It is striking that all of the texts included in this chapter begin with an epigraph, that is with citation from elsewhere that is somehow, if we follow the etymology of the word, written upon, yet also before, the text itself. The epigraph therefore offers a way into the text, as Derrida observes in *Archive Fever*: 'To cite before beginning is to give the tone through the resonance of a few words, the meaning or form of which ought to set the stage. In other words, the exergue consists in capitalizing on an ellipsis'.[22] Derrida's explanation of the exergue (a word he chooses over 'epigraph' — the two are fairly interchangeable in French, but the former contains the added referent of a space on a coin or medal, upon which a value/date may be inscribed) suggests that it constitutes both an inscription and a gap (upon which an inscription could be added). The exergue is, then, a form of ellipsis, an inscription that marks a gap between the text to follow and the intertext from which it is taken, yet which may also be located within the gap that makes space for potential inscription. It seems both to be located at a space of absence and to imply that something (or perhaps someone, in the case of the texts of parental mourning explored here) is missing. Finally, the exergue, in implicitly referring outwards to other texts or frameworks, also works as an address to the reader, framing the text and 'setting the tone' through citation.

The epigraphs to Laurens's *Philippe*, Adler's *À ce soir*, and Daull's *Camille, mon envolée* all invoke resistance. This is clear in the epigraph to Laurens's *Philippe*, taken from André Breton's *Arcane 17*, which suggests that even, and particularly, 'en présence de l'irréparable' [in the presence of the irreparable], rebellion (however futile it might be) is crucial: 'Elle est l'étincelle dans le vent, mais l'étincelle qui cherche la poudrière' [It is the spark in the wind, but the spark that seeks out the powder keg] (*Philippe*, p. 11). Laurens thus frames her memoir with the insistence that whilst rebellion (presumably in this text taking the form of an indictment of what she sees as the medical mismanagement of her son's birth and death and a refusal to accept the medical professionals' version of events) cannot heal the irreparable loss, it nonetheless constitutes a spark that may somehow succeed in finding ignition as it is tossed by the wind. Rebellion is bound up in writing in this text ('Écrire m'arme' [writing arms me], p. 79) in order to 'rendre justice' [restore justice] (p. 80); through writing, she can utter the cry of protest that she could not articulate before Philippe died in order to save him (p. 81). Adler's *À ce soir*, meanwhile, also has a figure of flight as epigraph, this time a quotation from Immanuel Kant featuring a dove: 'La colombe légère qui, dans son libre vol, fend l'air dont elle sent la résistance pourrait s'imaginer qu'un espace vide d'air lui réussirait mieux encore' [The light dove, cleaving the air in free flight, and feeling its resistance, might imagine that its flight would be more successful in airless space] (*À ce soir*, p. 9). The significance of this epigraph is less clear, but it appears to foreground resistance: the dove imagines that it could fly more easily in an airless space, without realizing that without the resistance of the air, it could not fly at all.[23] Writing in Adler's text is also implicitly constructed in and through resistance to irreparable loss: the same word used in Laurens's epigraph figures early in *À ce soir*: 'la déchirure était irréparable' [the tear was irreparable] (p. 14). Daull, meanwhile, again uses an image of flight in her title, *Camille, mon envolée*, and in the epigraph, a Chinese proverb ('Tu ne peux pas empêcher les oiseaux de la tristesse de voler au-dessus de ta tete, mais tu peux les empêcher de faire leur nid dans tes cheveux' [You cannot prevent birds of sorrow from flying over your head, but you can stop them from building their nests in your hair], *Camille*, p. 9). This acknowledges the inevitability of suffering, but also emphasizes rebellion and movement over resigned acceptance and stasis. These texts thus frame their accounts of irreparable loss in and through writing mired in resistance and/or rebellion.

The relation between the reader and these texts is, in turn, shaped by resistance rather than (for example) empathy or compassion. The reader is required to recognize the limits of our own understanding, as highlighted by the 'Vivre' [Living] chapter of *Philippe*, in which Laurens recounts the reactions of others to the death of her son, including those who fail to recognize his life (conceptualizing his death in terms of an early miscarriage), who utter platitudes, who avoid her, who seem puzzled when she continues to express her pain (pp. 67–71), or who never mention him. She ends this chapter with an account of a conversation overheard at an airport between tourists flippantly discussing a florist who decided to specialize in funeral flowers for a captive audience who could be fobbed off with second-rate flowers without complaint. In an italicized postscript to the 'Vivre' chapter she notes that a year later, rereading this chapter, '*la question se pose de supprimer ou non cette dernière anecdote, et, d'une façon plus générale, le* grief *qui anime ces pages*' [the question poses itself as to whether or not to delete this last anecdote, and more generally, the *grief* that underpins these pages]. She decides not to alter the text because '*je n'écris pas de tombeau*' [I am not writing a tomb/musical composition] (p. 73). This may be read as a refusal of the literary and musical tradition of creating a composition in memory of the dead, but it is also a rejection of the possibility of writing as preservation or containment of loss (a figurative tomb).[24] Laurens cites Comte de Lautréamont — 'Si vous êtes malheureux, il ne faut pas le dire au lecteur. Gardez cela pour vous' [If you are unhappy, you mustn't tell the reader. Keep it to yourself] (p. 20) — before observing that the issue at stake for her is not discretion, but rather the impossibility of articulating suffering: 'On ne peut pas dire le malheur [...]. Tous les mots sont secs. Ils restent au bord des larmes. Le malheur est toujours un secret' [One can't speak sadness [...]. All words are dry. They remain on the edge of tears. Sadness is always a secret] (pp. 20–21). The point here is that language cannot communicate sadness, the tears exceed the capability of words and the suffering remains silent. Yet also, the tears evoked here are ultimately projected onto the reader in the last line of *Philippe*, where Laurens urges the reader to bring Philippe back to life: 'Pleurez, vous qui lisez, pleurez: que vos larmes le tirent du néant' [Cry, you who are reading, cry: let your tears pull him from oblivion] (p. 81). The reader is not called upon to see the 'néant', nor to understand it, but is demanded to respond in such a way as to make a difference — not to empathize, but to fulfil an impossible request (to revive the child). The trace of loss, in this text, is somehow inscribed through the reader, rather than through the narrator, yet the exhortation to the reader which closes the narrative is also oddly adversarial, placing the burden of emotion upon the reader to rescue Philippe from the oblivion to which he seems to have been consigned.

Reading Traces of Absence, Absence of Traces

Evoking Philippe, Laurens observes: 'il est venu au monde, et le monde n'avait de cesse de l'oublier, de l'annuler, de n'en pas même garder la trace, tel un nom sur une tombe' [He came into the world, and the world kept forgetting him, deleting him, not even keeping a trace, such as a name on a tombstone] (*Philippe*, p. 71), his life, and death, frequently negated, the trace of his life under erasure.[25] In *Cet absent-là* [This Absent One], which invokes the absence of Philippe, amongst others, Laurens asks: 'Où vont les souvenirs dont on n'a plus la trace?' [Where do memories go once their trace is lost?].[26] The question is inextricably bound up in her subsequent references to Philippe in this text: whilst on the one hand, 'sur les tombes les morts gardent leur nom, on le grave dans le marbre et ça reste longtemps' [on tombstones, the dead keep their names, engraved in marble and remaining for a long time], on the other, language itself becomes as ephemeral as the body after death. She writes that:

> Il n'y a plus de mots pour les morts, les mots disparaissent en même temps que le corps qu'ils nommaient, ou juste après, juste après cadavres, après dépouille, après restes, os, reliques, squelette, il n'y a plus de mots, c'est innommable, cette houille, ça n'existe plus dans la langue, dans aucune langue, les morts n'ont plus de mots sur les os, c'est intraduisible. (*Cet absent-là*, p. 93)

> [There are no more words for the dead, words disappear at the same time as the body that they name, or just afterwards, just after corpses, body, remains, bones, relics, skeletons, there are no more words, it's unspeakable, this dust, it no longer exists in language, in any language, the dead no longer have words on their bones, it's untranslatable.]

Laurens's comment that bodies becomes disarticulated — just as words become disembodied — is undercut by her repetition of words that relate to bodies ('cadavre', 'dépouille', 'os', 'squelette', and so on) which paradoxically serves to lend her words some sort of materiality, or at least to invoke material traces, albeit ephemeral ones. It is through these ephemeral traces that Laurens attempts to remember her son in this text — through the evocation of the Polaroid photograph taken when Philippe was wired up to life-support technology, that developed, she imagines, while he was dying (*Cet absent-là*, p. 92). His image materializes, literally, while he dies, creating a trace of absence out of the absence of trace of his death (that she missed, because she was still in recovery from his birth).

Laurens's insistence on inscription and trace is echoed in Daull's *Camille, mon envolée*, in which writing is itself markedly ephemeral (she began writing in the bath: 'La vapeur rendait le papier poreux, et le stylo marchait mal' [The steam made the paper porous, and the pen didn't work very well], *Camille*, p. 11). Writing, in Daull's text, serves to suspend the acknowledgement of the finality of separation from her daughter; she states that it is when she finishes her letter to her daughter (a fantasized means of keeping communication open), that she must finally acknowledge her loss. Near the end of the text, Daull recounts deleting Camille's number from her mobile phone: 'Un clic pour Options, puis Répondre, Enregistrer, Modifier... La! Voila! Quatrieme clic: SUP-PRI-MER [...]. Et clic je t'ai supprimé.

Effacée. Erased' [One click for Options, then Answer, Record, Modify... There we are! Fourth click: de-le-te [...]. And click I have deleted you. Rubbed out. Erased] (p. 180). It is as though Camille herself, rather than her telephone number, has been deleted; this is emphasized through the use of the English word 'erased' which works both as a translation and a reiteration of the French 'effacée'. The analogy of deleting Camille's contact details from her mobile phone is interesting because it highlights the immateriality of the trace of Camille (which can be erased through four clicks), in direct contrast to the endurance of the inscription on a tombstone evoked by Laurens. Yet whilst the telephone number and contact can be deleted in seconds, this is experienced by Daull as a repetition of the severing of the umbilical cord ('la rupture du troisieme cordon, ombilical le 12 juin 1997, symbolique l'été 2009 (tu parlais toi-même d'une deuxième naissance [...]), mortel le 2 janvier 2014' [the rupture of the third cord, umbilical on 12 June 1997, symbolic in the summer of 2009 (you yourself talked about a second birth [...]), fatal on 2 January 2014] (p. 181)) that constitutes a very corporeal separation.

This is reinforced by the repeated references to Camille's remains, after her funeral. Daull compares Camille's death to the destruction of Pompeii by volcanic eruption, asking: 'Quel sera l'état des ruines après ton glissement de terrain? Zone non constructible. Mon enfant morte, ma si belle chérie, ne laisse rien, surtout, repousser sur ton Pompéi. On est bien dans tes cendres' (*Camille*, p. 164) [What state will the ruins be in after your earthquake? No-construction zone. My dead child, my so beautiful darling, don't let anything, above all, grow on your Pompeii. We are content in your ashes] (*Camille*, p. 164). Here Daull insists that they ('on', presumably she and Camille's father) are living inside Camille's ashes (the analogy is perhaps surprising as Camille was buried, not cremated), which, like the ash that preserved the town of Pompeii intact, will conserve Camille as well as her parents. Daull also, however, addressing both Camille and her own deceased mother, refers to 'mon corps entier comme une chapelle ardente, tout mon dedans façonné par la poussière de vos restes' [my whole body like a chapel of rest, all my insides shaped by the dust of your remains] (p. 167). Her body therefore forms the space of bereavement, her interior shaped by the remains of her daughter (as though the ash is not only covering Camille, but also constituting the narrator's identity). Her own survival is shaped entirely around the fantasized physical remainder of her daughter (ashes and/or dust). Whilst on the one hand, then, Camille's trace is speedily erased, on the other hand, the narrator clings to a fantasy of her physical trace, yet her own body (figured as 'chapelle ardente') is also by implication a space preserving the body pre-burial or cremation, in other words, before it has been converted into ashes or dust. The trace of loss is, then, bound up in a fantasized projection of Daull's own body, and her own self, as space of bereavement; it is also, however, impossible to delineate and can only be imagined, fantasized, or dreamed.

The relation between trace, ash, and dream/fantasy in the context of the death of a child evoked in *Camille, mon envolée* recurs curiously throughout the texts explored in this chapter as well as in Caruth's *Literature in the Ashes of History*. It is primarily the last chapter of Caruth's book, entitled 'Psychoanalysis in the Ashes of History', that interests me here; the substitution of the word 'Psychoanalysis' for 'Literature' in the book title highlights the close relation — at times, the interchangeability — of the two within her argument, particularly in the context of discussions of dream. In an account of Derrida's *Archive Fever*, Caruth writes:

> We turn back, in Derrida's 'Post-script' [...] to discover an encounter between Freud and a dream, or rather, between Freud and a literary text about dreams that returns us to the site of a disaster and to the site of literature, *to the site of literature as archive*. (*Literature*, p. 82)

Caruth's precision here — that Freud's encounter is with the text, rather than with the dream recounted in it — is crucial, underlining Caruth's awareness of the literary text as medium/mediator (and as archive, inscribing past trauma, if we are to follow Derrida's analogy). The dream in question is from Jensen's novella *Gradiva: A Pompeiian Fantasy*, in which an archaeologist dreams of a woman, Gradiva, who died in Pompeii in the eruption of Vesuvius; he subsequently travels to Pompeii in a quest to trace her toe-prints in the ashes.[27] Freud's essay, 'Delusion and Dream in Wilhelm Jensen's Gradiva', was later explored by Derrida as an example of *mal d'archive* [archive fever]; Caruth's chapter draws on both Freud and Derrida in order to rethink psychoanalysis, memory, and literature through traces in, and of, ash. Most striking here though is her insistence on dream and the relation between literature, dream, and ash, which emerges out of her reading of the accounts of Derrida, Freud, and Jensen.

Jensen's story recounts how the archaeologist Hanold travels to Pompeii in search of traces of Gradiva, the woman who appeared to him in a dream, walking through the streets of Pompeii and then lying down, 'as if to sleep', but actually to die. His trip is 'part of a complex scene of dreaming and awakening' (*Literature*, p. 85) because his 'memory' of Pompeii is mediated through a dream. His return to Pompeii thus repeats the quest in the dream to follow Gradiva's toe prints in the ash. Caruth asks:

> How can ashes sustain a print, when ashes are precisely that which may disperse and drift away? And what would it mean to leave a trace, or a remainder in that which it, itself, a remainder. the ash that is the burned up trace of what is incinerated? The figure of ash is, indeed, not only the substratum *for* a writing that has taken place but the figure *of* a writing that is burning up. (*Literature*, p. 87)

What is striking here is both that ash is itself already a trace (the trace of what has been burned) but also that Hanold's memory of ash originates in a dream. Thus the language of traces and burning ashes is inextricably bound up in figures of dreaming and lack of consciousness, echoing those deployed in Freud's analysis of Jensen. Caruth argues that Freud engages with this scene through compulsively repeating it in a quest to return to the origins of his own theory of psychoanalysis (because the archaeological figures of burial and preservation used here were also integral to Freud's early conception of the unconscious). The figure of Hanold 'represents his own unconscious processes' (*Literature*, p. 83) and Freud, like Hanold, appears to be 'dreaming' (p. 84). Caruth also observes that Derrida, meanwhile, repeats the words 'I dream' several times in *Archive Fever*, leading her to 'submit that the philosopher, in turn, can be said to be dreaming throughout the entire work of *Archive Fever*' (p. 89). Both Freud and Derrida, rather than simply analyzing Jensen's narrative of Hanold's dream, are thus, according to Caruth, themselves also dreaming. Yet Derrida at least also fails to reference Hanold's dream:

> Even while Derrida writes that Hanold 'dreams', the actual dream of Hanold, to which he alludes, is to a certain extent effaced from the philosopher's text, as the dream is also effaced from many critical texts on Jensen and Freud. It is, then, a dream that repeatedly recedes into unconsciousness, though it is, I would argue, at the very heart of Jensen's story. (*Literature*, p. 84)

The dream is thus both integral to and effaced from the subsequent reiterations of Jensen's story — like ash, it offers a trace of erasure, yet also a means through which knowledge of what has been effaced may be gained. Reading Derrida, Caruth asks, 'What, indeed, is the language, or figure, of cinders which is the language of Freud, and of Derrida, if it is "the annihilation of the capacity to bear witness?"' This, she insists, has implications for reading: 'What of the readers, for example, who read the figure of ash?' (p. 87). I would suggest that this question needs to be explored precisely through dreaming. Caruth notes:

> From following traces to writing in the ashes — this is not only the trajectory of the concept of the archive in its burning-dreaming conceptualization. It is also the trajectory of the very figures of these burning conceptualizations, all these authors as themselves signs or dreaming figures. (*Literature*, pp. 89–90)

What Caruth seems to mean here is not that literature is written in the ashes of history, as the trace of a past which can thereby be articulated via its trace, but that what is inscribed in and through the burning ashes is a story (or stories) of a past, and, she argues, a future, that resist knowledge, but that become accessible through dream. This may help us to approach (and to articulate our approach to) narratives that recount surviving the death of a child differently. Rather than assuming that we can somehow trace, through narrative, the child who has been lost, or indeed the impact of that loss on the surviving parent, instead we can focus on the ways in which writing in and through ash (and through dream) overlays a different story. Caruth writes that 'to search for traces in the ash: this is the story of an impossible quest, not for what lies buried beneath the ashes, but for what may be impossibly, evanescently, inscribed upon them' (*Literature*, p. 92). Hanold, followed by Freud, and later Derrida and Caruth, all search for traces in ash through creating more stories — they are writers and readers, and writing and reading here become synonymous. This suggests that reading itself also implies inscribing in ash and, by extension, that reading, too, is bound up in the structure of the dream through which the ash becomes site of inscription of loss.

This is perhaps clearer if we turn to Felman's chapter, 'Fire in the Archive: The Alignment of Witnesses', originally delivered at a conference as an oral response to Caruth's paper 'After the End', a revised version of which constitutes the fifth chapter of *Literature in the Ashes of History*. Felman begins:

> I hope you empathize with me [...] because the text that I was sent and was going to respond to got partially erased in the course of Cathy's revisions. So I'm responding to an erased archive of the first draft of this lecture, in which there was more Caruth that got partially erased today.[28]

Felman's original verbal response is therefore based on a text that was edited (and partly erased) before the conference audience heard a spoken version of it; Felman's chapter literally reads a text already under erasure, even before Caruth again reworked her paper for publication. Felman's invitation for the audience to 'empathize' with her — whilst clearly on one level a shorthand way of apologizing for the fact that her paper responds to a paper that has subsequently been edited — works to establish a relation of understanding, a connection between herself and the audience (and, given that the paper is subsequently published, the reader) that is oddly rooted in the acknowledgement of reading a text under erasure. Felman goes on to highlight the connections between Jensen, Freud, Derrida, and Caruth, describing them as a *'chain of witnesses'*, in an 'alliance',[29] an 'alignment of story-tellers',[30] yet who, beginning with Jensen, whose memories are located within a dream, tell the stories of what they do not consciously know.[31] Where Caruth emphasizes dream as a link between Jensen/Hanold, Freud and Derrida, Felman focuses instead on an autobiographical connection (in Caruth's case, the allusions to (the death of) her mother and in the case of Freud, the reference to the death of his daughter Sophie). For Felman, then, the chain of storytellers is bound together not by shared understanding of traumatic loss, but by the ways in which other people's stories — and more importantly, their sites of erasure — allow them to articulate something unspoken about their own lives. This is clearly not akin to empathy, but it may allow space for some sort of critical engagement with the text that could be fruitful in the context of autobiographical narratives of the death of a child, that does not involve identification or appropriation, but that offers the possibility of following other footsteps/words in the ash through dream.

Dreaming and the 'Real'

In an interview, Daull observes that whilst 'après un choc pareil, l'organisme met en place un système de refoulement [...] je veux rester en prise avec ce terrible réel' [after such a shock, the organism puts in place a system of repression [...] I want to stay in contact with this terrible real].[32] The desire to remain somehow in touch with the 'real' (the death of her daughter) implicitly evokes (and nuances) Jacques Lacan's commentary on the burning child dream first recounted by Freud in *The Interpretation of Dreams*. Freud narrates that a bereaved father, asleep in the bedroom next to the one temporarily accommodating his deceased child's body, dreamt that his son was standing by his bed, tugging his arm and asking, *'Father, don't you see I'm burning?'* The shock in the dream awakened him, whereupon he found that a candle had fallen in the neighbouring room, setting fire to the cloths wrapping his son's body.[33] Where Freud claims that the dream works to keep the father asleep and to protect him from the reality of his loss, Lacan argues rather that the father can see his child's death more clearly in dream than when he wakes up ('Il y a plus de réalité, n'est-ce pas, dans ce message, que dans le bruit, par quoi le père aussi bien identifie l'étrange réalité de ce qui se passe dans la pièce voisine' [There is more reality, isn't there, in this message, than in the sound, through which the father also identifies the strange reality of what is happening in the next room]), yet of course, the dream also enacts his failure to protect his son from burning.[34] Caruth argues that this story traces 'a double failure of seeing: a failure to see adequately inside and a failure to see adequately outside'.[35] In Daull's *Camille, mon envolée*, the 'real' is not simply the registration of the child's death, but is also her point of contact with her daughter: the use of the phrase 'en prise' with her death implies touch, yet also possession (of the loss rather than of the child?). This may be related to Freud's account of the father's dream in which the child grasps his father's arm as he whispers, 'Father, don't you see I'm burning?'. Dreaming of (and imagining) his child's touch becomes a way of registering the child's death (and of the limits of his own vision of his child), a marker of separation as well as of proximity. In analogous form, staying in touch with 'le réel' for Daull means a simultaneous articulation of proximity to and separation from her deceased child enacted through the act of writing the extended letter to her (a letter that is itself rooted in fantasy, since its addressee can never read it).

Adler's *À ce soir*, which recounts the respiratory illness and death of her young son, Rémi, seventeen years before the time of writing, also strikingly alludes to the loss of her child in relation to the 'real'. This text opens with the account of a narrowly avoided car crash in which the threat of imminent death appears oddly calming, a 'non évènement' [non-event], 'd'autant plus réel qu'il n'avait pas eu lieu' [all the more real because it didn't happen] (p. 15). The traumatic missed encounter with death (to borrow Caruth's formulation) acts as an encounter with the 'real' (is all the more 'real') precisely and paradoxically because the imagined crash did not happen. The 'real' is thus, oddly, experienced here through a trauma that nearly happened, but did not, and that somehow works to re-inscribe the death of her son. Here Adler echoes Caruth's observation that as trauma 'is not experienced as it occurs, it is fully evident only in connection with another place and in another time'.[36] This is highlighted in her observation that, after the near-crash, she discovered that her watch's face was 'embué' [misted up] and thus the inscription on her watch, 'À ce soir' [Until this evening], 'était comme effacé. La date, elle, était bien visible' [seemed to be erased. The date, though, was clearly visible], p. 15). The date and time remain visible, but her own perception of time is disrupted (later, she adds that 'il n'y avait plus ni jours, ni nuits' [there was no longer day or night], p. 187), whilst time as marker of relationality ('à ce soir' acts as an abbreviation for 'until I see you this evening') is blurred. At the end of the text, she repeats the word *embué* when she describes the consultant's face, 'embué de larmes' [brimming with tears] as he tells her that Rémi cannot survive, so that the indecipherable inscription on her watch works to recall the announcement of her son's impending death (that is also by implication somehow illegible, resisting comprehension).

Adler's account of the period during which her son was critically ill highlights her own, and her husband's, failure to register the severity of his condition: 'on prend son désir pour une réalité' [we take our desire for reality] (*À ce soir*, p. 146); 'J'ai honte d'avoir pu à ce point me cacher la vérité. Dans quel état d'inconscience me suis-je enfoncée?' [I am ashamed to have been able to hide the truth from myself to this extent. In what state of unconsciousness have I sunk myself into?] (p. 148). The language she uses to describe her self-denial is striking: they were 'bercés par nos illusions, dans un état d'hébétude hallucinée, persuadés que le cauchemar était terminé' [cradled by our illusions, in a state of hallucinatory daze, convinced that the nightmare was over] (p. 147); 'muets, emprisonnés dans un monde illusoire' [mute, imprisoned in an illusory world] (p. 177). Having been convinced that the 'nightmare' of her son's condition is ending and that he is recovering, she later realizes that they were deluded. She registers that the 'nightmare' in which his survival seemed impossible was closer to reality than fantasy, and that what she had perceived to be an escape from that nightmare (presumably by waking up) was another fantasized illusion — curiously aligned to the womb ('Comme un foetus, j'étais' [...] dans mon terrier liquide' [Like a foetus I was [...] in my liquid den], p. 95), a privileged pre-symbolic space of symbiosis. Adler's text thus offers an alternative means of approaching the burning child dream: here, the nightmare is experienced while they are awake, and before the child's death. Waking up, meanwhile, is also before his death and is explicitly not an encounter with the 'real', but simply a shift to another fantasy, one that is even less close to 'reality' than the apparent nightmare. There is no direct recognition of 'reality' (no encounter with the 'real'): even after Rémi's death, she recounts how she and her husband are alienated from their home in a space of exile for 'ces vagabonds chassés par la douleur' [vagabonds hunted by pain], wandering 'sans but ni destination' [with no aim or destination] (p. 187). This state of alienation is no more 'real' than the nightmare or the subsequent foetal space of self-delusion. The point here is that there is no 'real' as such, just a sequence of shifts from one space of illusion or alienation to another (after his death, she is 'dans l'espace abandonné par la mort' [in the space abandoned by death] (p. 188), left behind and displaced, in a peripheral space to which she cannot belong). For the reader, it is not a question of determining the boundaries between fantasy/ nightmare and reality, nor of seeing reality as somehow less 'real' than fantasy; Adler's text precisely interrogates the very possibility of comprehending the reality of her son's illness and death outside the overlapping and competing fantasies and dreams that structure her experience of it.

Adler's insistence that her experience of losing her child is mediated through fantasy (and no less 'real' for it) may help us to reread Caruth's account of the burning child dream differently. Caruth suggests that 'it is precisely the dead child, the child in its irreducible inaccessibility and otherness, who says to his father: '*wake up, leave me, survive; survive to tell the story of my burning*'.[37] Yet Caruth does not point out that within Freud's text, the plea itself, and the concomitant imperative to testify, originated from a projection of the child's voice within the parent's own dream, rather than coming directly from the child himself outside the father's dream (so it is not the dead child himself who speaks). It is impossible, within the multiple layers of interpretation that structure the account and reception of the burning child dream, to locate or pin down 'reality', let alone the 'real'. There can be no originary plea, only a fantasized projection of a plea to bear witness on the part of the father, ventriloquizing the words onto a dreamed apparition of his son. What is striking in the multiple psychoanalytic readings of the text is that they all fail to recognize that the child's voice in the father's dream is a projection, mediated through layers of narrative interpretations. Caruth, for example, is interpreting Slavok Žižek's reading of Lacan's reading of Freud's account of the dream (which was originally told by the bereaved father himself, to Freud). Through these multiple, overlapping narratives is inscribed the alterity not only of the dead child, but also the grieving father, rendering the distinction between 'dream' and consciousness (as well as any originary voice, of the child, but also of the bereaved parent) difficult to see.

Seeing Loss Differently

In Freud's burning child dream, it is the child who appears to the bereaved parent in the dream; in *Camille, mon envolée*, however, the appeal within dream comes from others (and the child is absent). Daull recounts a dream, in which she is in a house of bereavement (in contrast with the non-space of her own grief). A man whom within the dream she identifies as her brother (she notes that in reality, however, she has no brother) tells her to stop crying and look after her other two children (again, in reality, Camille was an only child): 'Ils ont besoin de toi' [They need you] (*Camille*, p. 111). He takes her into a different room where she finds 'deux enfants que je n'ai jamais vus' [two children I have never seen], to whom her brother introduces her as her own children ('voici ton fils, ta fille' [here are your son and daughter]) and whose names she forgets instantly. These unfamiliar children greet her with 'Bonjour madame, pas Bonjour maman' [Hello Madam, not hello Mum] (p. 112), whereupon the dream ends. In this dream, as in the burning child dream, the loss is implicit (both are specifically located in spaces of bereavement), whilst here, too, there is an appeal to the parent to tend to the child. Yet where in Freud's narrated dream, the appeal comes within the dream from the dead child who is fantasized alive, here there is no suggestion that Camille might be alive, so that the dream does not fulfil the wish fulfilment alluded to by Freud in restoring the child to life.[38] More, the characters in the dream are imagined: she can see these fantasized family members, but not Camille. The appeal to the bereaved mother in this dream is indirect (articulated by a (fantasized) brother, not a child) and urges her not to tend to Camille, but rather to turn away from her dead child in order to care for her living children (who are strangers to her and call her 'Madame' and who do not exist outside the dream). If, as Caruth argues, waking up means learning to construct an identity as bereaved parent, here it seems to mean registering not only the loss of Camille (of which she was fully aware even within the dream) but also that of other (fantasized) children, whose names she cannot remember, and who do not call her 'maman'. These children represent, in the framework of the dream, the (im)possibility of parenting after losing a child, as well as her sense of alienation (she does not recognize her supposed children, who treat her 'poliment' [politely], like a stranger): the space of grief is one in which she feels like an outsider and from which her dead child is absent.[39]

Daull suggests that Camille will appear in her dreams later, as her own mother now does, years after her death, suddenly ('Elle surgit comme ça, à l'improviste' [She appears suddenly like that, unexpectedly]), leaving her 'ahurie, stupéfaite' [flabbergasted, stupefied], (*Camille*, p. 112) to ask why she has appeared, whereupon her mother puts her index finger over her mouth and gently tells her to be quiet. In the dreams, her mother is an apparition whose spectral presence comforts her ('les fantômes sont ma seule couverture' [ghosts are my only cover]) and she imagines that Camille will protect her like a mother ('Je serai ton enfant' [I will be your child], p. 113). These dreams seem to be a reversal of sorts of Freud's account of the burning child dream, in which the child appears in order to ask the parent to open his eyes to investigate his suffering, whereas here the mother in the dream seeks rather to close her daughter's mouth (implicitly to silence her). Whilst the child in Freud's story is alive, moreover, Daull explains that her daughter almost never appears alive in her dreams. In one dream only, Daull states, she 'sees' Camille alive fleetingly, jumping on the bed in her own childhood bedroom, which makes her parents laugh but also makes them worry about her glasses breaking (p. 112). The futility of anxiety over broken glasses is poignant given Camille's death, but the emphasis on visual aids also foregrounds the risks of limited vision, implicitly echoing the child's question of his father, 'don't you *see* I'm burning?' (my emphasis). This reference to glasses also recalls the episode in which, half-asleep in bed, she saw her husband/partner up close minus his spectacles and believed she had seen Camille ('je croyais te voir' [I thought I could see you], 'Je l'appelais Camille' [I called him Camille], p. 25) because his eyes are reminiscent of Camille's eyes. Yet she has previously admitted that she very rarely saw her daughter without her glasses, until the last few days of her life during her fatal illness (p. 24): the vision of her husband, without glasses, thereby presumably evokes an image of Camille, sick, rather than as she was before her illness. On one level, then, she saw Camille more clearly during her illness than previously (without her glasses). On another level, of course, Camille at this point was unable to read or look at a screen, her lack of glasses underscoring her inability to survive, so that her mother, while looking at her without her glasses, was also not really seeing her alive in the way that she had been before her illness. At the end of the book, as she finishes her letter to her daughter, Daull states that 'Je ne te vois plus du tout [...]. Adieu, mon enfant' [I can no longer see you at all [...]. Goodbye, my child] (p. 186), as though once she can no longer see Camille clearly, she can no longer continue her letter. However, it is already clear that seeing has been rooted in fantasy: she has already failed to 'see' her daughter clearly, even when she was alive, whilst the end of the letter seems to mark the recognition of the closure of the fantasy of connection between herself and Camille ('Je ne te vois plus du tout' [I can no longer see you at all], p. 186). In other words, in this text, as in *À ce soir*, there is no possibility of seeing the suffering or deceased child clearly: the question posed by the child in Freud's text, 'Can't you see I'm burning?', is clearly answered in the negative, because seeing is described as impossible.

In *Cet absent-là*, Laurens comments that as she contemplates her own mirror reflection:

> Il y a l'enfant que j'ai été et celui qu'il ne sera jamais, il est là comme un mort à qui j'aurais donné des yeux pour se voir, il est là comme un mort à qui j'aurais donné des yeux pour me voir. (*Cet absent-là*, p. 39)

> [There is the child I was and the child that he will never be, he is there like a dead person to whom I would have given eyes to see himself, he is there like a dead person to whom I would have given eyes to see me.]

Philippe's lack of vision (of himself, and of her) is underscored as the following page of Laurens's text figures a photograph of a baby, looking up at the person holding him/her and supporting the baby's head; this cannot be a photograph of Philippe, who was photographed alive only whilst wired up to life support machines. In *Philippe*, Laurens asserts that 'Je ne veux pas fermer les yeux. J'écris pour *voir*' [I don't want to close my eyes. I am writing to *see*] (*Philippe*, p. 80): the italicization of the verb 'to see' highlights her insistence on vision, yet she cannot literally see her son (and she did not see him until he was deceased: she sees him alive only via the Polaroid photographs). If writing becomes a way of seeing, then, it is also, necessarily, a means of registering the limits of vision, in relation to the dying/deceased child. In *Cet absent-là*, Laurens describes how the nurse dropped the packet of photographs of Philippe as she handed them over ('Oh ça tombe, a-t-elle crié' [Oh, it's falling, she cried], *Cet absent-là*, p. 43), her carelessness and flippancy surrounding the value of the photographs echoing the negligence of the doctor whose failure to perform an emergency C-section (and whose disregard for the baby's wellbeing) led to Philippe's death. Laurens's own position in relation to the photographs is strikingly ambivalent: where Philippe's father keeps his son's photo in his wallet, she seems less protective of her own four photos of Philippe ('Elles sont dans une enveloppe, je sais où' [They are in an envelope, I know where]). The casual statement that she knows where the envelope is kept seems both careful — she knows where the pictures are — and careless (she does not state the actual location). Furthermore, she admits that 'Je ne les regarde jamais, je ne les soutiens pas du regard' [I never look at them, I can't hold their gaze] (*Cet absent-là*, p. 43). The implication here is that she cannot look the photographs in the eye, they seem to be looking at her and she cannot hold their gaze, so that there is some sense in which the photographs can somehow look (whereas Philippe could not), whereas she, again, cannot, except through writing. Writing, in this text, plays a similar role to dream or fantasy in *À ce soir* as both offer a means to 'see' through not seeing, or knowing.

The connection between writing and dreaming is underscored in these texts, as seeing the lost child seems to be possible only in and through dream and/or writing (and writing, in these texts, is bound up in dreaming). At the very end of *Camille*, Daull recalls how she loved seeing her daughter approach from a distance ('Tu me voyais te voir, et le fil entre nous, d'or celui-là, se tendait d'amour' [You saw me see you, and the thread between us, made of gold, was strained with love]) but, as she finishes her letter/text: 'Je ne te vois plus du tout' [I can no longer see you at all] (*Camille*, p. 186). The end of the text corresponds to the end of the fantasy of seeing (and of being seen by) the child: writing is, here (as, in Caruth's analysis, for Derrida and for Freud), a form of dream or fantasy in itself. If we return to Felman's reading of the dream of Gravida as inscribed in Jensen, Freud, Derrida, and finally Caruth, her emphasis on 'an alignment', 'an alliance', 'a chain of witnesses' requires nuance; the connections between these 'witnesses' is formed not through knowledge, nor reading in its most literal sense, but through dream. This is, moreover, a dream that, as Caruth notes, is also effaced even as it is inscribed, the narration of which is bound up in autobiographical self-revelation. Reading is also here aligned with dreaming, as Caruth, for example, reads Derrida reading (and dreaming about) Freud, in turn reading (and dreaming about) Jensen.

The texts analyzed in this chapter at once foreground and interrogate paradigms of sight and knowledge in the context of the death of a child, both on the part of the bereaved parent, who can 'see' reality only through fantasy, and on the part of the reader, who 'dreams' through layers of textual mediation of an origin (the child's death, or indeed the child's life) that cannot be grasped as such. Recognizing this may allow us to rethink empathy in reading differently: we can, perhaps, 'empathize with' Felman, as she struggles to respond to a text under erasure, but we cannot empathize with the mothers recounting the loss of a child. Yet, if we (are told that we) cannot know how they feel, what is striking in these texts is the extent to which the bereaved narrators also struggle with grasping the reality of their loss and, by extension, of knowing how they themselves feel. This suggests that we ought to shift our emphasis away from knowledge, or at least to acknowledge that it is rooted in fantasy, and try to renegotiate the encounter with the text rather around what is not known or seen (let alone understood), either by the bereaved narrator or by the reader.

Conclusion: Empathy in Other Words

Caruth ends her Afterword to *Literature in the Ashes of History* as follows:

> For these stories of trauma cannot be limited to the catastrophes they name, and the theory of catastrophic history may ultimately be written in a language that already lingers, in these texts, after the end, in a time that comes to us from the other shore, from the other side of the disaster. (*Literature*, p. 92)

There is still in this statement a recognition of sides — of subjects either side of trauma, divided by it — yet the focus is on seeking to hear and understand the words spoken from the other side, which relate not only to traumas that have already happened, but to the future. Caruth's 'parting words' are however somewhat over-generalizing (implying a singular language that can be identified and understood despite or across the divide), arguably themselves bound up in a fantasy of intelligibility and understanding that is predicated on a shift from the specific (the named catastrophes) to a future (disaster) that cannot yet be known or articulated, a generalization that might ultimately be meaningless.

It is useful to reconsider Caruth's 'language that already lingers' through the ending of Daull's *Camille, mon envolée*. Daull ends her text with the words. 'Adieu mon enfant' [Goodbye, my child], seemingly marking a straightforward and direct address to Sophie from her mother. Yet earlier on the same page, Daull notes that 'Avant-hier les derniers mots que j'ai dits sur scène cette saison théâtrale sont "Adieu, mon enfant"' [The day before yesterday the last words I spoke in this theatrical season are 'Goodbye, my child'] (*Camille*, p. 186). In other words, the parting words to her child are self-confessedly a quotation from a play, words she spoke in a role on stage, which she describes as 'de bons mots pour finir cette saison' [good words to finish this season] (p. 186), repeated as a means to end her book as well as her season. The end of this text thus constitutes yet another citation and another performance, suggesting that, if we return to Caruth, the 'language that already lingers, in these texts, after the end' is itself also a citation or an intertext, a different sort of relation with the other (in her case, bound up in her readings of Jensen, Derrida, and Freud, through which the death of her mother is inscribed).

As seen in the Introduction to this book, most discussion of the role of empathy in literature has focused on the assumption that 'literature [...] can prize [*sic*] us open in some profound way and allow us to imagine other lives and other worlds'[40] through 'the sharing of feeling and perspective-taking induced by reading'.[41] Debates have largely centred around whether or not (and how), as readers, we can in fact understand other (narrative) perspectives or share feelings, as well as the power structures underpinning the reading encounter. Whilst these questions remain crucial, they also require nuance in the context of narrators who do not, necessarily, 'know' how they feel themselves, and in narratives that underscore the limitations of their own articulation of feelings and that self-confessedly can express emotions only through citation. The 'trace', then, that Caruth tracks through ashes and dreams is also necessarily textual; reading these texts of seemingly unthinkable trauma is not (only) an encounter with experience that we cannot imagine, but also with previous texts, possibly, like Caruth's own, themselves under erasure; with other people's words, beyond the 'I' of the narrator. This calls for us to extend our conception of empathy in literature beyond the question of what we can understand or share with the narrating subject, to trace narratives of suffering that are themselves already textual, rooted as much in previous articulations of loss as they are in the lived experience of the death of a child that they seek to express. It is, then, important to reframe the reader's 'encounter' (to use Caruth's term) with traumatic loss in the text through recognition of its mediation in and through other texts which inscribe what we do not know about our own relation to trauma. Empathy, in this context, becomes a future possibility, founded not in shared experience or knowledge, but in dreams and fantasies that we cannot know, or share, and that are repeatedly inscribed and reiterated in and through other people's words.

Notes to Chapter 2

1. Camille Laurens, *Philippe* (Paris: P.O.L. 1995), p. 68.
2. Celia Hindmarch, *On the Death of a Child*, 3rd edn (Boca Raton, FL: CRC Press, 2009), p. 5.
3. Emma Wilson, *Cinema's Missing Children* (London & New York: Wallflower Press, 2002), p. 153.
4. Laure Adler, *À ce soir* (Paris: Gallimard 2001), Aline Schulman, *Paloma* (Paris: Du Seuil, 2001), Anne-Marie Revol, *Nos étoiles ont filé* (Paris: Stock, 2010), and Sophie Daull, *Camille, mon envolée* (Paris: Philippe Rey, 2015).
5. Hélène Cixous, *Le Jour où je n'étais pas là* (Paris: Galilée, 2002). See Gill Rye, 'Family Tragedies: Child Death in Recent French Literature', in *Affaires de famille: The Family in Contemporary French Culture and Theory*, ed. by Marie-Claire Barnet and Edward Welch (Amsterdam & New York: Rodopi, 2007), pp. 267–81, for a study of child death in recent French literature including *Philippe* and *À ce soir*.
6. Laurence Tardieu, *Puisque rien ne dure* (Paris: Stock, 2006), Anne Godard, *L'Inconsolable* (Paris: Minuit, 2006), and Marie Darrieussecq, *Bref séjour chez les vivants* (Paris: P.O.L., 2001).
7. See Darrieussecq's response to being accused of plagiarism in *Rapport de police*. Laurens also returns to this in *Romance nerveuse* (Paris: Gallimard, 2010).
8. Kathryn Robson, 'Psychic Plagiarism: The Death of a Child in Marie Darrieussecq's *Tom est mort* and Camille Laurens's *Philippe*', *French Studies*, 69.1 (2015), 46–59.
9. Gill Rye, *Narratives of Mothering: Women's Writing in Contemporary France* (Newark: University of Delaware Press, 2009), p. 41.
10. Wilson, *Cinema's Missing Children*, p. 157.
11. Paul C. Rosenblatt, *Parent Grief: Narratives of Loss and Relationship* (Philadelphia, PA: Brunner/Mazel, 2000), p. 227.
12. Cathy Caruth, *Literature in the Ashes of History* (Baltimore, MD: Johns Hopkins University Press, 2013).
13. Peggy Phelan, 'Converging Glances: A Response to Cathy Caruth's "Parting Words"', *Cultural Values*, 5.1 (January 2001), 27–49 (p. 28).
14. Ibid., p. 28.
15. Shoshana Felman writes that 'the woman she quotes so discreetly, the psychoanalyst (and psychoanalytic writer), Elaine Caruth, happens to be her own mother: her *late* (dead) mother' ('Fire in the Archive: The Alignment of Witnesses', in *The Future of Testimony: Interdisciplinary Perspectives on Witnessing*, ed. by Antony Rowland and Jane Kilby (New York: Routledge, 2014), pp. 48–68 (p. 63)).
16. This is also, of course, true of Freud's 'Beyond the Pleasure Principle', as Caruth points out in her analysis of Freud's autobiographical footnote: 'In noting the real death of the child's mother, Freud first explicitly links the child to himself, since the child's mother was also, in reality, Freud's daughter Sophie, who died toward the end of the writing of *Beyond the Pleasure Principle*' (*Literature*, p. 16).
17. Rye, 'Family Tragedies', p. 271.
18. Camille Laurens, *Encore et jamais* (Paris: Gallimard, 2013), p. 164.
19. Camille Laurens, 'Dans le poème, le son est comme la maman, on est content qu'il revienne' [In the poem the sound is like the mother, one is happy that it comes back] (*Encore et jamais*, p. 51). In her novel *Dans ces bras-là*, Laurens writes of Philippe: 'C'est l'enfant là-pas là, il va et vient comme la bobine qui roule et puis revient' [It's the child who is there-not there, he comes and goes like the cotton reel that rolls away and then comes back] (*Dans ces bras-là* (Paris: P.O.L, 2000), p. 219), thereby also implicitly placing the loss of her son in the context of Freud's theorization of traumatic repetition.
20. Jutta Fortin notes that 'le fantôme de Philippe fait retour dans pratiquement tous les textes que la romancière a publié après *Philippe*' [the ghost of Philippe returns in practically all of the texts that the novelist has published since *Philippe*] (*Camille Laurens: le kaléidoscope d'une écriture hantée* (Lille: Presses universitaires du Septentrion, 2017), p. 65), yet this ghost is as comforting, if we are to follow Laurens's logic, as it is haunting. Laurens observes that 'quelques lecteurs m'ont reproché d'évoquer trop souvent la mort de mon fils dans mes livres, d'y revenir sans cesse, de

radoter comme une vieille femme qui n'arrive pas à oublier — ou pire, qui reprend le crincrin de la corde sensible afin d'en tirer profit' [Some readers have reproached me for mentioning the death of my son too often in my books, for rambling like an old lady who can't manage to forget — or worse, who gets the violin out to tug at the heart strings to make a profit] (*Encore et jamais*, p. 157).

21. Clare Hemmings observes in an analysis of female genital mutilation that 'the repetition of the horror' within Western feminist representations of this both make her, as a reader, 'want to gag' and 'feel sick' yet also offer 'bodily satisfaction at the certainty of what I will find there' (*Why Stories Matter: The Political Grammar of Feminist Theory* (Durham, NC: Duke University Press, 2011), p. 222), highlighting that repetition, even of trauma or horror, can be comforting to read.

22. Jacques Derrida, *Archive Fever: A Freudian Impression*, trans. by Eric Prenowitz (Chicago, IL, & London: University of Chicago Press, 1995), p. 7.

23. There is also evident self-delusion here, as the easier flight that the dove imagines would be a logical impossibility: this echoes Adler's account of self-delusion during Rémi's illness, when she believes that her son is recovering.

24. The French *tombeau* implies both a tomb and a musical composition commemorating someone who has died.

25. This is echoed in *À ce soir* where the narrator describes how, when her passport expired and was replaced, 'DCD' (standing for *décédé*, or 'deceased') was written next to Rémi's name on the expired passport, whilst Rémi's name (and thus his existence, as her son) was omitted entirely from the replacement passport (p. 130).

26. Camille Laurens, *Cet absent-là* (Paris: Gallimard, 2004), p. 87.

27. Wilhelm Jensen, *Gradiva: A Pompeiian Fantasy*, trans. by Helen M. Downey, in Sigmund Freud, *Delusion and Dream: An Interpretation in the Light of Psychoanalysis of 'Gradiva', a Novel by Wilhelm Jensen* (New York: New Republic, 1927).

28. Felman, 'Fire in the Archive', p. 48.

29. Ibid., p. 54. Her term is drawn from Freud: 'For, when they cause the people created by their imagination to dream, they follow the common experience that people's thoughts and feelings continue into sleep, and they seek only to depict the psychic states of their heroes through the dreams of the latter. Story-tellers are valuable allies, and their testimony is to be rated high, for they usually know many things between heaven and earth that our academic wisdom does not even dream of' (Freud, *Delusion and Dream*, p. 123).

30. Felman, 'Fire in the Archive', p. 56.

31. Freud writes: 'The author has expressly renounced the portrayal of reality by calling his story a "phantasy"', yet 'all his descriptions are so faithfully copied from reality that we should not object if *Gradiva* were described not as a phantasy but as a psychiatric study' (Freud, *Delusion and Dream*, p. 41).

32. Flora Vandenesch, interview with Sophie Daull, 'Ce livre est un geste poétique, une posture par le haut', 20 August 2015, <https://toutelaculture.com/livres/interview-sophie-daull-ce-livre-est-un-geste-poetique-une-posture-par-le-haut/> [accessed 7 March 2019].

33. Sigmund Freud, *The Interpretation of Dreams*, trans. by James Strachey, ed. by Angela Richards, The Penguin Freud Library 4 (Harmondsworth: Penguin, 1991), p. 652.

34. Jacques Lacan, 'Tuché et Automaton', in *Le Séminaire, livre XI: Les Quatre Concepts fondamentaux de la psychoanalyse* (Paris: Du Seuil, 1973), p. 68.

35. Cathy Caruth, *Unclaimed Experience: Trauma, Narrative and History* (Baltimore, MD, & London: Johns Hopkins University Press, 1996), p. 103.

36. Caruth, *Unclaimed Experience*, p. 17.

37. Ibid., p. 105.

38. Freud, *The Interpretation of Dreams*, p. 653.

39. The alienation articulated here is echoed in the end of Adler's *À ce soir*, in which the death of Rémi turns his parents into vagabonds, displaced from their own home.

40. Anthony M. Clohesy, *The Politics of Empathy: Ethics, Solidarity, Recognition* (London: Routledge, 2014), p. 6.

41. Suzanne Keen, 'Narrative Empathy', in *The Living Handbook of Narratology* (Hamburg: Hamburg University, 2013), <http://www.lhn.uni-hamburg.de/article/narrative-empathy> [accessed 7 March 2019].

CHAPTER 3

❖

Beyond Compassion?
Maternal Filicide and the
Limits of Empathy

In an analysis of two recent French novels featuring mothers who kill their children, Natalie Edwards writes: 'Infanticide is often considered to be one of the most heinous crimes possible. It is a specific threat to the symbolic and social orders in which the mother operates'.[1] Yet although, on the one hand, incidents of mothers killing their children clearly inspire reactions of shock, disgust, and horror — challenging core cultural assumptions about the maternal figure as nurturer and protector: 'Mothers nurture; they do not destroy. The need to explain away the actions of violent mothers therefore proves even stronger than that of other violent women' — literary representations of these cases have also curiously invoked understanding and even empathy.[2] This chapter explores representations of maternal filicide in contemporary French women's (fictional) writing and in the highly-publicized cases that have occurred in France in this century and have in part inspired the fictional texts. Whilst narratives of child death unsurprisingly typically figure unthinkable traumatic loss that is difficult to articulate and to comprehend, infanticide seems surprisingly almost too easily recounted and understood in contemporary French writing. More, representations of maternal filicide are strikingly bound up in and framed by claims of empathy (often caught up in a self-consciously feminist agenda) which this chapter will seek to explore.

Novels recounting infanticide have proliferated in France in recent years,[3] including most famously Leïla Slimani's international bestseller, and Prix Goncourt-winning, *Chanson douce* [Sweet Song] which features a nanny murdering her two young charges.[4] This is in contrast with the United Kingdom and the United States, where, for example, 'relatively few contemporary literary works depict neonaticide as a thematic focus'.[5] This may reflect the somewhat surprising number of high-profile cases of mothers killing their young children that have hit the headlines in France in this century, including several instances of multiple neonaticides in which individual women managed to conceal (several) pregnancies, give birth alone, kill, and hide the baby without other family members finding out.[6] Whilst maternal filicide may seem unthinkable, 'a significant proportion (approximately half in most studies) of filicides are committed by the child's mother';[7] the younger the child victim of homicide in general, the more likely it is that the perpetrator will be the mother.[8] The different terms commonly used for child homicide (notably infanticide and neonaticide) are often used interchangeably. Jaclyn Smith observes that:

> If the murdered child is between 48 hours and 2 years old, then the term most often used to describe that crime is infanticide. If the child is younger than 24 hours, neonaticide is the term most frequently used. Caution must be taken, however, because there is no readily apparent principle to distinguish between infanticide and neonaticide.[9]

In common speech, the term 'infanticide' is also frequently applied to children above two years old, whilst in UK law (as in some other countries, including Australia, Canada, and Ireland) infanticide, which constitutes its own legal category separate from homicide, applies strictly only for children up to twelve months old. The Infanticide Act of 1938 decreed that mothers killing their babies of up to twelve months old could be convicted of infanticide, rather than murder, if deemed to be of unbalanced mind caused by childbirth and lactation.[10] In France, by contrast, since 1994 there is no legal distinction between child homicide and infanticide and legally no special consideration should be applied to mothers who kill babies (even new-born babies).[11] In practice, however, the highly mediatized neonaticide cases in France in this century have pivoted around claims of pregnancy denial (in which the mother is unaware of, or represses awareness of, her pregnancy) that work to negate agency and responsibility and thereby minimize the sentence given.[12] Neonaticide thus inspires different responses from the killing of an older child. If mothers who kill their children are typically assumed to be 'bad, mad, or sad', mothers who kill new-born babies are typically seen to fit into one of the latter two categories, whilst mothers who kill older children are more often vilified ('bad').[13] Christine M. Alder and June Baker note that:

> In the criminological literature, maternal filicide is most often represented as taking one of two forms: a psychologically disturbed young woman who kills her new-born or young infant, or a stressed mother who regularly loses control and abuses her children.[14]

These cases are shaped by wider cultural assumptions about maternal ideals that filicide would appear to undermine, yet also reinforce (for instance, the homicidal mother is often assumed to be mad, because a sane mother could not be imagined capable of killing her child, whereas different assumptions are typically made about fathers who kill). Heather Leigh Stangle's critique of the judicial handling of cases of infanticide in the United States points to 'the troubling possibility that preserving myths of female passivity has become more important than protecting children and disciplining those women who commit heinous crimes'; approaching cases of maternal filicide means unpicking these unspoken assumptions underlying attitudes to (and laws surrounding) infanticide.[15]

Maggie Inchley writes that 'the voices of women who commit such acts are rarely directly heard' as 'the voice of the transgressive female delinquent is subsumed by legal processes, distorted by the media and drowned out by the din of public discourse'.[16] This is certainly true of the recent French trials, where the accused mothers have strikingly been silent in court, unable, or unwilling, to speak in self-defence.[17] Examples of autobiographical accounts of infanticide are rare; in this chapter, therefore, I focus on fictional narratives, analyzed in the context of the real-life filicides that have inspired the fictional texts — yet clearly this is not to suggest a straightforward distinction between fiction and 'real life'. The reports on the high-profile cases of maternal filicide are equally framed by wider cultural expectations of mothers and by conventions of plot and character, such that the central figure within them (the mother accused of killing her child or children) is effectively represented as a heroine/villain, as mad/bad/sad, but always unable to speak for herself. The fictional texts explored here are, by contrast, written in the first person for the most part, giving voice to the infanticidal mother as subject. These fictional narratives of infanticide should be read, as Edwards notes in 'Babykillers',[18] as part of a wider tendency within contemporary French women's writing in particular to expose the difficulties of mothering in modern society, 'the darker side to mothering'.[19] Certainly, Véronique Olmi's *Bord de mer* [Beside the Sea] and Laurence Tardieu's *Le Jugement de Léa* [The Judgement of Léa] both feature depressed, alienated, and impoverished single mothers. Edwards shows how these texts challenge dominant assumptions that women who kill their children are either 'mad' or 'bad',[20] whilst Ruth Cain proposes that 'literature brings us to an acknowledgement of situations which I think that legal reports, media reports simply don't do' so that 'we need to engage on a literary level with these tragedies'.[21] The role of literary narratives of infanticide is perceived to be to challenge the overly schematic models evidenced in legal contexts and frequently sensationalized in media reports, to give voice to the mother who commits filicide, and to offer alternative versions that 'provide insight conducive to a more empathetic understanding of neonaticide'[22] and urge us 'to view this story, this mother, with empathy'.[23]

The notion that literary narratives of infanticide can promote empathy and/or understanding is implicit within most approaches to the texts discussed in this chapter, both on the part of the writers describing authorial intention and on that of critics analyzing the texts. Susan Ayres suggests that in the context of maternal filicide, 'literature can provide a complex story that allows readers to [...] view others with empathy and compassion', yet she does not address what is at stake in establishing empathy with mothers who kill their children nor what sort of 'complex story' this might be (let alone the possibility of plural stories).[24] Her passing reference to 'viewing others with empathy' is crucial here because, as we will see, images of sight (and problems of vision and visibility) are foregrounded in several narratives of infanticide; 'viewing others with empathy' is not as simple (nor indeed as straightforwardly positive) as it may seem. As Breda Gray observes, 'empathic relationships can force us to engage with how the boundaries of feminist solidarities are produced', highlighting the limits of feminist discourses and narratives.[25] Sara Ahmed writes that when subjects assume that they can empathize with others without registering the distance between their respective positions, 'empathy sustains that very difference that it may seek to overcome'.[26] Clare Hemmings observes that empathy is 'always marked by that which cannot be empathized with', a limit that acts 'as a self-evident boundary for what (and who) can be included in feminism itself'.[27] Within this language of limits and boundaries, maternal filicide necessarily occupies a liminal, yet crucial, position in relation to feminism, as well as empathy, as we shall see. Hemmings also notes that in feminist discourses (that tend to privilege agency), 'a focus on empathy [...] instantiates a dynamic between the empathetic subject and the other-subject (who can become a subject only under certain conditions'.[28] What she means here is that empathy can work only if the 'other' can be related to as 'other-subject', not 'other-object', but this is less simple than it seems: firstly because it is still predicated on the perspective of the self-nominated autonomous empathetic subject (typically the Western feminist, in Hemmings's analysis) and secondly because the other may evidently lack agency and autonomy (and, although Hemmings does not state this, voice). In the context of women who commit filicide, filicide may be prompted by precisely this lack of autonomy and voice, as this chapter will show. Hemmings suggests that empathy with the 'other-subject' frequently works to 'reproduce rather than challenge the amenability of Western feminist political grammar'; similarly, I will argue, feminist empathy with infanticidal mothers works to shore up rather than destabilize our assumptions about maternity and violence.[29]

Before moving on to look at contemporary narratives of maternal filicide, this chapter begins by discussing Marguerite Duras's notorious article 'Sublime, forcément sublime' [Sublime, Necessarily Sublime], which predates my corpus by several decades. This article is a useful point of departure because it raises questions that enable us to reflect on how an empathetic (and feminist) approach to representations of infanticidal mothers (fictional and otherwise) might be developed. My discussion also seeks to highlight key imagery and themes that recur in more recent representations of filicide, both in the media and in fiction, as well as to underscore the difficulty in establishing clear distinctions between these.

Marguerite Duras: Sublimating Infanticide

Duras's extraordinary article, 'Sublime, forcément sublime', on the case of four-year old Gregory Villemin who was found, hands and legs tied, drowned in the Valogne river in 1984, and whose killer has never been identified, appeared in *Libération* at a point when suspicions were centred around Gregory's mother, Christine.[30] In her article, Duras both accuses Christine Villemin of filicide and defends this alleged act. Duras's piece reads more like a short version of one of her novels, for example, like *Le Ravissement de Lol V. Stein* [The Ravishing of Lol V. Stein], the link reinforced by Duras's abbreviation of Christine's surname to its initial: 'In Duras's text, the fleshy woman, Christine Villemin, becomes Christine V., and is thus transformed from fleshy woman to textual figure',[31] a 'mythical character more like a figure from one of her own books'.[32] 'Sublime, forcément sublime' was later reprinted in Duras's *Cahiers de l'Herne*, this time including two prefatory lines that flag up the text's fictional status: 'Loin de toutes les polémiques qu'il a suscitées, cet article appartient à l'univers fictionnel de Marguerite Duras. Il rappelle qu'inlassablement l'écrivain s'empare du monde réel, le réinvente et le métamorphose par le seul pouvoir de son écriture' [Far from all the polemical debate that it has provoked, this article belongs to the fictional universe of Marguerite Duras. It reminds us that the writer tirelessly seizes the real world, reinvents it and transforms it through the power of her writing] (*SFS*, p. 69). Yet, as Elise Hugueny-Léger points out, 'Si cet article appartient au domaine de la fiction, sa publication dans un journal quotidien réputé, au plein cœur d'une affaire criminelle qui passionne l'opinion publique, ne peut que poser problème' [If this article belongs to the realm of fiction, its publication in a reputable daily newspaper, in the midst of a criminal affair that excites public opinion, can only cause problems].[33] This highlights the difficulty in distinguishing between fiction and non-fiction, as well as the impossibility of writing 'about' an alleged infanticidal mother without turning her into a textual character. Nancy Huston aptly observes that in this piece, Duras creates a story:

> Duras turned *The Death of Little Gregory* into a novel by Marguerite Duras. She invented a beginning and a middle and an end for it and rendered it more credible to the French public than Villemin had been able to do. Villemin herself became one of the characters.[34]

Duras's rewriting of Gregory's case and her construction of the character of Christine V., while rendering both credible, obviously raises ethical questions about creating a story out of someone else's tragedy and about the feminist solidarity or empathy that underpins this narrative projecting a woman damaged by sexual violation and led to kill out of desperation. In portraying Christine V. as 'une martyre de la condition féminine, un personnage durassien au destin brisé' [a martyr of the feminine condition, a Durassian character with a shattered destiny], as Hugueny-Leger puts it, Duras's empathy is projected not onto the individual woman (who Duras has never met and has knowledge of only through media reports), but onto an imagined violated woman whose alleged act (Duras suggests) constitutes a refusal of the condition imposed upon her by social and familial expectation.[35]

Whilst 'Sublime' creates a fantasized background to Christine V.'s act, it also, however, rejects logical explanations for it. As Andrew Slade remarks:

> Christine V is sublime in so much as she is the limit figure. Her act is incomprehensible and this should be understood in the technical sense; her act is not available to a judgment of understanding. It is unrecognizable and yields no truth.[36]

Duras does not attempt to understand the alleged murder that she recounts, nor does she judge it, but her self-positioning as narrator of Christine V.'s story (which is framed in feminist terms) is complex. Duras writes: 'Ce qui aurait fait criminelle Christine V. c'est un secret de toutes les femmes, commun. Je parle du crime commis sur l'enfant, désormais accompli, mais aussi je parle du crime opéré sur elle, la mère. Et cela me regarde' (*SFS*, p. 73) ('What would make Christine V. a criminal is a secret that all women share. I speak of the crime committed against the child, however it's accomplished, but also of the crime perpetrated on her, the mother. And that regards me', *SNS*, p. 17). It is unclear why the crime perpetuated on the mother 'me regarde'; the implication is that it is bound up in a shared female secret that links women together in unspeakable knowledge. Duras uses the first person frequently within the article, inserting herself into the other woman's story and setting up a connection (and a gesture of feminist solidarity?) with the other woman that suggests a parallel between the writer and the alleged infanticidal mother which finds echoes in Huston's proposal that 'a mother who is willing to kill her own child is pretty much the same thing as a novelist'.[37] The connection between Duras and Christine V. is constructed around images of seeing/not seeing. Alluding to women married to dominant men, Duras also writes that 'elles s'en servent pour ne pas voir, survivre' (*SFS*, p. 71) [they use all their power not to see, to survive] (my translation) whilst enquiring of the male partners, 'Comment ne les voient-ils pas, eux, les hommes?' (*SFS*, p. 72) ('How can they not see it, the men?', *SNS*, p. 15). The men who set the law have the power (yet do not see); the women have a different vision, one bound up in not seeing, which is seemingly rooted in a fantasized affiliation with other women and which, crucially, constitutes the basis for Duras's article. She begins her article with the statement that 'Je ne verrai jamais Christine V.' (p. 69) ('I will never see Christine V.', p. 9)], yet the subsequent paragraph starts, 'La maison, je l'ai vue' (p. 69) ('I saw the house', p. 9), and she goes on to reiterate positive images of seeing ('C'est ce que je vois'; 'Je vois ce crime'; 'Je ne vois qu'elle au centre du monde' (p. 69) ('This is what I see'; 'I regard this crime'; 'I see only her at the center of the world', pp. 9–10). The initial avowal of a failure to see is disrupted by her later insistence on what she can see (which should then be understood more in terms of imagination than of literal vision), which is repeatedly implied to be limited ('je ne vois qu'elle'). Duras states that 'je vois une photo d'elle dans l'auto qui l'emmène à la prison, je retrouve aussi cette absence, cette inexpressivité légère qui vitrifie le regard' (p. 69) ('I see a picture of her in the car taking her to the prison', p. 9). She never sees Christine Villemin in person, only a photograph (taken in the police car following her arrest, highlighting that Duras's image of her is already framed by the image of her as a suspect); the absence that Duras describes in her gaze underscores her inaccessibility.

Here, then, seeing is both framed and limited by a lack of knowledge and insight. This is reinforced as Duras recounts Christine V.'s own struggle to see (which should be contrasted with the women who strive not to see described earlier), evoking 'Christine V. innocente qui peut-être a tué sans savoir comme moi j'écris sans savoir, les yeux contre la vitre à essayer de voir clair dans le noir grandissant du soir de ce jour d'octobre' (p. 70) ('innocent Christine V. who had, perhaps, killed without knowing it, as I, I write without knowing, with eyes fixed at the window trying to see clearly in the growing dark of the evening, that day in October', p. 11). The eyes in question must be Christine's (it was October when her son was killed) but it is not clear when or why she is looking (out of a shuttered window, p. 69), although the implication is that she is seeking knowledge of what has happened to her son (having, Duras suggests, killed him without registering her act). Yet the eyes that struggle to see may also belong to Duras, whose difficulties in seeing (and knowing) are foregrounded throughout her article; the thwarted quest to see connects the two and indeed curiously forms the basis of Duras's empathetic depiction of Christine V., rooted precisely in the inability to see, or know, what happened to Gregory.

The above discussion of Duras's text raises questions that underpin my analysis of contemporary narratives of infanticide. Can empathy find origins in an explicit failure to see/know that could somehow be shared? Is it ethical to empathize without knowledge of the other? This question goes beyond the obvious criticism of Duras for projecting guilt upon a mother with no evidence — even if Christine V. had been proved beyond reasonable doubt to have killed her son, to what extent could Duras really 'know' why? Or would seeing (or assuming that one can see clearly) be equally if not more troubling in a context of a 'limit case' such as this? Can Duras's narrative model an empathy founded in recognition of lack of understanding and insight, rather than in an assumption of comprehension? The other ethical questions raised by 'Sublime, forcément sublime' pivot around the relation between fiction and the 'reality' it both reflects and constructs. The prefatory sentences added for the publication of this article in the *Cahiers de l'Herne* are somewhat misleading: the claim that Duras 's'empare du monde réel' [seizes the real world] is over-simplistic in its allusion to a 'monde réel' [real world] that can be neatly separated from fictional reconstructions of it. The difficulties in seeing that are emphasized throughout 'Sublime' also point to the difficulty in ever getting beyond a constructed image of an infanticidal mother, as in the judge's reported description of Christine Villemin's absent gaze, 'une légère absence dans le regard' (*SFS*, p. 69) ('a slight absence in the gaze', *SNS*, p. 9). Christine is oddly similar to Duras's protagonists: she is always already a character of sorts, even before Duras begins to (re)create her). Media reports, like novels, invent characters as mothers who kill (albeit in different conventions and rhetoric); what my reading of 'Sublime' shows is not only how difficult it is to see clearly beyond the narrative constructions, but also how assumptions of empathy are also bound up in the fictional representations, as I will show in representations of neonaticide in the press and in contemporary fiction.

Neonaticide: Empathizing with the 'Ordinary Mother'

While cases remain statistically very low, there have been a striking number of cases of multiple neonaticides in this century in France. The most well-known case, which inspired Mazarine Pingeot's novel *Le Cimetière des poupées* [The Doll Cemetery], is that of Véronique Courjault, who killed three new-born babies, burning the body of the first and freezing the bodies of the other two. There are other sensationalist cases: nursing assistant Dominique Cottrez, for instance, was found guilty in 2015 of killing eight of her new-born babies (between 1988 and 2000), whilst Céline Lesage was convicted in March 2010 of smothering four babies and strangling two others between 1999 and 2007. In 2002, Audrey Chabot was imprisoned for killing her new-born baby; she was later released and subsequently convicted of killing a second new-born baby in 2011 and a third in 2012 (burying both bodies in the freezer). Sophie Marinopoulos suggests that serial neonaticide is bound up in traumatic repetition: 'l'acte non pris en compte par la réalité, jamais

entendu ou réperé, se répète [...] tel un symptôme qui attend d'être entendu'
[the act not taken into account by reality, never heard or grasped, is repeated [...]
like a symptom waiting to be heard], because the pregnancy and childbirth have
never been acknowledged or assimilated.[38] This is bound up in, but not bound
to, conceptions of pregnancy denial (which may have surprising physiological
effects such as delayed abdominal weight gain, possibly the continuation of regular
bleeding mimicking menstrual periods, and so on).[39] Debates around pregnancy
denial figured particularly prominently in discussions of Véronique Courjault's
high-profile case, to which I now turn.

Courjault's husband, Jean-Louis, reported the discovery of two infant bodies
in the freezer in their family home in Seoul, South Korea, in 2006; DNA tests
confirmed that these were the offspring of the Courjaults. Later, when the case
had been transferred to France, Véronique Courjault admitted that she had given
birth to and killed the babies in secret in 2002 and 2003, before putting their bodies
into the freezer. She also confessed to having killed another baby in France in 1999
and burnt its body. In 2009, the case against her husband was dismissed and she
was found guilty of killing the three babies. Courjault's case attracted widespread
media attention in France and internationally, including regular newspaper updates,
television and radio coverage. These represented her either as a loving mother
suffering from mental health issues (*The Irish Times*, for instance, as Lynsey Black
points out, describes her as a '*devoted wife and mother*') or as '*freezer baby mum*'; both
of these representations work to minimize her multiple crimes.[40] The violence of
the triple murder is somehow contained within mocking discourses around 'freezer
babies', evidenced in the surprising number of blog posts and cartoons including
caricatured drawings of Courjault looking in the freezer, eating an ice lolly within
which a baby's body has been frozen, pushing a supermarket trolley to hunt out
babies in industrial-sized freezers, and so on. On the one hand, what is shocking
here seems less to be the murder than the storage of the bodies in the freezer,
whilst on the other, focus on the freezer images allows the killing of the babies to
be somehow trivialized (likened to frozen meat) and the violence therefore to be
minimized.[41] Courjault's story has also been turned into a docufiction produced
by Jean-Xavier de Lestrade, entitled *Parcours meurtrier d'une mère ordinaire: l'affaire
Courjault* [The Murderous Journey of an Ordinary Mother: The Courjault Affair],[42]
including both archival footage and reconstruction of events with actors and
drawing on court transcripts to copy the original words spoken ('Il fallait restituer
la parole de Véronique Courjault' [We had to reproduce Véronique Courjault's
words], insisted the producer).[43] Yet the media frenzy prompted by Courjault's case
offers so many competing versions of Courjault herself that her perspective remains
difficult to understand. The news of maternal filicide, Marinopoulos suggests,
'nous aveugle' [blinds us] (the allusion to blindness here recalls Duras's insistence on
the limits of vision in 'Sublime'), impeding our vision by haunting us ('Obsédants
sont les crimes sur les enfants' [crimes against children obsess us]), and drawing us in
as agents, rather than spectators, of the drama ('le fait divers nous rend acteurs d'une
mauvaise pièce de théâtre' [news reports turn us into actors in a bad play]).[44]

Marinopoulos writes that 'sur les photos des mères néonaticides, on remarque ce gel des affects: on peut lire un vide, une absence dans l'expression de leur visage. Ces femmes ont peu d'estime d'elle-même et on retrouve toujours, dans leur histoire, des manques affectifs' [on photos of neonaticidal mothers, you can see frozen emotion: you can read an emptiness, an absence in their facial expressions. These women have little self-esteem and have always experienced a lack of emotional attachment].[45] Like Villemin, Courjault is described as having 'le regard vide' [an empty expression] which makes her equally hard to see and to 'read'.[46] This is compounded by the contradictions marking her self-representation. In court, she states of her babies that, on the one hand, 'ils n'avaient pas pour moi d'existence réelle' [they didn't really exist for me], whilst on the other, 'je n'aurais pas pu les jeter dans une poubelle' [I couldn't have thrown them in the bin]; 'Je voulais les garder avec moi' [I wanted to keep them with me].[47] She seems caught between being unable to acknowledge her babies as real and feeling desperate to keep them close to her. Similarly, when asked in court why she had not cremated her babies' bodies, Cottrez replied, 'Parce que ça leur aurait fait mal' [Because it would have hurt them] and commented that 'L'hiver, je pensais à eux, j'enlevais les pots de fleurs et je leur mettais une couverture' [In the winter, I thought about them, I lifted up the flowerpots and put a cover on them]. In both cases, neonaticide seems to constitute an illusory means of preserving the maternal bond with the babies after their birth and death.[48] Chabot, meanwhile, claimed that 'Quand j'ai tué et congelé les bébés j'allais leur parler, ça me semblait important et je m'en voulais' [When I killed and froze the babies I went to talk to them, it seemed important to me and I was angry with myself]; and, 'Parfois, j'ouvrais la porte du congélateur pour les toucher, leur dire que je les aimais, pour m'excuser, mais c'était trop tard' [Sometimes, I opened the freezer door to touch them, to tell them I loved them, to apologize, but it was too late].[49] Her recognition of her babies is self-consciously belated, as though she could only register their existence once she has killed them, but, like Cottrez and Courjault, her (limited) self-representation in relation to the babies she killed is that of a loving mother intent on preserving the maternal connection with the child.

The delayed recognition of the dead baby is explored in Marinopoulos's novel, *La Vie ordinaire d'une mère meurtrière* [The Ordinary Life of a Murderous Mother], from which the later docufiction on Courjault derived its title: the insistence on the mother who commits infanticide as 'ordinary' (rather than monstrous) already signals Marinopoulos's intention to promote understanding of pregnancy denial and neonaticide.[50] In this text, the protagonist, Éva, unaware that she is pregnant, gives birth suddenly and secretly in the bathroom and places the baby's body in the freezer before continuing her normal daily life; it is only in prison that she begins to recognize the baby's existence. Éva is represented as a model wife and mother, whose own feelings and desires are subjugated entirely to the needs of her family ('elle est là, toujours là' [she is there, always there] but 'si effacé' [so effaced] (*La Vie*, p. 9), 'une mère aimante, vide' [a loving, empty mother], p. 30). She constructs a sense of self only after her arrest (p. 94) at which point she also begins to register the existence of her baby. This novel presents a psychoanalytically coherent model of pregnancy denial, neonaticide, and subsequent self-realization; it constitutes an alternative form of psychoanalytic case history. Elsewhere, Marinopoulos insists on the need to approach infanticidal mothers with 'un regard empathique' [an empathetic regard], but she fails to explore what this might mean.[51] In this novel, it seems to mean constructing a coherent explanation of neonaticide and a rehabilitation of the infanticidal mother (Éva becomes aware of her crime and takes responsibility for it at the end of the text) even as she is found guilty. Yet this is more complex than it first seems. As her judgement is announced, 'Éva la meurtrière, Éva la mère, reste énigmatique pour le plus grand nombre' [Éva the murderer, Éva the mother, remains enigmatic for the majority] (p. 119): whilst the narrative renders her character legible (through the portrayal of pregnancy denial), others cannot understand her or indeed see her other than as a mother who killed her baby. This is compounded because Éva in court retains the 'visage impassible, vide d'expression' [impassive face, devoid of expression] (p. 106) reminiscent of the descriptions of Courjault and of Villemin.

The 'regard empathique' is, then, fraught with the difficulty in seeing (beyond) the infanticidal mother (and her blank, empty expression) whose viewpoint is simultaneously constructed, exposed, and occluded by the third-person narrative. For instance, in court, following the descriptions of Éva giving birth to a living baby, the rhetorical question 'Est-ce nécessaire de le redire cinq, six fois?' [Is it necessary to repeat it five, six times?] (p. 109) could express either Éva's own perspective or that of the narrator; the confusion between the voices here may mark the empathetic approach that Marinopoulos advocates (as the narrative interprets the mother's emotion), but it may also imply silencing the mother who has killed her baby by projecting onto her particular words and emotions (and fitting her into a set psychoanalytic mould). This is not to dismiss the form of *La Vie ordinaire*; on the contrary, Marinopoulos uses fiction as a means of illustrating her experience of working with infanticidal mothers and to try to explain their motivations. But its blurring of different subject positions (as in Duras's text) underscores the difficulty of recounting infanticide empathetically in the third person without silencing the women whose voices the text is attempting to represent. Lorraine Code writes that 'empathy at its best preserves yet seeks to know the "strangeness", respects the boundaries between self and other that the "forbiddenness" affirms'.[52] Here, the boundaries between narrating voice and neonaticidal mother are obscured, whilst the attempt to represent the latter as 'ordinary' may work to efface the 'strangeness' that might offer a more productive means of establishing an empathetic relation. This text, like 'Sublime, forcément sublime', attempts to explain the perspective of the infanticidal mother even as it foregrounds the difficulty of comprehension; where Duras assumes the possibility of connection with Christine V., here the subject position of the narrating voice (in relation to Éva) is difficult to locate. The problem of giving voice to infanticidal mothers is played out differently in the other texts discussed in this chapter, which are all written (predominantly) in the first person, yet in which, inevitably, the mother's voice is also always mediated and framed by other discourses. These texts do, however, renegotiate the relation between empathy and understanding, as we see in Pingeot's *Le Cimetière des poupées*.

Le Cimetière des poupées: Complying with Empathy

Pingeot's *Le Cimetière des poupées* takes the form of an extended letter written by a woman awaiting trial for killing her new-born baby to her husband, who had been unaware of the pregnancy or the child's birth and death. The novel finds its origins, Pingeot states, in 'la série d'infanticides, pas seulement l'affaire Véronique Courjault, mais tous ceux dont on a pu lire les comptes rendus dans la presse' [the series of infanticides, not only the Véronique Courjault affair, but all those reported in the press], but the fact that the narrator preserves her baby in the freezer inevitably recalls the Courjault case.[53] The novel courted controversy even before it was published, as Courjault's mother-in-law claims that she wrote to Pingeot to urge her to delay publication until after the trial, but the author did not reply, whilst her publishing house, Julliard, responded by denying any straightforward connection between Courjault's case and Pingeot's novel.[54] Pingeot's aim in writing this novel was to try to understand the inexplicable: 'Pour une mère [...] l'infanticide est vraiment l'acte le plus incompréhensible qui soit. Et je pense que la littérature, c'est justement d'aller dans l'inconcevable' [For a mother [...] infanticide is really the most incomprehensible act ever. And I think that literature means exploring the inconceivable].[55] The act of neonaticide is never explicitly recounted in the novel and the narrator's account of putting her baby's body in the freezer is also indirect (she makes a reference to the freezer at the very end of the penultimate chapter, then begins the last chapter by admitting that 'je l'ai mis là' [I put it there] (*Le Cimetière*, p. 154), the abbreviated 'l'' implicitly referring to her unnamed child and the 'là' a somewhat vague allusion to the freezer). Nathalie Morello notes that 'l'ellipse finale confine l'acte dans le domaine du tabou, non-dit *et*, voire même ici *parce que*, non dicible' [the final ellipsis confines the act in the realm of the taboo, non-spoken *and*, indeed even here *because*, unspeakable].[56] The question remains however as to how neonaticide — the 'non dicible' — can be recounted through Pingeot's self-consciously empathetic approach: 'je n'ai pas voulu faire une enquête journalistique ou porter un jugement moral, je suis, au contraire, dans une démarche d'empathie' [I didn't want to do a journalistic investigation or pass moral judgement, I am, on the contrary, approaching through empathy].[57] This opens up the question of what an empathetic approach to infanticide might mean, both on the part of the writer who creates an infanticidal narrator, and on the part of the reader, seeking to understand why a mother would kill her child.

Within the narrative economy of this text, neonaticide is surprisingly logical, an act 'dont le but principal était de faire advenir un sujet autonome' [the main aim of which was to produce an autonomous subject][58] committed by a 'Sujet-enfant' [child-Subject] struggling to assert autonomy and agency. The preservation of the baby's body in the freezer represents the mark of 'l'amour le plus absolu que plus rien n'entacherait' [the most absolute love that nothing more could sully] (*Le Cimetière*, p. 155) as it allows her to keep her baby close to her.[59] Elissa Marder, in a psychoanalytic reading of maternal mourning, cites cases of neonaticide, including that of Courjault, in which babies' bodies are buried in freezers, to conclude that 'the babies are suspended in a time of perpetual birth-death. As such, the freezer can be read as a replacement for and extension of the mother's body', standing in for both the womb and for the crypt.[60] This is reinforced in Pingeot's novel as the narrator describes herself kneeling before 'le cercueil blanc' [the white coffin] — located in the cellar, another image of the womb/tomb — to pray (p. 154). For Marder, the freezer is emblem of a particular kind of (failed) mourning, as the mother attempts to refuse loss of (or separation from) her child by preserving the child intact. Pingeot's narrator is seeking to retain the integrity of the mother/child bond, 'la pureté du lien qui nous unissait' [the purity of the link that united us] (p. 155), thereby denying the separation and individuation that would usually begin at birth. Apparently a model mother of her two sons, she struggles with separation from them, fearful that they will not return (she refers to 'cette panique en moi quand je les laissais à l'école' [this panic inside me when I left them at school], p. 71). Julia Kristeva writes that 'neonaticide and infanticide do not *give* death: they are the work of *possession*'.[61] Like Olmi's narrator, who suffers from jealousy at her younger son's affectionate relationship with his teacher and fears her older son growing up, Pingeot's narrator seeks above all to possess her child, to avoid letting go. Her final revelations about preserving the baby in the freezer, the mother's domain, are almost too easy to integrate into a coherent psychoanalytic model of maternal possessiveness as sketched out by Marder, yet Pingeot's narrator is motivated less by possession and the refusal of separation and mourning, and more by fantasies of (self-) sacrifice.

In the famous story of Solomon's two would-be mothers fighting over a child, where the 'real' mother was (decided to be) the one who would let the child go rather than cut the child in half, Elaine Tuttle Hansen writes that 'The "good" woman and mother can speak only to erase her authority, to renounce possession, to disown her desire; a mother is someone who sacrifices something she has or wants, or is willing to do so, for the good of another'.[62] Pingeot's narrator, seemingly driven by the desire to possess her child, is the antithesis of the 'good mother', yet she also presents her act as sacrificial, as, like Solomon's 'good mother', she can 'speak' (write) only to assert her act as one of maternal sacrifice, this time to save her child (and thereby herself) from her husband's control. Joubi observes that in this text 'néonaticide est un double sacrifice', of the child but also of the self, even as it also allows the narrator to (temporarily) 's'affirmer en tant qu'agent' [affirm herself as an agent]. The title, alluding to her childhood games with Ken and Barbie dolls in which she ritually made Ken violate and murder a succession of Barbie dolls before burying the dolls (that clearly represent herself: 'je m'étais tant de fois tuée dans d'atroces souffrances' [I had killed myself so many times in atrocious suffering], p. 80) ascribes a certain inevitability to her subsequent crime which is figured as a form of self-harm/suicide as well as murder, a sacrifice/self-sacrifice.[63]

The narrator's striking failure to recount the birth and death of her child is described as being deliberately intended to refuse to allow her husband a satisfying story ('Satisfais-toi de l'innommable. J'ai voulu pour toi la faillite des mots' [Content yourself with the unspeakable. I wanted for you the failure of words], *Le Cimetière*, 153) rather than a mark of her inability to put trauma into words.

The incomprehensibility of neonaticide here is inextricably bound up in her claustrophobic marriage, as her attempt to possess and preserve her child is less a failure to accept separation and loss than a perverse power game with her husband. Even the final account of burying the baby's body in the freezer, and the use of the singular possessive in her claim that 'j'avais sauvé *mon* fils' [I had saved *my* son] (p. 155) defiantly claims possession over the baby to spite her husband. Whilst the neonaticide is surprisingly easy to understand and explain, then, the novel displaces the 'inconcevable' [inconceivable] from neonaticide to the claustrophobic marriage. The repeated use of the singular 'tu' [you] in address to the husband as projected intratextual reader works both to exclude the reader and to emphasize this exclusion. The only possibility of empathy (as opposed to understanding) would be through becoming complicit in the narrator's damaging relationship and following her lead in underplaying the murder of a new-born baby (likened to a doll), as opposed to being able both to understand her crime and register its severity. However, the text also works to foreclose empathy precisely by emphasizing its own foregrounding of the narrator's marriage over her child, and by highlighting that which is most 'inconcevable' (and uncomfortable) here is precisely how easy it might be to understand (and minimize) the killing of a baby. The possibility of empathy here is troubling because it seems bound up in complicity in a violent and damaging relationship within which the (murder and) preservation of the baby is (are) intended to hurt his father, and thus the baby is effectively once more denied and erased. This text thereby points to potential risks of empathy, which I explore further in another celebrated first-person narrative of child filicide (here the double murder of older children, rather than neonaticide), Olmi's *Bord de mer*.

Bord de mer: Feminist Empathy and Community

Where *Le Cimetière des poupées* seems to work to foreclose empathy, critics and readers of *Bord de mer* have emphasized how the text induces sympathy and indeed empathy for the narrator: as Cain observes, '*Beside the Sea*'s evocation of the experience of a woman whose sanity and personhood are unravelling may enable empathy, or at least comprehension, rather than (simply) repulsion or pity'.[64] In the words of Adriana Hunter, who translated the novel into English:

> It gets right inside the head of someone who does the unthinkable, and you come out of it sympathising with her, rather than hating her [...]. All parents will have moments of despair and feelings of inadequacy, though not all will admit to them.[65]

The implication here is not only that the reader ends up feeling sympathy for the narrator, but also that the reader understands her actions through shared experience of parenting. Cain asserts that 'this woman is definitely one of us', 'I didn't read her as separate from me';[66] whilst Edwards writes that in this text and in Tardieu's *Le Jugement de Léa*, 'the narrating mothers show the possibility of being us'.[67] Yet Olmi's narrator, economically deprived, isolated, and (possibly) mentally ill, is not only a parent struggling to do her best: she neglects her children (her elder son gets her younger son ready for school while she stays in bed; she habitually arrives late to collect the boys from school, for instance) even before she kills them. The reader's empathy for her is triggered by her lack of support: the structures of social intervention (health visitors, social workers, and so on) seem to judge rather than help, focusing on minor, even irrelevant issues such as allowing the boys to scribble on the wall, rather than helping her to look after her children. Cain asks, referring to the double murder, 'whose responsibility is this?', a question that is surprisingly easy for the liberal (feminist) reader to answer, as the narrator herself can clearly not be held totally responsible, in moral, if not in legal, terms, given the lack of support for her (not to mention the strong suggestion of mental illness).[68] For the reader, then, empathy for the narrator is entwined with judgement of the society that offers her inadequate support.

If we pause here, however, the implications of occupying an empathetic position in relation to Olmi's narrator are intriguing. Edwards opens a study of infanticide in two French films with two provocative questions: 'How can one sympathise with a murderer of children? And furthermore, how can one sympathise with a mother who has murdered her own child?'[69] In *Bord de mer*, sympathy for (or empathy with) the infanticidal mother is possible partly because maternal filicide — described in strikingly maternal terms — does not undermine dominant cultural ideals of maternity. The narrator recounts in detail how she suffocates each sleeping child with a pillow: as she smothers her youngest son, she recalls him writing 'Maman' (*BM*, p. 75) ('mommy', *BS*, p. 108) on the wall and calls him 'mon Kevin' (*BM*, p. 75) ('my Kevin', *BS*, p. 107), 'mon petit garçon' (*BM*, p. 78) ('my little boy', *BS*, p. 107) (the insistence on 'my' here again marks the desire for maternal possession) before ruffling his hair and kissing him. She sits very close to Stan — 'tout près de son visage pour ne pas le lâcher, jamais' (*BM*, p. 81) ('right next to his face so I wouldn't let him go, not ever', *BS*, p. 117) as she holds the pillow over his face — and then kisses him gently, just as a mother might kiss her sleeping child goodnight. She recounts infanticide as an act of maternal love and sacrifice, allowing her sons to move together to a better place. Thus the reader can sympathize, or indeed empathize, with Olmi's narrator precisely because — even as she kills her children — her love and maternal urge to protect them (as well as possess them) are evident; empathy here does not require dismantling ideals of maternity.

More, however, empathy in this context is bound up in assumption of commonality. Both Cain and Edwards refer to the narrator as 'one of us': who exactly is 'us' and who is the implied 'other' (them?) in this formulation? This imagined community of mothers, readers, or both, or neither, is constructed in implicit opposition to the society that has failed Olmi's narrator. The empathy shown to the narrator is tied up in a judgement of society; by aligning oneself with her, the reader is not only taking the risk of acknowledging infanticide as a perpetual maternal possibility, but also abdicating responsibility (which is effectively deferred to the anonymous 'them'). This reading of *Bord de mer* thus risks becoming complacent because it is rooted in an identification with the struggling mother that is based on self-distancing from the society that offers inadequate support to mothers in difficulty.

It projects responsibility elsewhere through the assumption of commonality that the narrative undermines (in her account, other mothers ignore her and she mocks their performance of public parenting) Critical readings of this novel have also aligned the reader with the children, as well as with their mother. Anne Mairesse writes that at the end of *Bord de mer* 'Le lecteur s'y trouve sans recours, abandonné comme l'enfant, victime et témoin impuissant d'une souffrance provoquée par un acte injustifiable' [The reader ends up with no recourse, abandoned like the child, victim and powerless witness of a suffering caused by an injustifiable act].[70] Edwards, meanwhile, claims that in this text and in *Le Jugement de Léa*, 'The reader is at once in the same position as the children, unable to understand or alter the events, and in the position of the onlookers who are asked to voice their stance'.[71] The reader's powerlessness is induced by the inevitable ending (predictable from the first page when the narrator mentions an unfinished pot of jam that they will never return to eat) of a claustrophobic story recounted with few chapter breaks and sparse dialogue, which leaves no respite for the narrator or for the reader until the end. The reader cannot, however, be in the same position as the children, not only because the children are victims rather than onlookers, but also because the children's perspective is limited (they are unaware of their mother's plans) whilst the reader's frustration lies partly in having anticipated the ending from the start and being unable to prevent it.

Empathizing with a mother who kills her children might seem shocking (and it clearly risks minimizing the children's deaths), yet here readers of this text have assumed a connection to the mother even while positioning themselves in the place of the children (without noting the cognitive dissonance that this requires). This may be because the novel stops abruptly when the narrator registers that her sons are dead and screams — at this point the reader shares her horror at the children's deaths and does not (as is the case in *Le Cimetière des poupées* and in *Le Jugement de Léa*) see the infanticidal mother survive the loss of her children. Perhaps what is most difficult to imagine and understand, then, is not the murder itself, but surviving it, the notion of a maternal subject who killed her children without subsequently killing herself. Empathizing with the infanticidal mother in *Bord de mer* is not as risky as it seems, it does not challenge dominant cultural ideals of maternity, and it projects blame onto an anonymously indifferent society from which the reader, seemingly aligned with the mother *and* with the children, can keep a safe distance. This is problematized in the final novel explored in this chapter, Tardieu's *Le Jugement de Léa*, which recounts a mother's wait in court to hear the verdict on the death of her son.

Le Jugement de Léa: Wrong-footing Judgement

Le Jugement de Léa recounts (for the most part in the first person) a mother's wait in the court antechamber to discover if she has been found guilty of killing her four-year-old son (by pushing him down a flight of steps). Léa recounts being judged harshly by fellow prisoners and by a prison nurse (*Le Jugement*, p. 10), reflecting societal contempt for child-killers, but she is treated kindly by the guard; it is his willingness to interact with her that enables Léa — who has been silent throughout her trial — to speak. Edwards notes that 'in the position of judge and jury, of those who ordinarily hear the plea of the accused, is the reader, who "hears" the narrator's story and who is invited not to pass judgement but to view this story, this mother, with empathy'.[72] Since the judge and jury have not heard Léa's perspective, it is clear that their judgement will be impaired; the reader, who along with the guard, is given privileged insight into her version of events, is implicitly urged to adopt a different position in relation to this story and to Léa herself (although it is important to unpick the connections and differences between 'this story' and 'this mother') by seeking to understand Léa's struggle, like the guard. She recounts her troubled childhood with emotionally distant parents, traumatized by the death of her brother, which evidently led to her dysfunctional relationships as an adult, beginning with a sexless marriage and a series of anonymous sexual encounters, one of which involved the conception of her son. Léa describes her isolation, poverty, and anxiety as a single parent; her insomnia, which causes her (like Olmi's narrator) to fall asleep during the day while her son plays in another room, and her struggle to show love for him, because cuddling him reminds her painfully of the affection that her mother in particular failed to give her. Her account is stumbling and incoherent, suggesting that she was depressed and exhausted; the account of her son's death emerges in jerky, awkward sentences and questions, often interrupted by ellipses, so that it is difficult for the reader to determine whether or not she (deliberately) pushed her son, let alone why. It is tempting to guess, based on her story, that she felt defeated and overwhelmed by her own poverty and alienation, and pushed her son because she could not in that moment cope with mothering him, but this is not explicitly stated. The reader's sympathy for Léa's lonely struggle is, however, not synonymous with empathy, which would mean being able to project oneself into her position, mainly because that position shifts throughout the narrative, as we shall see.

Even from the beginning, Tardieu's narrative is disruptive: the opening statement, 'Je m'appelle Léa' [My name is Léa] (*Le Jugement*, p. 9) is already false, as we later learn that her name is Marie when she is referred to in court. This initial introduction founds her story in deception, although she does later admit her real name and that 'Léa' was a pseudonym chosen for her brief sexual encounter with Théo's father. The title, then, displaces the question of judgement: it is not (only) Marie, who is being judged for infanticide, but Léa, for having sex with a stranger without contraception and, in her mind more culpably, without finding out his name. Part of Léa's anxiety lies in her shame at the circumstances of her son's conception; when he asks about his father, she grabs and shakes him because she has no idea how to tell him about his origins (p. 90), no way of making sense of her past ('Je perdais le fil. Je perdais le sens. Ma vie se rédusait à des miettes' [I lost the thread. I lost the meaning. My life was becoming reduced to crumbs], p. 95). The loss of coherence in her life story is part of her struggle to exist. She seems shaky, confused, and disorientated ('Tout tourne autour de moi, chavire' [Everything is turning around me, swaying]; 'Je vacille' [I wobble], p. 99), which also marks the point at which Théo falls (or she pushes him) down the steps. While the reader sympathizes with her, it is impossible to empathize because the text itself becomes disorientating at this point — ('Non, je ne l'ai pas poussé. Tu l'as poussé, Léa' [No, I haven't pushed him. You pushed him, Léa], p. 101) — and it is unclear whose voice is being reported. This is mirrored following the jury's verdict, at which point Léa/Marie describes her son falling, then herself ('C'est lui qui crève, c'est toi qui tombes' [It's him who dies, it's you who falls], p. 106), so that subject positions become blurred as she dissociates herself from her own body ('ce corps, là, assis, avachi, ce n'est plus elle' [this body, there, sitting, slumped, it's no longer her], p. 106), watching her own body fall just as she watched her son. This is compounded as the narrative abruptly shifts following the announcement of the jury's verdict, from the first person subject position of Léa to the third person, implying that since she has been found guilty of infanticide, she can no longer be allowed a subject position as such. If the reader, like Léa herself, is destabilized by the shifting narrative frame, the effect of this is not to gain insight into Léa's feelings, or to empathize with her, but to register the limits of our understanding of Léa's act. The guilty verdict is reached by judge and jury without hearing Léa's own testimony, but her account of her life does not make judgement easier; instead, it disrupts the reader's attempts to either judge or understand.

This is compounded by the final encounter of the novel, between Léa and her estranged parents; her mother does not look at her, but her father puts his hand on her shoulder, and 'leurs regards se fondent l'un dans l'autre' [their gazes melt into each other] so that 'tous deux se noient dans ce regard' [Both are drowning in this gaze]. The emphasis is again here on vision: the reference to drowning highlights that both are destabilized, reinforced by the statement that 'Léa vacille' [Léa wobbles]. She then hears a voice, presumably her father's, murmuring 'Pardonne-moi' [Forgive me] (p. 107). This final request for absolution — it is not an apology as such — jars, because it comes not from the infanticidal mother, but from the neglectful father to the mother who has killed her own child; it also highlights Léa's own lack of apology and sets this in the context of her background of emotional deprivation. The reader is left entirely disorientated as the description of Léa's meeting with her parents (particularly her father) displaces the story of the relationship between Léa and Théo and erases Théo completely from the narrative frame, as the reader focuses on Léa as (neglected) child rather than on Léa as infanticidal mother. The text ends with the brief admission that Léa is unsure as to whether she has heard or understood her father's words correctly (p. 107), thereby reinforcing the lack of clarity framing its narrative, which begins with a simple identification that turns out to be false and ends with a confused lack of certainty. The text disorientates the reader through its representation of a narrator whose viewpoint we can never entirely share, yet equally cannot separate ourselves entirely from, as the reader — like Léa, and like her son before her — is destabilized. The reader's lack of stability in relation to the text both mirrors and is markedly different from Théo's fatal fall and Léa's faint (which are also, of course, dissimilar), underscoring the disjunction between the child who has been killed, the mother who cannot make her life story cohere, and the reader. The reader is prevented from judging (because judgement within this text is shown to be misplaced, unable to take Léa's perspective into account) and from understanding (due to the lack of coherence at key points in the text) but this is of course less disempowering than Léa's position (let alone that of her son). The distance between the reader and the infanticidal mother may however itself offer an alternative approach to empathy that in Anne Whitehead's words 'does not claim to know or to understand the other, but remains alert to her distance and her difference'.[73]

This model of empathy may be related to Hemmings's notion of 'affective dissonance', which implies a recognition of the disjunction between one's own position (and social value) and someone else's that can point up the injustice in the respective social positionings. The example Hemmings uses in her article 'Affective Solidarity: Feminist Reflexivity and Political Transformation' is that of a house-owner and her cleaner, who have very different knowledge of and power within the house (the latter has knowledge that the former wishes to suppress and thereby has power; the former has the clear socio-economic advantage). They may, at some point, register the disparities in their situations, recognition of which could have multiple ramifications playing out different potential power permutations: the cleaner could blackmail her employer; the cleaner could be sacked, for example. As Hemmings notes, 'That moment of affect — anger, frustration or even rage — [...] is of course an unstable entity and its impact cannot be controlled', but it carries potential for transformative action and possibly even 'mutual recognition and affective solidarity' between the two women.[74] The role of empathy here lies precisely in the simultaneous realization of connection with and distance from the other. Hemmings does not interrogate the notion of 'affective solidarity', assuming it to be positive, but if we turn back to *Bord de mer*, it is clear that the roots of affective solidarity, rather than being located in commonality, may be located in a disavowal of other suffering subjects. It is striking in Olmi's text that it is only once the narrator has killed her sons that she can make herself heard: she registers that they are dead and states baldly, 'J'ai hurlé' (*BM*, p. 82) ('I screamed', *BS*, p. 119). The double infanticide is not itself a cry for help, but an acknowledgement that she has nobody to cry to; the scream supplements the murder, suggesting that as a struggling mother in poverty, she cannot speak until infanticide makes her suddenly visible and audible through, effectively, creating a story that can be told and received.

Without the dramatic denouement, there would be no story, yet the traumatic unspeakable here is not the maternal filicide (which she recounts in painstaking detail), but is inscribed in her subsequent wordless scream, which indicates both her desperation at registering the loss of her sons and the indifference of society. The scream highlights that the narrator's difficult experiences of motherhood, although not unspeakable in the sense of a traumatic gap rupture in narrative, are nonetheless critically unspeakable in the sense that they become narratable, and audible, only through the plot device of infanticide (and it is worth pointing out here that while recently we have seen a number of narratives of infanticide by French women, we have seen notably fewer stories of more common suffering such as poverty, homelessness, or hunger). Laura Brown has criticized the tendency within trauma studies to define trauma as an event 'outside the range of human experience'[75] (such as infanticide, perhaps) at the expense of insidious, typically invisible everyday trauma (that she theorizes might disproportionately affect socially disadvantaged subjects and women).[76] In *Bord de mer*, the truly unspeakable is arguably not the double murder (after which she can scream, even if not speak coherently) but the neglect and alienation that the mother and particularly her children suffer beforehand and that become narratable (and readable) only thanks to the filicide, not only in society itself, but also as a literary plot.[77] In other words, far from limiting empathy, filicide generates the possibility of empathy (for mothers who might otherwise be culturally invisible), not by giving a voice to these mothers, but by allowing their social or emotional alienation to become belatedly visible and audible. Yet they become narratable only when it is too late, as is also evident when Léa's father asks for forgiveness in Tardieu's novel.

Elsewhere, Hemmings has observed that whilst empathy is most frequently defined as 'bridging a gap' through establishing shared subject positions, it might work more effectively through acknowledging (as opposed to trying to erase) what she calls the 'discomfort of distance'.[78] Her use of the term 'discomfort' chimes with my analysis of *Le Cimetière des poupées*, in which empathy would be possible only through complicity, and with my reading of *Bord de mer*, in which empathy risks complacency (where critics have repeatedly asserted that the narrator is 'one of us', might it be more productive to interrogate the 'us' rather than assume commonality?). In relation to the narratives of infanticide analyzed here, working through the 'discomfort of distance' means unpicking ideals of maternity, on the one hand, and of feminist solidarity on the other, as well as reflecting on what allows us (or compels us) to understand or empathize with a seemingly unspeakable atrocity like infanticide. This does not, however, mean aligning the reader with either the mother who has committed filicide or the child (or children) killed; the point here is precisely the misalignment through which the reader is destabilized. This dislocation may constitute a means through which empathy (understood in terms of distance and difference, as well as proximity) may be rethought as both a response to and a producer of narrative. In Tardieu's novel, it is clear that empathy is not generated as a response to a narrative (that is, the guard does not listen to Léa's story and then react with empathy) but is part of what prompts the story (it is the possibility of empathy that causes the guard to invite Léa to speak, and thus that produces the narrative). Put otherwise, empathy generates as well as emerges from narrative; more, it is part of the act of telling that opens up the possibility of renewed stories told by subjects who, like Léa, hitherto did not/could not speak, but whose voices can emerge through the empathetic relation created by the other's invitation to tell their story.

Conclusion: The Discomfort of Distance and Empathy

If the infanticidal narrators whose stories are analyzed here might initially seem to be 'beyond' empathy (through their seemingly unthinkable acts), infanticide is surprisingly easy to understand in these texts. Part of this is the language used — Pingeot's narrator avoids a direct account of her neonaticide, while Léa's account of her filicide is hesitant and fragmentary, and Olmi's narrator describes her double filicide in notably maternal terms — so that the violence of the murder in each case is somehow minimized. As critics we also need to be aware of how we conceive of maternal filicide: it is noticeable how critics (myself included) hesitate to describe it as 'murder' or even 'killing', using euphemisms such as 'tragic act' which serve to minimize the violence (and erase the mother's responsibility) and evoking shared values and ideals of maternity to connect mothers who kill to an assumed community of readers.[79] Empathy is, in this context, not particularly risky, as shown in my reading of *Bord de mer*. Yet as the analysis of Tardieu's novel highlights, what matters here is understanding that empathy is not a definable response to a closed narrative, but a renegotiated relationship through which alternative narrative versions might be opened up.

In all of these texts, filicide constitutes a (troubling) attempt to assert oneself as (visible and audible) subject. Pingeot's narrator writes:

> Aujourd'hui on me regarde, n'est-ce pas? On me regarde quand je me suis retirée de la scène, lors même que je n'apparaîtrai plus. Tu ne peux plus détourner les yeux, tu ne peux plus faire semblant, aujourd'hui j'existe, mais hier? (*Le Cimetière*, p. 114)

> [Today people look at me, don't they? They look at me when I have left the stage, even though I will not reappear. You can no longer look away, you can't pretend, today I exist, but yesterday?]

Becoming visible, as Morello observes, is not analogous to becoming a subject. Yet the use of visual imagery once again is striking: she is not looked at until her crime is discovered (and when she will no longer appear). Whilst she is addressing her husband, the jump between 'on' and 'tu' highlights that she is also referring to other people who look at her only now that she is no longer present (and still see her only as a mother who killed her baby). Part of what is difficult in these texts is that empathy is inevitably too late for the children who have been killed and for the women who are struggling (but have not (yet) committed filicide) and whose stories remain largely untold. If, following these texts, empathy is bound up in what we can see (or not see), what is it that we do not notice when we are looking so obsessively at infanticide? Here it is worth noting Marinopoulos's observation that 'on voit si mal quand on est collé à ce que l'on regarde!' [We see so badly when we are glued to what we are looking at].[80] The 'discomfort of distance' may not only apply to individuals like Hemmings's two women occupying the same domestic space with dissonant positions but also to the relation between different stories, some of which are more permissible than others, and some of which generate empathy bound up in an assumption of commonality that works to conceal other subjects of suffering.

Hemmings's evocation of 'the discomfort of distance' does not, I would suggest, necessarily imply a fixed and stable distance, because positions shift and the possibility of commonality is destabilized. Hemmings suggests that empathy 'is a relationship between subject and other-subject, then, in which I use the term "other-subject" to describe this process of the other's becoming, a process that the empathetic subject has by definition already achieved'.[81] Yet her assumption that the empathetic subject has already 'achieved' a stable subject position is itself troubling in assuming the possibility of a fixed identity or even location — it might be more productive to envisage both subjects as 'becoming', not necessarily moving closer, but recognizing their own difference and distance. This might respond to Hemmings's rhetorical (and slightly awkward) question as to:

> What it would be like as a Western feminist theorist to be prepared to sit with the discomfort of distance rather than trying to move to a kind of bridging of distance before in fact [...] the discomfort of that was fully in some senses inhabited.[82]

The point is not to deliberately refrain from attempting to bridge the gap, but to avoid the temptation to assume that the gap can be bridged without registering the discomfort — or awkwardness — that it generates.

The title of this chapter is 'Beyond Compassion', but I am not arguing that mothers who commit filicide should not (or indeed do not) receive empathy or compassion; rather, I am suggesting that as readers we evaluate more critically what assumptions and beliefs an empathetic response to infanticide might work to protect and what is at stake in assuming positions of empathy in relation to filicide (and again, of course, if the word were replaced by 'murder', perhaps responses would play out differently). Lauren Berlant's observation that 'the modern social logic of compassion can as easily provide an alibi for an ethical or political betrayal as it can initiate a circuit of practical relief' may be paraphrased here as empathy, like compassion, may also serve to conceal disregard for certain types of suffering or social alienation.[83] To conclude, then, this chapter suggests rethinking empathy beyond understanding and cohesion and beginning to consider what a model of empathy rooted in cohesion might mask; this in turn leads to the possibility of developing different models of empathy allowing for (and wrong-footed by) discomfort and distance, which I shall explore in Chapter 4.

Notes to Chapter 3

1. Natalie Edwards, 'Babykillers: Véronique Olmi and Laurence Tardieu on Motherhood', in *Women's Writing in Twenty-first-century France: Life as Literature*, ed. by Amaleena Damlé and Gill Rye (Cardiff: University of Wales Press, 2013), pp. 98–110 (p. 99).
2. Heather Leigh Stangle, 'Murderous Madonna: Femininity, Violence, and the Myth of Postpartum Mental Disorder in Cases of Maternal Infanticide and Filicide', *William and Mary Law Review*, 50 (2008), 699–734 (p. 708).
3. Edwards, 'Babykillers', p. 99.
4. Leïla Slimani, *Chanson douce* (Paris: Gallimard, 2016).
5. Susan Ayres, 'Who is to Shame? Narratives of Neonaticide', *William and Mary Journal of Women and the Law*, 14.1 (2007), 55–105 (p. 78). See for instance Paule Constant, *La Bête à chagrin* (Paris:

Gallimard, 2007), Marie Darrieussecq, *White* (Paris: P.O.L., 2003), Ying Chen, *L'Ingratitude* (Arles: Actes Sud, 1999), Nancy Huston, *Instruments des ténèbres* (Arles: Actes Sud, 1996), as well as the texts discussed in this chapter: Sophie Marinopoulos, *La Vie ordinaire d'une mère meurtrière* (Paris: Fayard, 2008); Mazarine Pingeot, *Le Cimetière des poupées* (Paris: Julliard, 2007); Véronique Olmi, *Bord de mer* (Arles: Actes Sud, 2001), and *Beside the Sea*, trans. by Adriana Hunter (London: Pereine Press, 2012); and Laurence Tardieu, *Le Jugement de Léa* (Paris: Éditions Arléa, 2004).

6. Statistics on neonaticide are unreliable; one population-based study of neonaticide in France in 2010 observes a clear 'underestimation of neonaticide in official mortality statistics' (Anne Tursz and Jon M. Cook, 'A Population-based Survey of Neonaticides Using Judicial Data', *Archives of Disease in Childhood — Fetal and Neonatal Edition*, 96.4 (July 2011), 259–63 (p. 261).

7. Christine M. Alder and June Baker, 'Maternal Filicide: More Than One Story to Be Told', *Women and Criminal Justice*, 9.2 (1997), 15–39 (p. 17).

8. Alison Wallace, *Homicide: The Social Reality* (Sydney: New South Wales Bureau of Statistics and Research, 1986), p. 113. A study in the United Kingdom found that 'infants less than 1-year old are at 4 times greater risk of being murdered than any other age group, with the 1st day of life being the highest risk', Helen Gavin and Theresa Porter, 'Infanticide and Neonaticide: A Review of 40 Years of Research Literature on Incidence and Causes', *Trauma Violence Abuse*, 11.3 (July 2010), 99–112 (p. 100).

9. Jaclyn Smith, 'Infanticide', in *Different Crimes, Different Criminals: Understanding, Treating and Preventing Criminal Behavior*, ed. by Doris Layton MacKenzie and others, 2nd edn (New York: Routledge, 2015), pp. 11–34 (p. 12).

10. Nicola Monaghan, *Criminal Law Directions*, 4th edn (Oxford: Oxford University Press, 2016), p. 130.

11. Tursz and Cook, 'A Population-based Survey of Neonaticides', p. 259.

12. 'Neonaticide is strongly associated with pregnancy denial' (Laura J. Miller, 'Denial of Pregnancy', in *Infanticide: Psychosocial and Legal Perspectives on Women who Kill*, ed. by Margaret G. Spinelli (Washington, DC: American Psychiatric Association, 2003), 81–104 (p. 94)); 'Pregnancy denial has recently received media coverage following a series of French cases of neonatal killing' (Angela Jenkins, Simon Millar and James Robins, 'Denial of Pregnancy — a Literature Review and Discussion of Ethical and Legal Issues', *Journal of the Royal Society of Medicine*, 104.7 (2011), 286–91 (p. 286)).

13. Siobhan Weare, 'Bad, Mad or Sad? Legal Language, Narratives, and Identity Constructions of Women Who Kill their Children in England and Wales', *International Journal for the Semiotics of Law — Revue internationale de sémiotique juridique*, 2016, 1–22, <https://link.springer.com/article/10.1007/s11196–016–9480-y> [accessed 7 March 2019].

14. Alder and Baker, 'Maternal Filicide', p. 22.

15. Stangle, 'Murderous Madonna', p. 733.

16. Maggie Inchley, 'Hearing the Unhearable: The Representation of Women Who Kill Children', *Contemporary Theatre Review*, 23.2 (2013), 192–205 (pp. 192–93).

17. In the case of Véronique Courjault, her husband Jean-Louis (who supported her throughout, having proved his own innocence) wrote his perspective on her story, in *Je ne pouvais pas l'abandonner* (Paris: Michel Lafon, 2010), yet the wording of the title positions him as magnanimous husband, unable to 'abandon' her; this is less an explanation of her story than a self-representation of a husband as loyal protector.

18. Edwards, 'Babykillers', p. 98.

19. Gill Rye and Amaleena Damlé, 'Women's Writing in Twenty-first-century France: Introduction', in *Women's Writing in Twenty-first-century France*, ed. by Damlé and Rye, pp. 3–16 (p. 8).

20. Edwards, 'Babykillers', p. 100.

21. Ruth Cain, 'Véronique Olmi's *Beside the Sea*: Law, Psychiatry and the Moral Dilemmas of Filicide' (podcast), Institute of Modern Languages Research, lecture given 11 May 2012, <https://www.sas.ac.uk/videos-and-podcasts/culture-language-and-literature/veronique-olmi-s-beside-sea-law-psychiatry-and> [accessed September 2017].

22. Ayres, 'Who is to Shame?', p. 61.

23. Edwards, 'Babykillers', p. 106.

24. Ayres, 'Who is to Shame?', p 90.

25. Gray, 'Empathy, Emotion and Feminist Solidarities', p. 227.

26. Ahmed, *The Cultural Politics of Emotion* p. 30.

27. Hemmings, *Why Stories Matter*, p. 197.

28. Ibid., p. 212.

29. Ibid., p. 226.

30. Marguerite Duras, 'Sublime, forcément sublime', in *Marguerite Duras*, ed. by Bernard Alazet and Christiane Blot-Labarrère (Paris: L'Herne, 2005), pp. 69–73, hereafter referred to as *SFS*; 'Sublime, Necessarily Sublime', trans. by Andrew Slade, *Janus Head*, 9.1 (2006), 8–18, hereafter referred to as *SNS*.

31. Andrew Slade, 'Differend, Sexual Difference, and the Sublime: Lyotard, Irigaray, Duras', in *Gender After Lyotard*, ed. by Margret Grebowicz (New York: SUNY Press, 2007), pp. 171–83 (p. 180).

32. Leslie Hill, *Marguerite Duras: Apocalyptic Desires* (London: Routledge, 1993), p. 34.

33. Elise Hugueny-Léger, 'Duras ou les contradictions d'une intellectuelle aux prises avec l'espace public', *French Cultural Studies*, 22.4 (2011), 321–31 (p. 326).

34. Nancy Huston, 'Novels and Navels', *Critical Inquiry*, 21.4 (Summer 1995), 708–21 (p. 712).

35. Hugueny-Léger, 'Duras ou les contradictions d'une intellectuelle aux prises avec l'espace public', p. 326.

36. Slade, 'Differend, Sexual Difference, and the Sublime: Lyotard, Irigaray, Duras', p. 180.

37. Huston, 'Novels and Navels', p. 713.

38. Sophie Marinopoulos, *Infanticides et néonaticides* (Paris: Fabert, 2011), p. 55.

39. A distinction is usually drawn between pregnancy denial (in which the mother may be unaware of her pregnancy or repress her knowledge of it) and pregnancy concealment, in which the mother is aware of pregnancy but chooses to conceal it from others (see Susan Ayres and Prema Manjunath, 'Denial and Concealment of Unwanted Pregnancy: A Film Hollywood Dared Not Do', *Journal of Civil Rights & Economic Development*, 26 (2012), 197–221 (pp. 202–03).

40. Lynsey Black, 'Paper Women: The Representation of Female Offenders in Irish Newspapers' (Masters dissertation, Dublin Institute of Technology, 2009), p. 39.

41. The mocking references to the mother and the freezer also potentially evoke the concept of the 'mère réfrigérateur', the cold mother once thought to be responsible for children developing autism (see Jacques Hochmann, *Histoire de l'autisme* (Paris: Odile Jacob, 2009), p. 250).

42. The docufiction was broadcast on France 3 on 7 December 2009.

43. Isabelle Hanne, 'Dans l'abîme d'un "parcours meurtrier"', *Libération*, 7 December 2009, <http://www.liberation.fr/medias/2009/12/07/dans-l-abime-d-un-parcours-meurtrier_597795> [accessed 7 March 2019].

44. Marinopoulos, *Infanticides et néonaticides*, p. 6.

45. Delphine Chayet, 'Ces mères infanticides sont incapables de s'expliquer', *Le Figaro*, 29 July 2010, <http://www.lefigaro.fr/actualite-france/2010/07/29/01016-20100729ARTFIG00580-ces-meres-infanticides-sont-incapables-de-s-expliquer.php> [accessed 7 March 2019].

46. Léa Danilewsky, 'Le Traitement médiatique de l'affaire dite "des bébés congelés": représentations des figures de "femme" et de "mère" à travers le discours médiatique; Véronique Courjault, monstre ou martyre?', <http://doc.sciencespo-lyon.fr/Ressources/Documents/Etudiants/Memoires/Cyberdocs/MFE2010/danilewsky_l/pdf/danilewsky_l.pdf> [accessed 7 March 2019]. Danilwesky also claims: 'je garde comme ideal feministe une certaine empathie pour les femmes en souffrance' (p. 5).

47. Cited in Stéphane Durand-Souffland, 'Véronique Courjault: la détresse et la confusion', *Le Figaro*, 11 June 2009, <http://www.lefigaro.fr/actualite-france/2009/06/11/01016-20090611ARTFIG00004-veronique-courjault-la-detresse-et-la-confusion-.php> [accessed September 2017].

48. Elsa Vigoureux, 'Dominique Cottrez tue ses petits', *Le Nouvel Observateur*, 2 July 2015, <http://tempsreel.nouvelobs.com/justice/20150702.OBS1907/dominique-cottrez-tue-ses-petits-l-hiver-je-pensais-a-eux.html> [accessed September 2017].

49. Frédéric Boudouresque, 'Procès Chabot: "J'avais les jambes qui tremblaient"', 3 March 2015, <http://www.leprogres.fr/ain/2015/02/27/suivez-en-direct-le-proces-des-bebes-congeles> [accessed September 2017].

50. Cathérine Vincent, 'Sophie Marinopoulos: portrait psychique et romancé d'une mere infanticide', *Le Monde*, 20 March 2008, <https://www.lemonde.fr/livres/article/2008/03/20/sophie-marinopoulos-portrait-psychique-et-romance-d-une-mere-infanticide_1025298_3260.html> [accessed 7 March 2019].

51. Marinopoulos, *Infanticides et néonaticides*, p. 57.

52. Lorraine Code, 'I Know Just How You Feel: Empathy and the Problem of Epistemic Authority', in *Rhetorical Spaces: Essays on Gendered Locations* (London & New York: Routledge, 1995), pp. 120–43 (p. 141).

53. Olivia Lambeterie, 'Le Crime de Mazarine Pingeot', interview with Mazarine Pingeot, *Elle*, 29 August 2007, <http://www.elle.fr/Societe/Interviews/Le-crime-de-Mazarine-Pingeot-147544> [accessed September 2017].

54. Pascale Robert-Diard, 'Mazarine Pingeot, le roman et le congélateur', *Le Monde*, 25 July 2007, <http://www.lemonde.fr/societe/article/2007/07/25/mazarine-pingeot-le-roman-et-le-congelateur_938976_3224.html#RYtGFjZ1UTP1UWU1.99> [accessed September 2017].

55. Lambeterie, 'Le Crime de Mazarine Pingeot'.

56. Nathalie Morello, 'Écrire le néonaticide maternel dans *Le Cimetière des poupées* de Mazarine Pingeot', *Modern and Contemporary France*, 19.1 (2011), 53–68 (p. 64).

57. Lambeterie, 'Le Crime de Mazarine Pingeot'.

58. Pascale Joubi, 'La Trace de Médée dans *Le Cimetière des poupées* de Mazarine Pingeot', 2015, <http://musemedusa.com/dossier_3/joubi/> [accessed July 2018].

59. The 'Sujet-enfant' is a term coined by Marinopoulos (*Infanticides et Neonaticides*, p. 48).

60. Elissa Marder, 'The Sex of Death and the Maternal Crypt', *Parallax*, 15:1 (2009), 5–20 (p. 10).

61. Julia Kristeva, 'Reliance, or Maternal Eroticism', *Journal of the American Psychoanalytic Association*, 62 (2014), 69–85 (p. 79). 'Reliance' as theorized here encapsulates multiple meanings in both English and in (old) French (including notions of binding and un-binding) that has been explored from the child's perspective (both connecting to and separating from the mother) but less so from the mother's position; the mother who kills her child to preserve the child is refusing reliance.

62. Elaine Tuttle Hansen, *Mother Without Child: Contemporary Fiction and the Crisis of Motherhood* (Berkeley: California University Press, 1997), p. 23.

63. The cover of the paperback *Points* edition of this novel shows a woman walking away, through a grassy park or garden: peering out from the back of her head (the hair framing her face) is a doll. The hair is styled around the doll's face, so that it might appear to be the woman's face, except that it is recognizably the face of a doll and that the woman is clearly facing the opposite direction. The image suggests both that the doll represents the 'other side' to the woman and that the doll is somehow part of the same body; the fact that the mother's face is turned away from the camera also emphasizes the limits of the reader's ability to see her.

64. Ruth Cain, ' "How to Say Hello to the Sea": Literary Perspectives on Medico-Legal Narratives of Maternal Filicide', in *Motherhood in Literature and Culture: Interdisciplinary Perspectives from Europe*, ed. by Gill Rye and others (London: Routledge, 2017), pp. 223–37 (p. 224).

65. Bidisha, ' "It Unlocks You From the Inside": Staging Véronique Olmi's Infanticide Novel', *Guardian*, 18 February, 2012, 'Guardian Books', <https://www.theguardian.com/books/2012/feb/18/beside-the-sea-veronique-olmi-monologue> [accessed 28 February 2019]. Quotations from *Bord de mer* are abbreviated as *BM* in the main text; those from *Beside the Sea* as *BS*.

66. Cain, 'Véronique Olmi's *Beside the Sea*'.

67. Edwards, 'Babykillers', p. 109.

68. Cain, 'Véronique Olmi's *Beside the Sea*'.

69. Natalie Edwards, 'Obliged to Sympathise: Infanticide in *Il y a longtemps que je t'aime* and *A perdre la raison*', *Australian Journal of French Studies*, 52.2 (2015), 174–87 (p. 174).

70. Anne Mairesse, 'Le Roman spectaculaire à l'épreuve du quotidien: l'œuvre de Véronique Olmi', *Contemporary French and Francophone Studies*, 10 (2006), 491–98 (p. 491).

71. Edwards, 'Babykillers', p. 108.

72. Ibid., p. 106.

73. Anne Whitehead, *Medicine and Empathy in Contemporary British Fiction: A Critical Intervention in Medical Humanities* (Edinburgh: Edinburgh University Press, 2017), p. 2.

74. Hemmings, 'Affective Solidarity', p. 157.

75. This definition follows that given in the *Diagnostic and Statistical Manual of Mental Disorders* (DSM) 3; DSM 4 in 1994 changed this stipulation to avoid referring to the 'usual range of experience'.

76. Laura Brown, 'Not Outside the Range One Feminist Perspective on Psychic Trauma', *American Imago*, 48.1 (1991), 119–33.

77. Whilst we should be wary of conflating nanny with mother, as they are culturally coded quite differently, the nanny in Slimani's *Chanson douce* is also poor, lonely, and alienated, and, like Olmi's narrator, becomes visible only when she kills her two charges.

78. Gunaratnam, 'Interview with Clare Hemmings'.

79. Rye, *Narratives of Mothering*, p. 109.

80. Marinopoulos, *Infanticides et néonaticides*, p. 6.

81. Hemmings, 'Affective Solidarity', p. 203.

82. Gunaratnam, 'Interview with Clare Hemmings'.

83. Berlant, *Compassion*, p. 11.

CHAPTER 4

❖

Responsibility, Reading, and Dispossession in Autofiction

My account of myself is partial, haunted by that for which I can devise no definitive story. I cannot explain exactly why I have emerged in this way, and my efforts at narrative reconstruction are always undergoing revision. There is that in me and of me for which I can give no account. But does this mean that I am not, in the moral sense, accountable for who I am and for what I do? If I find that, despite my best efforts, a certain opacity persists and I cannot make myself fully accountable to you, is this ethical failure? Or is it a failure that gives rise to another ethical disposition in the place of a full and satisfying notion of narrative accountability?[1]

If, according to Diana Holmes, 'the dominant genre in contemporary French women's writing is undoubtedly auto-fiction, with its strongly autobiographical dimension, its single, intra-diegetic narrative voice, its confessional rather than strictly narrative structure', the recent prevalence of autofictional texts also raises questions about the ethics of the reading encounter in the context of texts that simultaneously recount suffering rooted in lived experience and interrogate their own veracity.[2] Autofiction is often described as ludic because it plays with the relation between fiction and reality,[3] and frequently creatively reworks linguistic structures too, but it is also commonly a frame for articulations of pain and suffering.[4] What ethical demands do autofictional texts place upon readers, and how is the reader situated in relation to these texts? How can empathy be negotiated in relation to texts that self-consciously question the truth of their own accounts, even as they narrate experiences of suffering that require acknowledgement? This chapter addresses these questions through analyzing autofictional texts by Chloé Delaume and Delphine de Vigan, taking as point of departure Judith Butler's *Giving an Account of Oneself*, which explores what is at stake in the attempt to narrate, and account for, oneself. This may seem an odd choice, as Butler's text alludes neither to autofiction nor to empathy, yet Butler's model of giving an ethical account of oneself resonates strikingly both with contemporary French women's autofiction and with questions raised by the notion of empathy. This is summarized in the epigraph above, which asks whether the inability to account for oneself can become a basis for a different ethical relation to the other; this might, in turn, be conceived of as an alternative conceptualization of empathy. Butler's theoretical examination of what it means to 'give an account of oneself' (motivated by, and addressed to, the other) also, although Butler does not frame it in these terms, relates to the relation between text and reader (as other). Through reading recent French autofiction by Delaume and Vigan in and through Butler's *Giving an Account of Oneself*, this chapter seeks to rethink the relation between reader and text and the limits of empathy in terms of the 'opacity' of what cannot be incorporated into the narrative of the self.

Giving an Autofictional Account of Oneself

According to Butler, 'the "I" has no story of its own that is not also the story of a relation — or set of relations — to a set of norms' (*Giving*, p. 8). That is, not only is there no pre-discursive self, but furthermore, the act of recounting oneself as an individual subject is necessarily dependent upon inserting oneself within 'social norms, a domain of unfreedom and substitutability within which our "singular" stories are told' (p. 21). The construction of the 'I' that constitutes giving an account of oneself is also, both because it develops through shared linguistic and social structures and because it is implicitly or explicitly addressed to another, founded in unacknowledged alterity. The 'I' as marker of an individual subject is, then, a fictional construct that individuates and demarcates the self only through creating a relation with another. Butler differentiates between telling a story about the self and giving an account of the self: 'Telling a story about oneself is not the same as giving an account of oneself [...] the kind of narrative required in an account we give of ourselves accepts the presumption that the self has a causal relation to the suffering of others' (p. 12). She explains giving an account of the self both in terms of accountability to the other and as a response to the other ('I begin my story of myself only in the face of a "you" who asks me to give an account', p. 11)). Her focus is on how to give account of oneself ethically, being mindful of the impact upon the other, the 'you' whose 'face' (following Emmanuel Levinas) should not be erased or ignored. For Butler, this means allowing the narrative, and by extension the self, 'to be undone by another' (p. 136), by rejecting the fiction of a fully cohesive and completed account and making space for interruptions and gaps. In her words:

> If the other is always there, from the start, in the place of where the ego will be, then a life is constituted through a fundamental interruption, is even interrupted prior to the possibility of any continuity. Accordingly, if narrative reconstruction is to approximate the life it means to convey, it must also be subject to interruption. (*Giving*, p. 52)

The 'self' that is constructed or represented in the narrative account is necessarily incomplete, not entirely known or knowable even to itself. The 'I' constitutes a fictional construct, the delineation of which, paradoxically, simultaneously requires the other within the self:

> I speak as an 'I,' but do not make the mistake of thinking that I know precisely all that I am doing when I speak in that way. I find that my very formation implicates the other in me, that my own foreignness to myself is, paradoxically, the source of my ethical connection with others. (*Giving*, p. 84)

Butler does not, however, go further in exploring how else the narrative of the self can be interrupted or 'undone' by the other, nor does she show how an ethical account of the self should or could address the other (as other, as well as the other that is part of the self, and the difference here presumably also needs to be elaborated) in and through the acknowledgement of alterity. As J. Aaron Simmons observes, Butler's text refuses to establish a prescriptive model of ethics which would risk reproducing the normative violence that constitutes the formation of subjectivity; Butler deliberately leaves open the question of what an ethical account of oneself might look like.[5] In a reading of *Giving an Account of Oneself*, meanwhile, Catherine Mills notes that 'the recognition of vulnerability and relationality does not itself guarantee ethical responsibility. While this recognition might be a necessary condition for responsibility, it is not sufficient in itself to breach the ambiguities of ethics and violence'.[6] The question as to whether the acknowledgement of mutual vulnerability is enough to create an ethical relation that can circumvent violence should be framed by the acceptance that this ethical relation is, precisely, founded in violent wounding. Butler suggests in her response that violence cannot be avoided: 'it may be that precisely because — or rather, when — someone is formed in violence, the responsibility not to repeat the violence of one's formation is all the more pressing and important'.[7] More than this, her politics of vulnerability 'is not a principle of nonviolence, but a practice, itself fallible, of trying to attend to the precariousness of life' because 'nonviolence', in her analysis, is also violent.[8] The emphasis on respecting the 'precariousness' of life, of the subject, and of the relation between self and other potentially offers another take on the notion of empathy. Christa Hodapp writes that Butler's model can 'assist us in understanding the necessity of our connections to others and undo some of the damage caused by the lack of empathy and relationality resulting from our insular definitions and understandings of ourselves'.[9] Hodapp does not, however, expand on how Butler's ideas might relate to or even facilitate empathy. This chapter explores to what extent Butler's theories of giving an ethical account of oneself may be seen to reflect upon questions of (the lack or failure of) empathy through reading Butler's theory in and through recent French autobiographical fiction.

Butler's insistence on the primordiality of the acknowledgement of the other in the account of the self offers a means to approach contemporary French women's autofiction — which, as I shall show, explicitly evokes alterity in its inscription of the self — whilst these texts also enable us to think further about the ethics of self-representation through (semi-)fictional writing.[10] Certainly, as a point of departure, autofiction clearly fits with Butler's insistence that:

> The ethical valence of the situation is thus not restricted to the question of whether or not my account of myself is adequate, but rather concerns whether, in giving the account, I establish a relationship to the one to whom my account is addressed and whether both parties to the interlocution are sustained and altered by the scene of address. (*Giving*, p. 50)

The autofictional texts analyzed in this chapter shift notably from attempting to establish, measure, or reflect a 'truth' or reality and focus instead on precisely this notion of relationality, 'the scene of address'. Marie Darrieussecq states that:

> Si l'autobiographie instaure un pacte de confiance avec le lecteur, l'autofiction, elle, invente un nouveau genre de pacte, un pacte de défiance assumée: 'lecteur, ne me crois pas. Ne sois pas assez naïf pour adhérer, ne sois pas dupe. L'écriture n'est pas la vie.'[11]

> [If autobiography establishes a pact of confidence with the reader, autofiction invents a new sort of pact, a pact of assumed defiance: 'reader, don't believe me. Don't be so naive as to concur, don't be duped. Writing isn't life'.]

Autofiction sets up a relation with the reader founded in an avowal of deceit on the one hand, and disbelief and doubt on the other. As Delaume notes, 'L'autofiction implique un pacte extrêmement particulier entre l'auteur et le lecteur. L'auteur ne s'engage qu'à une chose: lui mentir au plus juste' [Autofiction involves a very specifc pact between the author and the reader. The author only commits to one thing: lying to the reader as much as possible].[12] For Delaume, the reader is not called upon to assess the truth or fiction in the account, but to register the extent to which the basis for the relationship between text and reader is founded in deception. The relation here is, of course, not as negative as the word 'deception' implies: the popularity of autofiction as genre points also to the reader's willing collusion in shared fantasy. Drawing on Butler, it would be better to move away from reading these texts to determine their respective veracity/fictionality and to focus instead on how they address the reader, considering how both text and reader 'are sustained and altered by the scene of address'.[13] Part of this is, of course, bound up in their claims of a basis, however unstable, in lived experience. If these autofictional texts give an account of themselves, it is necessarily in and through the relation with the other (both within and beyond the self), as we see in the case of Delaume's *Le Cri du sablier* [The Cry of the Hourglass], in which the subject of trauma shifts, and in Vigan's *Rien ne s'oppose à la nuit* [Nothing Holds Back the Night], which tells the story of the (m)other rather than of the self. In Vigan's *D'après une histoire vraie* [Based on a True Story] and in Delaume's *Une femme avec personne dedans* [A Woman with Nobody Inside], the other is inscribed textually in the form of a reader, depicted as stalker/double/victim, to whom, and through whom, the writing subject must give account of herself.[14] The relation between writing subject and textually inscribed reader is framed in and through violence, rather than empathy; these texts interrogate the very possibility of giving account of oneself ethically. Yet they also, I will suggest, allow us to rethink how we conceive of empathy as a relation between self and other and make way for alternative and potentially more productive and open-ended conceptualizations of empathy.

Narrative Interruptions and Alterity in Chloe Delaume's *Le Cri du sablier*

Butler's description of giving an ethical account of oneself resonates intriguingly with the model of autofiction developed by Delaume. Delaume, daughter of a French mother and a Maronite Lebanese father, was born Nathalie Abdallah, a name that her family later changed to Nathalie Dalain to sound more 'French' and that she herself subsequently altered to Chloé Delaume — the forename derived from Boris Vian's *L'Écume des jours* and the surname from Antonin Artaud's rewriting of *Alice in Wonderland*, entitled *La Larve et l'aume* — a self-consciously literary and fictional marker of constructed identity. In an interview, Delaume states that:

> Il était nécessaire de me créer une nouvelle identité, qui porterait mon propre Je, l'imposerait dans le réel. Se définir comme personnage de fiction, c'est dire je choisis qui je suis, je m'invente seule, moi-même, jusqu'à l'état civil. Je ne suis pas née sujet, mais par ma mutation en Chloé Delaume, je le suis devenue. Puisque le réel n'est qu'une somme de fictions collectives, de la cellule familiale à la saturation des fables médiatiques, politiques, sociales, économiques, écrire sa fiction propre, dans ce même réel, pas seulement par le biais de la littérature, était la seule réponse efficiente, le seul geste, la seule action possible.[15]

> [It was necessary for me to create a new identity, which would bear my own 'I', and would impose it in the real. Defining oneself as a fictional character, that is to say I choose who I am, I invent myself, just me, myself, including in my official documentation. I wasn't born a subject, but through my mutation into Chloé Delaume, I have become one. Since the real is just a set of collective fictions, from the family unit to the saturation of media, political, social and economic fables, writing my own fiction, in this same real, but this time from a literary angle, was the only efficient response, the only gesture, the only action possible.]

Delaume's insistence that the Real is constituted of collective, shared fictions — that her own fictional self-reconstruction is thus no less 'real' than the identities imposed upon her by her family beforehand — chimes with Butler's point that 'we are constituted in relationality: implicated, beholden, derived, sustained by a social world that is beyond us and before us' (*Giving*, p. 64). In Delaume's case, the words that shaped her identity as a child were violently imposed by both parents: her abusive father, whom she witnessed kill her mother then himself when she was ten years old, and her negligent mother.[16] *Le Cri du sablier* highlights the child's subjugation to words imposed by others, firstly through the use of third person narrative until near the end of the text, and secondly through the repeated incorporation of other people's (frequently incongruous) words without standard punctuation conventions for reported speech. The description of the discovery of the wounded bodies in the account of the murder scene, for instance, is disrupted by disconcertingly mundane reported speech: 'L'un d'entre eux au salon saisit le téléphone. Chérie je rentrerai tard, fais-les dîner sans moi' [One of the people in the living room grabbed the telephone. Darling I'll be late home, have dinner without me] (*Le Cri*, p. 9). Similarly jarring interventions interrupt the narrative from the very beginning: there is no singular narrative voice or corresponding narrative subject that is not interrupted by another voice.

Le Cri du sablier, which opens with the aftermath of the murder and suicide, is literally structured as an account addressed to the other. The narrative is repeatedly interrupted by questions from an unnamed 'vous' (labelled as one in a line of psychoanalysts) demanding that the narrator tell the story of her trauma and its consequences ('Combien de temps demanda-t-il' [How long, he asked], 'Quels jeux demanda-t-il' [What games, he asked] (p. 15); 'Quel mal demanda-t-il' [What evil, he asked] (p. 16), for instance). Yet this text also frames the relation with the other in terms of resistance and refusal to tell ('Non je ne dirai rien me voilà résolue' [No I won't say anything I'm resolved], p. 11). The narrator recounts a nine-month period of mutism following her parents' deaths — the time frame evoking the gestation period of pregnancy, implying the creation of a new self — in which the child not only could not, because language is inevitably inadequate faced with such trauma, but also deliberately would not, speak. The narrator continues this resistance as she refuses to tell the therapist the story he demands ('Je ne vous dirai rien. Vous ne sauriez qu'en faire' [I won't tell you anything. You won't know what to do with it] (p. 16); 'Je ne vous dirai rien' [I won't tell you anything], 'Je ne veux pas vous dire' [I don't want to tell you] (p. 19); 'Je ne vous dirai rien' [I won't tell you anything], p. 26). If, as Butler observes, 'the refusal to narrate remains a relation to narrative and to the scene of address' (*Giving*, p. 12), the rejection is imbricated in the relation to the other. In *Le Cri*, the 'il' [he] ('Racontez-moi, demanda-t-il' [Tell me, he demanded], p. 20) that invokes the analyst may also, of course, refer to the father; the narrator's refusal to narrate to the analyst is also a rejection of the father's violence and the father's language.[17] Butler notes that

> Learning to construct a narrative is a crucial practice, especially when discontinuous bits of experience remain dissociated from one another by virtue of traumatic conditions. And I do not mean to undervalue the importance of narrative work in the reconstruction of a life that otherwise suffers from fragmentation and discontinuity. The suffering that belongs to conditions of dissociation should not be underestimated. Conditions of hyper-mastery, however, are no more salutary than conditions of radical fragmentation. It seems true that we might well need a narrative to connect parts of the psyche and experience that cannot be assimilated to one another. But too much connection can lead to extreme forms of paranoid isolation. In any event, it does not follow that, if a life needs some narrative structure, then all of life must be rendered in narrative form. (*Giving*, p. 52)

There is no hyper-mastery in Delaume's text; it is structured around multiple interruptions exemplified in the repeated, mocking references to the lovely weather in June, the month of the father's murder and suicide. According to Butler, the interruption not only marks the presence of the other within the self and within the narrative of the self, but also allows for an alternative model of narrative of the self that rejects 'hyper-mastery' or a coherent and cohesive narrative and 'I' without disregarding the need for some sort of narrative formulation in a context of trauma and dissociation. The narrative of *Le Cri du sablier* is self-confessedly motivated by the imperative to respond to and exorcize the father and his violence, figured in the recurring references to grains that embed themselves within the narrator's body and mind ('Le grain du père. Toujours et encore' [The father's grain. Again and again] (p. 85); 'les grains tarés du père' [the mad grains of her father], p. 25) and that her relatives describe her as inheriting ('c'est elle qui a *un grain*' [she is the one who has a grain [is mad]]; 'Elle a un grain comme son père' [she has a grain [is mad] like her father] (p. 85). Thus the text invokes the figurative expression 'avoir un grain' (meaning 'to be mad') through the figure of the grain of sand, representing parts of the father that infiltrate themselves painfully into the narrator and that she seeks to expel through writing. Initially, the narrator refers to 'l'enfant' [the child], the 'je' [I] used only to affirm her refusal to tell the analyst the story he demands; by the end of the text, the 'Je' (note the capital) has emerged: 'Et puis un jour le Je. Le Je jaillit d'une elle un peu trop épuisée de se radier de soi' [And then one day the I. The I sprang out of a she slightly too tired of writing itself off] (p. 107), as the father has been exorcized. On the one hand, then, this text follows a fairly conventional structure, as the narrator moves from literal silence — an inability or refusal to tell — to smashing the hourglass and the father's power over her through her writing, yet it is through fragmentary, incoherent prose that she becomes able to reinvent herself, as an incoherent subject. It is through the refusal to give the 'other' (the analyst, who troublingly seems to stand in for the father) the words he demands that the account of the self can be constructed in and through acknowledgement of its own alterity. This is compounded as the analyst does not exist ('Puisqu'à aucun moment à aucun je vous dis j'ai depuis des années trépassé le seuil rance d'un cabinet [...]. Vous n'existez donc pas et j'en suis désolée' [Because I tell you at no point have I for years crossed the rancid threshold of a consulting room [...]. You don't exist and I am sorry about that], p. 116) other than as a fantasized projection through which she can perform her own narrative of resistance. The 'I' that recognizes its own alterity and its dependence upon a (fantasized) other thus emerges out of the self-erasing (or 'undone', to borrow Butler's term) 'she'.

The reader's position here is difficult to pinpoint: does the reader assume the position of the 'vous' (the analyst) or the 'tu' (the father), or that of a witness to the resistance to the 'vous'/'tu'? The text opens with the discovery of the murder/suicide: 'Les hommes nombreux forcèrent la porte' [the many men forced the door], 'se gorgèrent du réel avec satisfaction' [gorged on the real with satisfaction], 'aspiraient chaque goutte' [sucked up each drop], 'salivaient chaque touffe de cervelle échevelée' [salivated over each tuft of dishevelled brain] 'pour vaincre et non pour regarder' [to conquer and not to watch] (p. 9). The first sentence, in which the men force down the door, foreshadows the violence underpinning their subsequent greedy salivation at the spectacle of the wounded bodies. Later, other people visiting the girl 'commentèrent l'orpheline étonnant spécimen' [commented on the orphan, astonishing specimen], approaching the child 'pour bien palper le mal' [to feel the damage] and 's'approprier une bribe de douleur inédite' [to claim a scrap of previously unseen pain] (p. 10): they come closer to her to appropriate her suffering. Valérie Dusaillant-Fernandes observes that 'il n'est pas question de faire du pathos dans la description des personnages et de la scène' [there is no question of producing pathos in the description of characters and decor].[18] Compassion is depicted as a sickly-sweet violation, following, but also repeating, rape, constituting an unwanted and forced intrusion: 'Comme la sainte biblique violée par les soldats qui creva au matin l'utérus gangrené, sur le matelas percale ils écartèrent chaque pli fouillant au plus profond pour y gicler bien fort leur fructose compassion' [Just as soldiers raped the biblical saint leaving her to die in the morning from a gangrenous uterus, they tore apart each fold of the thick cotton mattress, reaching far inside it to spurt out their saccharine-sweet compassion] (p. 10). *Le Cri du sablier* thus warns the reader of the risks of both witnessing and feeling compassion towards the child's trauma. The text avoids placing the reader in an analogous situation to those who first attend the scene of the crime, however, through a fragmented perspective that details different, disparate wounded body parts (p. 9) and through a subject position split between 'l'enfant' [the child], 'elle' [she], and 'je' [I] that can never fully reconcile itself into one fixed and stable entity and location. Definitions of empathy tend to portray the person we empathize with as a fixed entity — as Carolyn Pedwell notes, empathy is 'understood in shorthand as the ability to "put oneself in the other's shoes"' — which implies that 'oneself' and 'the other' can be neatly defined.[19] My reading of Delaume's text suggests that it might be more productive to rethink empathy not in terms of the over-prevalent analogy of stepping into someone else's shoes, not least because this assumes two coherent, cohesive, and stable subjects (both the subject and object of empathy), which is clearly resisted in *Le Cri du sablier*. Instead, perhaps, it is through what the subject does not know about him/herself, or what seems to remain 'other' to narrative articulations of the self (and the fracture of the self/other binary), that empathy can possibly emerge. Butler muses:

> But is there an ethical valence to my unknowingness? If I am wounded, I find that the wound testifies to the fact that I am impressionable, given over to the other in ways that I cannot fully predict or control. I cannot think the question of responsibility alone, in isolation from the other. If I do, I have taken myself out of the mode of address (being addressed as well as addressing the other) in which the problem of responsibility first emerges. (*Giving*, p. 84)

Butler's argument must be nuanced in the context of narratives like *Le Cri du sablier*, wherein being 'given over to the other' might mean submitting to the violent control of the father, or to the psychoanalyst's repeated demands for a particular story. The notion of giving oneself over to the other cannot be extricated from the structures of violence that construct and frame the self in relation to the other. *Le Cri du sablier* articulates the wound through fragmented, incoherent, and disrupted prose in a way that gestures towards a different relation with alterity, both in terms of what is unknown and unexpressed within the 'Je', and in connection with the reader. Butler does not refer to reading in *Giving an Account of Oneself*, yet the question of how one can write from a position of woundedness with a recognition both of the other within the self and of the other to whom the account is addressed must also be explored in relation to the addressee. In *Le Cri du sablier*, this means both the analyst (to whom the narrator refuses to speak) and the reader, whose encounter with a fragmentary, interrupted narrative is inevitably played out differently, through an explicit refusal of compassion and an implicit rejection of empathy.

Alternatively, one could conceive of empathy differently from the violating yet sweet compassion described in this text, by rethinking it in relation to the interruptions that punctuate it. Lindsay B. Cummings suggests that:

> Empathy's interruptions challenge us to engage others *even when we cannot understand*, to make room in our dialogue for gaps and fissures. But we are

also reminded that our empathetic engagement impacts the other and that we cannot always assume the impact is positive.[20]

This model of empathy is potentially set up in *Le Cri du sablier*, through the repeated interruptions that emphasize the extent to which others '*cannot understand*', and through the gaps and contradictions that structure the narrative. The question of how empathetic engagement might impact upon the other is complex. Hemmings observes that 'it is always assumed that "good" empathy would be appreciated', neglecting the possibility that 'to be empathized with could be a horrific prospect, one resulting in the dissolution of self' if, for instance 'the empathizer is associated with violence'.[21] In *Le Cri du sablier*, the father who is addressed embodies violence, whilst the fantasized psychoanalyst who is attempting to enter into dialogue with the narrator — and who also represents the reader, approaching the story of someone else's pain — is also associated with violence through the insistent, insensitive interrogations. Yet the extra-textual reader is clearly not in the same position as either the father or the analyst within the text: the frequent interruptions to the narrative implicitly compel the reader to think more critically about what it means to read representations of suffering that preclude comprehension. To think further about the positioning of the reader and the potential of empathy with the other in relation to an autofictional account of oneself, I turn now to Vigan, whose work explores what it means to write oneself in relation to the other (and the other in relation to the self) by focusing specifically on the way in which this constructs and impacts upon the reader

Writing, Reading and the (Failed) Response to the Other in Delphine de Vigan's *Rien ne s'oppose à la nuit*

Vigan's critically acclaimed and prize-winning *Rien ne s'oppose à la nuit* explores how one can write — in response to the other — in and through the mutual recognition of injury, but in this case through giving an account of the other, not the self.[22] If, 'Depuis 2001, l'écrivaine française Delphine de Vigan [...] ne cesse de faire parler d'elle' [Since 2001, the French writer Delphine de Vigan, [...] hasn't stopped getting herself talking about],[23] the main character in *Rien ne s'oppose à la nuit* is her mother, named Lucile here, who suffered from bipolar disorder and eventually committed suicide.[24] Yet this semi-fictional, semi-biographical narrative, labelled 'roman' [novel] on the cover, is also 'giving an account of' the narrator herself, who asserts that she writes as a response to a psychotic episode of her mother, when a naked and manic Lucile tried to insert acupuncture needles into her younger daughter's eyes ('J'écris à cause du 31 janvier 1980' (*R*, p. 280) ('I write because of 31 January 1980'), *N*, p. 216). Writing is figured as a response to the other, specifically to the incomprehensibility of a mother who both loved and wounded her daughters. *Rien ne s'oppose à la nuit* finds its origins in Lucile's suicide; the narrator is 'giving an account of' herself both in terms of her inability to prevent Lucile's suicide and in relation to her own decision to attempt to recount Lucile's life, which she repeatedly interrogates.

Rien ne s'oppose à la nuit is written in the first person, from the perspective of the daughter; the first part of the novel, after opening with Lucile's suicide, imaginatively reconstructs Lucile's childhood, while the second and third parts of the novel are rooted in the narrator's memories of her mother during her own lifetime. This narrative is repeatedly interrupted by the narrator's worries about her inability to capture her mother's experience and voice. The effect of the repeated narrative interjections, highlighting the impossibility of representing Lucile adequately, is to distance the reader from the character of Lucile and block assumptions of empathy. This text raises ethical dilemmas around responsibility and autobiography, as the narrator rhetorically questions herself whilst she interviews family members to uncover trauma, including the premature deaths of three of Lucile's siblings, and Lucile's father's possible sexual abuse, and as she tries to narrate her mother's life while remaining mindful of the potential impact her project might have on others (*R*, pp. 44–45; 181; 186–87). Thus *Rien ne s'oppose à la nuit* constitutes, to return to Butler, 'the kind of narrative required in an account we give of ourselves' that 'accepts the presumption that the self has a causal relation to the suffering of others' (*Giving*, p. 12). For the narrator, this is not only guilt at not having pre-empted and prevented her mother's suicide, but a burden of responsibility both for her current project to narrate her mother and indeed for her existing published texts. After the publication of her first novel *Jours sans faim*, which includes descriptions of a bipolar, negligent, and silent mother strikingly similar to the character of Lucile as recounted in *Rien*, the narrator acknowledges an awareness, 'même à travers la fiction, d'agiter le couteau dans la plaie' (*R*, p. 14) ('even through fiction, of turning the knife in the wound', *N*, p. 4):

> Lorsque j'ai su que *Jours sans faim* allait paraître, je lui ai donné à lire le manuscrit. Un samedi soir où elle devait venir chez nous pour garder nos enfants, Lucile est arrivée ivre, le regard dilué. Elle avait passé l'après-midi à lire le roman. Elle l'avait trouvé beau mais injuste. Elle a répété: c'est injuste. Je me suis isolée avec elle, j'ai tenté de lui dire que je comprenais que cela puisse être douloureux, que j'en étais désolée, mais il me semblait que le livre révélait aussi, si besoin en était, l'amour que j'éprouvais pour elle. Dans un sanglot, Lucile a protesté: ce n'était pas vrai, même au pire de la torpeur, elle n'était pas comme ça. Je l'ai regardé, j'ai dit: si.
> Je ne lui ai pas dit qu'elle avait été pire, pire que ça. (*R*, p. 381)

> [When I found out that *Days Without Hunger* was going to be published, I gave her the manuscript to read. One Saturday evening when she was due to look after the children, Lucile turned up drunk, her eyes watery. She had spent the afternoon reading my novel, and thought it was beautiful but unfair. She repeated: it's not fair. I took her into another room and tried to tell her that I understood that it could be painful for her, that I was sorry, but it seemed to me that the book also showed — if it were necessary — how much I loved her. With a sob, Lucile protested: it wasn't true, even at the worst of her torpor, she hadn't been like that. I looked at her and said: yes, you were.
> I didn't say she had been worse, worse than that.] (*N*, p. 297)

In some ways, *Rien ne s'oppose à la nuit* rewrites the character of Lucile represented in *Jours sans faim*: this text may be construed as an ethical attempt to re-create a relation with the mother in writing. Yet it also portrays Lucile as inadequate reader, who denies the veracity of the representation of the negligent mother in *Jours sans faim* without acknowledging the suffering that her behaviour potentially engendered: as a reader, Lucile fails to take responsibility for the causal relation between herself and the suffering of others, to rephrase Butler. 'Giving an account of oneself', then, has ethical implications for the reader, as well as the writer. Lucile is not the only inadequate reader in *Rien*. She writes a letter to various family members — including her mother and daughters — recounting being raped by her father when she was sixteen years old ('Il m'a violée pendant mon sommeil' (*R*, p. 237) ('He raped me while I was asleep', *N*, p. 184) and receives no responses. Vigan writes that, 'Le texte est resté lettre morte et Lucile n'a reçu en retour qu'un silence pétrifié' (p. 241) ('The text remained a dead letter and all Lucile received in return was frozen silence', p. 187), her readers avoiding engaging with her suffering and, by extension, resisting any sort of empathy. Lucile later retracts her statement, rebranding her relationship with her father as 'inappropriate' rather than 'incestuous' (*R*, p. 241), prompting family members to refer dismissively to 'un viol fantasmé par Lucile' (p. 242) ('Lucile had simply imagined she had been raped', p. 187). Vigan later discovers, when interviewing Lucile's sibling Justine and her childhood friend Camille, that Georges was clearly guilty of more than one sexual assault.[25] If, as Butler puts it, 'the refusal to narrate remains a relation to narrative and to the scene of address' (*Giving*, p. 12), the frozen silence — the refusal to engage — on the part of Lucile's readers must also be understood in relation to narrative, the readers' response (as much as Lucile's own words) formulating the 'dead letter' that silences her admission of violation.

After Lucile's death, her daughters find several variations on that letter: 'J̶e̶ ̶n̶e̶ ̶s̶a̶i̶s̶ ̶p̶a̶s̶ ̶s̶'̶i̶l̶ ̶m̶'̶a̶ ̶v̶i̶o̶l̶é̶e̶. Il m'a violée pendant mon sommeil' (*R*, p. 250) ('I̶ ̶d̶o̶n̶'̶t̶ ̶k̶n̶o̶w̶ ̶i̶f̶ ̶h̶e̶ ̶r̶a̶p̶e̶d̶ ̶m̶e̶. He raped me while I was asleep', *N*, p. 194); 'il m'a peut-être violée. Je ne sais pas. Tout ce que je sais c'est que j'ai eu très peur et que je me suis évanouie' (p. 251) ('he may have raped me. I don't know. All I know is that I was very afraid and fainted', p. 194). The certainty of the accusation in the letter is literally effaced here as Lucile states that she lost consciousness (and thus cannot narrate reliably). The narrator states that concerning the alleged rape, 'nous ne saurons jamais' ['we will never know'], 'Lucile nous a laissé ce doute en héritage, et le doute est un poison' (p. 252) ('Lucile bequeathed this doubt to us, and doubt is a poison', p. 195), but adds:

> Quelques mois après la rédaction de ce texte, et le silence qui entoura sa diffusion, Lucile fut internée pour la première fois [...]. Telle que j'écris ces phrases, telles que je les juxtapose, je donne à voir ma vérité. Elle n'appartient qu'à moi. (*R*, pp. 252–53).

> [Some months after she wrote this text and the silence which surrounded its distribution, Lucile was committed for the first time [...]. The way I write these sentences, the way I place them, reveals my truth. It is mine alone.] (*N*, p. 195)

For the narrator, then, Lucile's illness can be linked to her (alleged) rape, and this is compounded when, referring to a documentary made about Georges and Liane's family, the narrator wonders what went wrong: 'Que s'est-il passé, en raison de quel désordre, de quel poison silencieux?' (R, p. 179) ('What happened? What disorder or silent poison caused it?', N, p. 136). The word 'poison' points back to her account of the ambiguity surrounding the narrative of rape: it is both rape and the uncertainty around its account that 'poison' the family and the family narrative.[26] In effect, then, the 'poison' (of not knowing) leaks through the family narrative, through the autofictional frame of Rien itself, which reiterates its own fictionality: 'La vérité n'existait pas. Je n'avais que des morceaux épars et le fait même de les ordonner constituait déjà une fiction' (p. 47) ('The truth didn't exist. I had only scattered fragments and the very fact of arranging them already constituted a fiction', pp. 30–31); 'Incapable de m'affranchir tout à fait du réel, je produis une fiction involontaire' (p. 151) ('Unable to free myself completely from reality, I am involuntarily producing fiction', p. 114). In relation to Lucile's own stories, the narrator refers to 'les fictions de Lucile' (p. 350) ('Lucile's fictions', p. 274) and observes that 'j'ai compris combien l'écriture, mon écriture, était liée à elle, à ses fictions' (p. 18) ('I realised how much writing, my writing, was linked to her, to her fictions', p. 7). What is not addressed in Rien, however, is the impact of the narrator's autobiographical fiction on the reader — if Lucile's ambiguous narratives 'poison' her readers through their lack of certainty, so, presumably, could Rien itself, particularly for those readers whose lives are in some way implicated within the family narrative.

If we return to Butler, her point that the very act of giving an account is bound up in the relation with the other is particularly pertinent here. In her words:

> After all, when one gives an account of oneself one is not merely relaying information through an indifferent medium. The account is an act — situated within a larger practice of acts — that one performs for, to, even on an other, an allocutory deed, an acting for, and in the face of, the other and sometimes by virtue of the language provided by the other. This account does not have as its goal the establishment of a definitive narrative but constitutes a linguistic and social occasion for self-transformation. (Giving, p. 130)

Despite Butler's repeated focus on giving an account of oneself as a form of performance 'for, to, even on an other', she defines the account entirely in terms of 'self-transformation', without exploring the possibilities of transformation of the other. The impact on the other in empathy is similarly often disregarded, as noted earlier in the discussion of Delaume's Le Cri du sablier. Vigan's writing does effectively explore the impact on the other of giving an account of oneself, firstly through the focus on the (insufficient) readers in Rien ne s'oppose à la nuit, as we have seen, but more extensively in the extended narrative of the relation between writer and reader in her later text, D'après une histoire vraie.

Reading and Possession in Delphine de Vigan's *D'après une histoire vraie*

D'après une histoire vraie, which was adapted into a film directed by Roman Polanski in 2017, deals with the aftermath of the success of the narrator Delphine's previous book about her bipolar mother (which is unnamed but implied to be *Rien ne s'oppose à la nuit*).[27] Delphine's encounters with her readers — who recount their own struggles with mental health and identify with the bipolar mother, leaving Delphine with the urge to hug them (*D'après*, p. 17) — are repeatedly described in terms of proximity and distance. She states that she has initially created for herself 'un imperceptible rempart' [an imperceptible rampart] enabling her to 'rester à la bonne distance' [stay at a safe distance] (p. 18) from her readers, but a relentless series of bookshop signings exhausts her, rendering her 'perméable. Vulnérable' [permeable. Vulnerable] (p. 19); the readers' over-proximity is experienced as a physical assault, breaking down the carefully constructed borders of the self and threatening her with bodily dissolution ('je vais me fendre en deux' [I'm going to split in two], p. 20).[28] Her increased sense of physical vulnerability here is partly due to the intimacy of the subject of her book, figured by the cover photograph of her mother, a private image 'reproduite par centaines puis par milliers [...] qui avait largement contribué à la propagation du texte' [reproduced by hundreds then by thousands [...] which had largely contributed to the propagation of the text] (p. 16). This photograph, which promises readers the possibility of getting to know her, simultaneously, she recognizes, 's'était dissociée d'elle et désormais n'était plus ma mère mais le personnage du roman' [had dissociated from her and was no longer my mother, but the character of the novel] (p. 17). Here the 'face' of the other to which Butler refers is literally reproduced and multiplied, exposing her mother to the gaze of the reading public, yet these readers encounter only the character of the mother in the novel in an illusion of intimacy. Similarly, Delphine herself, asked by readers to sign her book, registers her signature as 'une imposture, une mystification' [a fake, a hoax] (p. 20) because she feels distanced both from the author whose name figures on the book cover and from the narrator who recounts her mother's life. She seems paralyzed by the awareness that whilst her last book was (necessarily) a fictional construct, its success with readers seemed to depend upon them believing in its veracity. Her readers are seduced by the promise of intimacy, offered firstly by the cover photograph of Lucile and the textual markers of autobiography (the narrator of *Rien* names her first novel as *Jours sans faim*) and secondly by the physical encounter with the writer in the bookshop. The readers seek to impose the 'hyper mastery' alluded to by Butler onto the fragmented narrative of *Rien*; they are not allowing the text to wound them, to borrow Butler's phrase, but see their own lives reflected through the textual mirror (the book acting as 'une sorte de miroir', 'renvoyant le lecteur [...] à sa propre histoire' [a sort of mirror, returning the reader to [...] his/her own history], p. 18). There is no space for empathy here, because the emotions stirred up by the suffering within the text are shown to relate more to the readers' own lives than to the text itself; the readers' assumption of continuity between life and text also leaves little room for incoherence or discontinuity. If *D'après une histoire vraie* plays repeatedly and self-consciously with the relation between fiction and 'reality', it sets up a different relation between reader and text, rooted in uncertainty and doubt.

Delphine's vulnerability as a writer faced with readers who demand continuity between her textual narrator and herself is aggravated when she encounters L., initially depicted as the ideal reader. L. takes control of her email, impersonates Delphine at an invited talk, even ghost-writes an entire book in her name, before vanishing completely, leaving no physical trace of her overwhelming, suffocating presence in Delphine's life. It is unclear in *D'après* whether L. is real or a fantasized double, a projection of Delphine herself: nobody else meets her and she leaves no proof of her existence, other than the ghost-written manuscript submitted to Delphine's editor, that we are led to surmise is the text that we are now reading. As an 'other', however, L. is oddly close to Delphine herself: she dresses like her and copies her mannerisms and their relationship is strikingly claustrophobic (even when L. has a dinner party, Delphine ends up being the only guest).[29] The narrative of *D'après* is apparently ghosted, but by a character who may be fantasized by Delphine or may represent a part of Delphine herself.[30] Alluding to Franz Kafka's story 'The Judgement', Butler writes: 'It is unclear in Kafka's story whether the characters are separate entities or function as porously partitioned parts of a self that is no entity, bears no core, constituted only within a field of fragmentation' (*Giving*, p. 46). This is strikingly also true of L. in Vigan's novel: the abbreviated name, homonym of *elle*, an unnamed 'she', also, curiously, invokes the initial of several of Vigan's characters — Lucile, in *Rien*; Laure and her sister, Louise, in *Jours sans faim*; Lou, in *No et moi* — as well the pseudonym 'Lou Delvig', used for the first published edition of *Jours sans faim*. It is entirely plausible that L. and indeed Delphine constitute 'porously partitioned parts of a self' with 'no core'.

Butler's suggestion that 'something is being done with language when the account that I give begins: it is invariably interlocutory, ghosted, laden, persuasive, and tactical' finds echoes in the account of the self in *D'après*: it is ghosted (yet possibly by the self taking the form of a fantasized other or by a bipartite self created through dialogue between self and other). In *Giving an Account of Oneself*, Butler (without acknowledging this) repeats spectral imagery of ghosts, haunting ('My account of myself is partial, haunted', p. 40), and possession, suggesting that:

> To be undone by another is a primary necessity, an anguish, to be sure, but also a chance — to be addressed, claimed, bound to what is not me, but also to be moved, to be prompted to act, to address myself elsewhere, and so to vacate the self-sufficient 'I' as a kind of possession. If we speak and try to give an account from this place, we will not be irresponsible, or, if we are, we will surely be forgiven. (*Giving*, p. 136)

The process of being undone and vacated is exemplified in *D'après une histoire vraie*, as L. gradually comes to 'possess' Delphine. Delphine notes that 'je voudrais [...] décrire avec précision le contexte qui a permis à L. de pénétrer dans ma sphère privée et, avec patience, d'en prendre possession' [I would like [...] to describe with precision the context that allowed L. to invade my private sphere and, patiently, to take possession of it] (p. 13) and that 'un genre de surmoi [...] avait pris possession de mon esprit' [A sort of superego [..] had taken possession of my mind] (p. 154), referring also to 'cet espace dont elle a pris possession' [this space she had taken possession of] (p. 266). Her partner comments, 'Tu sais parfois, je me demande s'il n'y a pas quelqu'un qui prend possession de toi' [You know, sometimes I ask myself if there isn't someone taking possession of you] (p. 325). Delphine increasingly vacates herself and allows L. to possess her, but L. is not only the writer's alter ego but also her reader. This has implications for the relation between reading and giving an account of oneself: if there are ethical imperatives on the writer, these must also affect the reader, given the imbrication of reading and writing here. There are two potentially wounding readers in *D'après*: the first is the anonymous poison-pen letter-writer, who accuses Delphine of 'selling' her mother (p. 45) and hurting family members through publishing aspects of their experiences, and who, like L., does not sign his/her own name (which initially implies that L. is the letter-writer, until near the end when the writer signs the letter). Whereas L. appears to seek to become or to possess Delphine, the correspondent writes partly to articulate the pain that Delphine's previous novel inflicted upon family members and partly to wound her in return ('Tu es une grande malade. Et en plus, c'est contagieux' [You're very ill. And moreover, it's contagious], p. 121), so that reader and writer injure each other reciprocally. This mutual wounding is in part a refusal to allow the self to be undone by the other, to paraphrase Butler; there can be no forgiveness, highlighted by the final (signed) letter, which hints threateningly at future violence ('Tu n'es pas tirée d'affaire. Crois-moi' [You haven't escaped completely. Believe me], p. 467). The relation between writer and reader here (Delphine is figured both as writer, author of the damaging book, and as reader of the angry letters; the letter-writer, in turn, is both reader of the book and author of the letters) is thus underpinned by violence, which suggests the difficulty in both reading and writing, ethically, in the model charted by Butler. The second potentially wounding reader is obviously L., whose overwhelming proximity to Delphine induces in Delphine writer's block, and who towards the end of the text (in a clear nod to Stephen King's *Misery*, quotations from which are cited as epigraphs to parts one and three of the novel), both looks after and seemingly poisons the injured Delphine (J'ai eu la certitude que L. m'empoisonnait' [I was sure that L. was poisoning me], p. 424). Within the text, then, the relationship between reader (of Delphine's novel and of the letters), writer, and text is repeatedly underscored by violence; the recurring image of poison (echoing that in *Rien*) points to a much less positive model of reading and writing an account of the self/other than that given by Butler.

If we read *D'après une histoire vraie* as an example of giving an account of oneself, what is striking is the extent to which text inscribes a subject who recounts herself in and through another whose boundaries she cannot control (L.). This is compounded by the final revelation that L.'s autobiographical stories were entirely comprised of scenes taken from books on Delphine's shelves, constituting 'un écho qui me laissait croire que nous avions en commun quelque chose de profondément intime' [an echo which let me believe that we had something very intimate in common] (p. 471) that resonates with Delphine as reader through evoking books she had read. Bearing in mind that there is no evidence that L. exists, this would mean that Delphine has effectively created L. out of her own reading; to follow this through, if L. may possibly be read as part of the 'je' who gives an account of herself in this text, this 'je' is itself also constructed and shaped out of prior reading. The 'other' as reader cannot be pinned down; it is ambiguously part of the construction of the self. At the end of *D'Après*, the narrator recounts the one story told by L. that she has been unable to source in a book, an alleged memory of L. of her father telling her at fourteen years old that 'elle est bizarre' [she is strange] (p. 478). At school where she was withdrawn and awkward, a concerned teacher kept her behind and encouraged her to talk about her feelings; when she remained silent, he suggested that she could write instead. L. did not answer:

> Elle ne dit rien. Elle pense très fort ces mots qu'elle ne peut pas dire, elle pense le plus fort possible pour qu'il l'entende, suis-je si laide, si ridicule, si différente, si voûtée, si mal coiffée, si méchante? J'ai peur de devenir folle. (*D'après*, p. 479)

> [She says nothing. She thinks very hard those words that she can't say, she thinks as hard as possible so that he can hear her, am I ugly, so ridiculous, so different, so hunched, with such bad hair, such a bad person? I am afraid of going mad.]

It is striking that this text ends with a story of L., a story that begins in the third person as though Delphine is re-telling it, but ends in the first person, seemingly in L.'s own voice. This text ends by giving voice to the other (albeit another who may be a projection or part of the self), expressing in writing a fear that she is unable to speak. The voice of the other, then, both marks the impossibility of defining and demarcating the self through the text and impacts upon how we read *D'après*. The uncertainty that the text emphasizes sets up a relation with the reader which shifts away from the attempt to establish the boundaries between self and other, fiction and reality that are shown to be underpinned by violence.

These two novels by Vigan do not elicit empathy from the reader, at least not in the form that we might anticipate or expect, given the subject matter (and despite the emotive reactions of readers to *Rien ne s'oppose à la nuit* as narrated in *D'après une histoire vraie*, whose response is clearly identification, rather than empathy). Yet Vigan's texts do explore what it means 'to be undone by another' and what position(s) the reader can adopt in relation to narratives that both recount and invent suffering. *D'après* in particular may be seen to draw out the fault-lines in Butler's focus on the other, firstly because it opens up the violent, as well as creative, potential of this encounter: L. as a reader, for example, is possessive and stifling, yet whilst she silences Delphine she is also clearly a source of creativity. Secondly, the refusal to fix the identity of the 'je' (is it Delphine, or is it L. ghost-writing as Delphine, or is it indeed Delphine imagining herself as L. ghost-writing as Delphine?) also opens up the relation with the reader through recognition of mutual uncertainty. Whilst the relation between self and other (of which empathy is clearly one example) is most frequently defined by location, echoed in Butler's reference to 'this place' ('If we speak and try to give an account from this place, we will not be irresponsible'), the place in question here is perpetually being vacated and the subject is perpetually 'being undone', unsure of its own boundaries in relation to the other. What is not clear in *D'après*, however, is the extent to which the extra-textual reader is also potentially 'undone' through the encounter with an unstable, incomplete narrative. To think further about this, I now turn back to Delaume, but this time to her more recent text, *Une femme avec personne dedans*, which explores precisely this question.

Dispossession and Violence in Chloe Delaume's *Une femme avec personne dedans*

Une femme avec personne dedans opens with a question beginning a telephone call: '*Vous êtes Chloé Delaume?*' [Are you Chloé Delaume?] (*Une femme*, p. 7), a deceptively simple question that, of course, has no straightforward answer in Delaume's autofiction. The question is posed by the mother of one of Delaume's readers, Isabelle, who has committed suicide. Isabelle Bordelin is figured as both reader (of Delaume) and writer, who had previously sent Delaume a manuscript of her own. Describing Isabelle's text as a weak imitation of her own (a 'décalque malsain de mes trois premiers livres' [poisonous copy of my first three books], p. 8), Delaume recounts telephoning Isabelle to recommend that she find her own literary voice and style; to think about whether she was motivated by writing or by being published; to seek further advice (p. 11). Her seemingly rational response fails to account for the violent structures that underpin her encounter with Isabelle, who had sent her manuscript only to Delaume, positioning her as ideal, and singular, reader, on whom she confers a hitherto unspoken story of an adolescence marked by paternal sexual abuse unacknowledged by her mother. In this way, Isabelle's text posed a double demand upon Delaume: not only to consider the manuscript for publication, but also to recognize Isabelle's previously unspoken childhood trauma. To disregard this would effectively mean collaborating in the silencing of Isabelle's suffering. In this context, being constructed in the place of ideal reader is akin 'd'etre prise en otage, brutalement impliquée, une position étrange' [being taken hostage, brutally implicated, a strange position] (p. 10); the manuscript that reveals suffering 'n'etait pas vraiment un appel au secours' [wasn't really a call for help] (p. 10) (because it is too late to save the victim of abuse) but rather a demand for recognition. Delaume notes:

> Elle voulait que je la reconnaisse elle qui affirmait sa souffrance. Que je la reconnaisse comme écrivain, parce qu'elle ne pouvait être que cela, son statut de victime légitimait sa démarche autant que le résultat. Elle prenait le trauma comme une preuve implacable: puisque l'horreur est vraie, il y a littérature. (*Une femme*, pp. 10–11)

> [She wanted me to recognize her, she who was stating her suffering. She wanted me to recognize her as a writer, because she could only be that, her status as a victim legitimated her approach as much as the result did. She took her trauma as an inescapable truth: because the horror is true, literature is confirmed.]

Isabelle's wish to have her suffering acknowledged becomes confounded with her desire to be recognized as a writer, the formulation echoing Darrieussecq's observations in *Rapport de police* on how narratives of suffering are seen to give credence and authority to the writing subject. Yet what is different here is that Isabelle roots her narrative not only in her own experience, but in her reading of Delaume (who also recounts childhood trauma in her work); Isabelle's writing constitutes one kind of reading of Delaume's own texts, while requiring Delaume to shift from the position of writer to that of reader. At stake here are not accusations of plagiarism, nor even of ownership of narrative, as in the Darrieussecq/Laurens debate, but the shifting relation between writer and reader. Delaume admits to feeling guilty ('Je ne peux qu'être responsable. Oui, je suis responsable' [I can only be responsible. Yes, I am responsible], pp. 14–15), but it is not as an inadequate reader, but as a writer.

A couple of pages after the mother's question '*Vous êtes Chloé Delaume?*', the narrator answers: 'Je suis Chloé Delaume [...] un personnage de fiction. Un être d'autofiction. Qui à maintes reprises engage son lecteur à s'écrire par lui-meme, à donner à sa vie une forme inédite dont il est le héros' [I am Chloé Delaume [...] a fictional character. A being of autofiction. Who repeatedly invites the reader to write for him/herself, to give his/her life a hitherto unseen form in which he/she is the hero] (p. 13). The case of Isabelle Bordelin, however, undermines this self-identification because Delaume's texts inspired clumsy imitation rather than the desired creative invention. She therefore holds herself responsible for Isabelle's suicide not because she failed to acknowledge the suffering that underwrote Isabelle's writing, but because 'ma fiction l'a rejetée' [my fiction rejected her] (p. 15), that is, it did not make it possible for Isabelle-as-reader to construct a more enabling self-narrative. Delaume feels guilty in relation to Isabelle not — as Isabelle's mother implies — because Delaume's texts tackle violence (p. 9), nor because she did not respond adequately as reader to Isabelle's own articulation of suffering, but because her text(s) did not create sufficient space to facilitate a more open narrative response from their reader. Delaume's text thereby shifts the ethical location of textual ethical obligations from the subject-matter (for example, whether or not it is appropriate to write fiction about trauma, or the extent to which any autofictional narrative corresponds to some sort of real-life event or experience) to the ways in which the text sets up a relation with its reader. What matters here, ethically speaking, is not whether or not the writer has experience of losing a child, or how 'true' details are, but the ways in which the narrative impacts upon the reader. In other words, where Laurens accuses Darrieussecq of reading *Philippe* and subsequently trespassing on her space, the issue here is not about taking the writer's place by appropriating her story, but rather one of making space from which the reader can speak in his or her own voice (in which case perhaps *Tom est mort* might be read as a creative readerly response to *Philippe* rather than plagiarism). This refutes the 'certificat doloriste', as the reader is shifted from one who must acknowledge the subject of suffering in writing, to one who should be given space from which to create his or her own stories. The reader still has an ethical obligation: to create another story, without denying or erasing the suffering expressed in the text. Both reader and writer are conferred with, or constrained by, the requirement to give space to the other's voice; this chimes with Butler's analysis of giving an ethical account of oneself, which now must be understood in terms of both writing and reading.

Whilst *Une femme avec personne dedans* opens with this reductive example of reader and writer unable to give voice to each other, the text develops out of this lack of engagement an open-ended structure that potentially enacts the relation with the reader differently. This text seeks explicitly to drive the reader to be creative, and the language deployed uncannily echoes Butler's in *Giving an Account of Oneself.* The narrator asserts: 'Je ne suis plus dans mon corps. Quiconque peut s'introduire et en prendre les commandes. Quiconque possède ce petit livre' [I am no longer in my body. Anyone can come in and take the reins. Whoever possesses this little book] (p. 113), inviting the reader to literally occupy — possess — her body via the reading encounter with the book (that seems to stand in for and point back to the body). She insists: 'Voyez, dedans il n'y a personne, aussi installez-vous, le cortex est confortable' [See, inside there's nobody, so settle in, the mantle is comfortable] (p. 113). *Une femme* includes a quiz on the reader's preferences, modelled on the kind of multiple choice quiz found in popular magazines, and offering the reader a different concluding chapter depending on whether the reader has scored mostly a) for a reader motivated by identification with the narrator/heroine, b) for a demanding and attentive reader, or c) for the reader who seeks 'reality' in fiction. The three alternative endings all, however, highlight the risks of reading and of attempting to identify or empathize with the narrator. Referring to her own character, she challenges: '*Prends-le, et avale-le; il sera amer à tes entrailles, mais dans ta bouche il sera doux comme du miel*' [*Take it, and swallow it; it will be bitter to your innards, but in your mouth it will be sweet as honey*] (p. 113). The relation with a potential reader is defined by resistance or conflict ('La question du pour qui, du pour qui on écrit, ne s'était jamais posée: je n'écrivais que contre' [The question of for whom, for whom one writes, had never been asked: I only wrote against], p. 130): the three endings are more accurately three different staged encounters with the character of Chloé Delaume that prevent the reader from identification, transference, or, indeed, empathy. Before introducing the quiz, the narrator observes to the reader: 'Vous êtes en empathie avec le personnage, sinon pourquoi poursuivre' [You're feeling empathy with the character, otherwise why continue] (p. 111); the subsequent quiz — and invitation to occupy or possess her vacant person — however undermines any assumption of empathy. This is not least because there is nobody present to empathize with, given that the self-defined character, Chloé Delaume, is always vacating itself whilst drawing the reader's attention to the self-vacating, which again echoes Butler in *Giving an Account of Oneself.* The chapter to which reader a) is directed highlights a violent relation between text and reader: 'je vais vous décevoir' [I am going to disappoint you]; 'vous voilà menotté' [here, you're handcuffed]; 'le piège s'est refermé, l'acier mord votre gorge, vous êtes à ma merci' [the trap has closed again, the steel bites your throat, you are at my mercy]; 'poignets liés au chapitre une consentante victim, taisez-vous, écoutez' [wrists tied to the chapter a consenting victim, shut up, listen] (p. 119). The illusion of identification is therefore shown to be structured by violence. The shorter chapter aimed at reader b) proposes a different relation between author/text and reader — 'le Nous sera si dense, multitude collectif, le Nous sera une kyrielle, pas un ogre de Je' [the We will be so dense, collective multitude, the We will be a group, not a terrifying I] — yet that is equally framed by violence and violation (the narrator invites the reader to become vampiric: 'bois mon sang, s'il te plaît' [drink my blood, please], p. 133). In the final chapter, aimed at those readers who wish to anchor the text in 'reality', the character Chloé Delaume is assaulted by an avenging angel in a form of Apocalypse ('je gis en trinité, auteur narratrice heroine' [I lie dead in the trinity, author narrator heroine], p. 137) that echoes the Book of Revelations, and thereby anchors the narrative not in real life, but in a biblical, apocalyptic intertext. In all of the three encounters, then, the encounter between the fictionalized construct, Chloé Delaume, and her reader, is underwritten by potential violence: empathy is precluded by the self-consciously ludic narrative structure. The violence, however, perhaps paradoxically, because it is explicit and highlighted, may also work to enable the reader to take up Delaume's final challenge: 'je vous lègue la formule, quelle vie en ferez-vous?' [I bequeath the method to you, what life will you make of it?] (p. 140). Yet this is partly dependent upon both occupying, and vacating, the apparently empty subject position offered by the text; if, as Butler writes, 'I am, as it were, dispossessed by the language that I offer' (*Giving*, p. 26), the same dispossession of the self is at stake in reading, as well as writing, ethically.

This reading of Delaume's text raises several questions about what it might mean to conceive of reading, like writing, as a form of giving an account of oneself. It does not, I would suggest, mean producing a literal narrative self-representation; following Butler, and indeed Delaume's own inscription of reading, it involves establishing a relation that 'sustains and alters' (*Giving*, p. 50) both text and reader. Part of what is at stake here is in recognizing, and taking responsibility for, the violence that subtends the relation between text and reader (and that is evident in all four of the literary texts examined above), and it is the importance of responsibility in reading, as in writing, to which I turn by way of conclusion.

Taking Responsibility: Reading Out of Empathy

In *Une femme avec personne dedans*, Delaume cites the *Petit Robert* in her interrogation of her own responsibility as a writer: 'Responsabilité, obligation de réparer une faute' [Responsibility, obligation to fix a fault]; 'faute, le fait de manquer, d'être en moins' [fault, missing something, being lacking] (p. 15). She takes this description of being lacking literally in the notion of a body lacking its subject and locates responsibility in terms of the double meaning of *faute*: 'fault' and 'lack'. The notion of being lacking chimes with Butler's notion of being incomplete or undone: one's responsibility is located in and through one's alterity. The texts analyzed in this chapter do not solicit empathy from their reader(s), but interrogate the very basis on which a subject can give account of him/herself that is self-consciously rooted in uncertainty and fragmented identity. Whilst Butler's text focuses on the writing/accounting subject, these texts also foreground the positioning of the reader as other, not only to highlight the ethical questions of how texts impact upon readers, but also to show the reader as inevitably already part of the production of giving account of oneself. If one writes to, for, and upon an other, to paraphrase Butler, the reader is not an external agent receiving or assessing a complete entity, but is always already bound up in the conditions of production of the text itself. 'Giving an account of oneself' ethically means being mindful of the other, both within and outside the self; this chapter has argued that this applies equally to the position of the reader.

If we turn back to the question of empathy in reading, my readings of these texts suggest that we shift away from the notion of putting oneself in someone else's shoes, and explore what it means to approach the other not through assuming a singular and coherent entity, but as an incoherent and incomplete subject whose formation as 'I' already implicates us in ways that we do not necessarily apprehend. Empathy should not, then, be understood in terms of one discrete, bounded subject being projected into the position of the other. In a reading of empathy in fiction after the atrocities of 9/11, Tim Gauthier writes that 'empathy effectively serves to bridge the gap, for example, in circumstances where the margin of overlap between the two parties may appear minimal or virtually non-existent'.[31] My point is not that empathy can or cannot 'bridge the gap', but that empathy is not most productively understood in terms of connecting a gap between two discrete subjects. Instead, perhaps we can rethink empathy through Butler's model of the relation between self and other founded in mutual woundedness and dispossession: 'If I am wounded, I find that the wound testifies to the fact that I am impressionable, given over to the other in ways that I cannot fully predict or control'. The adjective 'impressionable' implies a negative judgement — being susceptible, suggestible, easily led — yet in Butler's formulation, to acknowledge oneself as impressionable means to recognize the imprint ('impressionable' is derived from the French *impressionner*, which in turn comes from the Latin *impressio*) of the other upon the self, which is figured through the wound, and which offers the basis for a potentially ethical encounter with the other. The wound, in Butler's discussion, does not denote specific past trauma, but violability or vulnerability (and responsibility) in relation to the other. The wound also marks the other's violence upon the self: Butler, reading Levinas, suggests of the other that 'although he wounds us here or, perhaps, precisely because he wounds us, we are responsible for him' (*Giving*, p. 95). Empathy may also, I would suggest, be rethought in terms of imprints or wounds that mark the relation between self and other. This is not because one's own woundedness offers privileged access to or understanding of the wounds of another — or even because it underscores what we cannot access or understand about the wounds of another — but because it denotes a responsibility to the other founded in a lack of cohesion, through which one can begin to approach the suffering of the other. This responsibility is necessarily bound up in violence and violability that mark not only the limits, but also the very possibility, of empathy.

Notes to Chapter 4

1. Judith Butler, *Giving an Account of Oneself* (New York: Fordham University Press, 2005), p. 40.
2. Diana Holmes, 'To Write is a Transitive Verb: Nancy Huston and the Ethics of the Novel', *Contemporary French and Francophone Studies*, 14.1 (2010), 85–92 (p. 87).
3. Elise Hugueny-Léger alludes to 'the ludic facet of autofiction' in 'Filatures de soi: Detectives, Deception and Deceit in the Crime-fictions of Calle, Laurens and Nothomb', in *Rewriting Wrongs: French Crime Fiction and the Palimpsest*, ed. by Angela Kimyongür and Amy Wigelsworth (Newcastle upon Tyne: Cambridge Scholars Publishing, 2014), pp. 145–61 (p. 156), whilst Liesbeth Korthals Altes states that 'autofiction is the genre in which this self-interrogation is pushed to its highest — ludic or anxious — degree of reflexivity', *Ethos and Narrative Interpretation: The Negotiation of Values in Fiction* (Lincoln: University of Nebraska Press, 2014), p. 192.
4. Shirley Jordan refers to 'the privileged connection between women's autofiction and trauma' ('Autofiction in the Feminine', p. 79), which is also shown in Suzette Henke's Shattered Subjects: Trauma and Testimony in Women's Life-writing (London: Palgrave Macmillan, 2000) and Kathryn Robson, Writing Wounds: The Inscription of Trauma in Post-1968 French Women's Life-writing (Amsterdam: Rodopi, 2004).
5. J. Aaron Simmons, 'Giving an Account of Oneself', *Journal for Cultural and Religious Theory*, 7.2 (Spring 2006), 85–90 (p. 89).
6. Catherine Mills, 'Normative Violence, Vulnerability, and Responsibility', *differences*, 18.2 (2007), 133–56 (p. 153).
7. Judith Butler, 'Reply from Judith Butler to Mills and Jenkins', *differences*, 18.2 (2007), 180–95 (p. 181).
8. Ibid., p. 190.
9. Christa Hodapp, 'Giving an Account of Oneself by Judith Butler (Review)', *The Pluralist*, 8.1 (2013), 115–18 (p. 118).
10. The imbrication of self and other in autobiographical writing is highlighted in Annie Ernaux's notion of the 'je transpersonnel' [transpersonal I], in 'Vers un je transpersonnel', in *Autofiction et cie.*, ed. by Serge Doubrovsky, Jacques Lecarme, and Philippe Lejeune, Cahiers du RITM 6 (Nanterre: Université de Paris X, 1993), pp. 219–21.
11. Marie Darrieussecq, 'Je est unE autre', in *Ecrire l'histoire d'une vie*, ed. by Annie Oliver (Rome: Edizioni Spartaco, 2007), pp. 105–21, <http://www.mariedarrieussecq.com/autres_textes> [accessed 8 March 2019].
12. Chloé Delaume, *La Règle du jeu* (Paris: Presses universitaires de France, 2010), p. 67.
13. There is an additional ethical question raised here in relation to the other people whose lives are also evoked, albeit in fictional form, in these texts. The texts analyzed in this chapter explore this through focusing on how autofictional writing impacts upon its reader; there are of course also wider questions about rights and responsibilities in exposing other people's lives in print, which have notably been raised in the autofiction of Christine Angot and Camille Laurens, for instance. See Gisèle Sapiro, 'The Legal Responsibility of the Writer Between Objectivity and Subjectivity: The French Case (Nineteenth to Twenty-first Century)', in *Literary Trials: Exceptio Artis and Theories of Literature in Court*, ed. by Ralf Grüttemeier (London: Bloomsbury Academic, 2016), pp. 21–47.
14. Chloé Delaume, *Le Cri du sablier* (Paris: Folio, 2003; first published Farrago/Léo Scheer, 2001) and *Une femme avec personne dedans* (Paris: Du Seuil, 2012); Delphine de Vigan, *Rien ne s'oppose à la nuit* (Paris: Jean-Claude Lattès, 2011) (hereafter referred to as R), and *Nothing Holds Back the Night*, trans. by George Miller (London: Bloomsbury, 2013) (hereafter referred to as N); *D'après une histoire vraie* (Paris: Jean-Claude Lattès, 2011).
15. Barbara Havercroft, 'Le Soi est une fiction', *Fictions de soi*, special issue of *Revue critique de fixxion française contemporaine*, 4 (2012), <http://www.revue-critique-de-fixxion-francaise-contemporaine.org/rcffc/article/view/fx04.12/671> [accessed 8 March 2019].
16. Addressing her father in *Le Cri du sablier*, the narrator asserts that 'Tu m'as sali des mots' [You sullied me with words] (p. 124), words which he used to threaten her with violence and to erase

her existence ('Jamais tu n'aurais dû naître' [You should never have been born], p. 46).

17. The narrator addresses her father as 'tu', the analyst as 'vous'; her interjections to her father, later in the text, are angry and violent, whereas she simply refuses to respond to the analyst, but both may be referred to as the 'il' whose commands she seeks to resist.

18. Valérie Dusaillant-Fernandes, 'Dérouter le lecteur: procédés stylistiques dans *Le Cri du sablier* de Chloé Delaume', in *Aventures et expériences littéraires: écritures des femmes en France au début du vingt-et-unième siècle*, ed. by Amaleena Damlé and Gill Rye (Amsterdam: Rodopi, 2014), pp. 43–54 (p. 44).

19. Carolyn Pedwell, 'Economies of Empathy: Obama, Neoliberalism, and Social Justice', *Environment and Planning D: Society and Space*, 30.2 (2012), 280–97 (p. 280).

20. Lindsay B. Cummings, *Empathy as Dialogue in Theatre and Performance* (London: Palgrave Macmillan, 2016), p. 76.

21. Hemmings, *Why Stories Matter*, pp. 203–04.

22. *Rien ne s'oppose à la nuit* won the following prizes: Prix du roman Fnac, Prix Renaudot des lycéens, Prix France Télévisions (2011), and Grand Prix 'roman' des lectrices de Elle (2012).

23. Valérie Dusaillant-Fernandes, 'Au fil du temps, les masques tombent: mémoire familiale et vérité chez Delphine de Vigan', *French Forum*, 40.2–3 (Spring/Fall 2015), 111–25 (p. 111).

24. The narrator of this latter text is clearly identifiable, from the references to her published novels, amongst other details, as Vigan herself, yet she repeatedly insists upon the fictionality of the text, as well as upon the impossibility of capturing her mother accurately in writing.

25. When Vigan later interviews Lucile's siblings, they minimize it ('toutes les filles ne sont-elles pas amoureuses de leur père?' (*R*, p. 222) ('aren't all girls in love with their fathers?', *N*, p. 188), yet Lucile's sister Justine recounts her father's repeated pestering to be allowed to take topless photographs of her and to teach her to masturbate, whilst Lucile's old friend Camille recounted being assaulted and raped by Georges too.

26. Untrustworthy narratives mark and define the family myth: when Lucile's adoptive brother Jean-Marc dies of autoerotic asphyxiation, the children are told that he accidentally suffocated himself because, as an abused child, he had become accustomed to covering his face to sleep; later, after Lucile's suicide, Delphine tells her children that her mother 'a choisi de s'endormir' (*R*, p. 16) ('decided to go to sleep', *N*, p. 6). Her son, however, corrects her version, asking if his grandmother committed suicide, the interrogation underscoring the inadequacy of his mother's explanation.

27. This text also won critical acclaim and literary prizes: the Prix Renaudot and the Prix Goncourt des lycées (2015).

28. Towards the end of *D'après une histoire vraie*, Delphine accepts an invitation to speak at a literary festival. As she approaches the guests, she recalls crying the first time that she presented her book in public and notes that since then, 'j'avais pris du recul' [I had stepped back]; 'j'étais, enfin, à la bonne distance' [I was finally a safe distance away] (p. 445), again figuring her relation to her text and her readers in terms of distance.

29. The intimacy is reflected in the repeated interior scenes in which Delphine and L spend time together — Delphine's home, the car, the cinema, the remote country house where Delphine is bedridden — that reflect her reclusion from the world outside/from other people.

30. Delphine's lover, François, whose job as a high-profile book critic (like Vigan's real-life partner, François Busnel, literary critic, journalist and television presenter) identifies him as another ideal reader, suggests that Delphine fantasized L. as inspiration to write (p. 465).

31. Tim Gauthier, *9/11 Fiction, Empathy, and Otherness* (Lanham, MD: Lexington Books, 2015), p. 31.

AFTERWORD

❖

Uncomfortable Empathy

Elizabeth V. Spelman, reading Hannah Arendt, warns of the risks of 'proclaiming to understand and know how to respond to the suffering of other people'; this recognition of the impossibility of understanding other people's pain has underpinned the analyses in this study.[1] This book does not seek to propose a model for reading narratives of suffering: instead, I have attempted to rethink the ways in which we approach both narratives of other people's pain and the notion of empathy. Two key points emerge here. Firstly, whilst empathy is typically defined as standing in someone else's shoes, which presupposes discrete identities and locations, it may be more productive to approach other people's pain through recognition of the impossibility of establishing such fixed positions. Secondly, as I argued in Chapter 4, reading narratives of suffering also means moving away from assumptions of commonality to attempt instead to address and take account of the violence and wounding that shape the encounter between self and other.

Acknowledging the impossibility of 'fellow feeling', to borrow Sara Ahmed's formulation below, does not mean discarding the concept of empathy entirely, but reformulating it in and through the impossibility of reconciliation between self and other. Ahmed writes:

> The impossibility of 'fellow feeling' is itself the confirmation of injury. The call of such pain, as a pain that cannot be shared through empathy, is a call not just for an attentive hearing, but for a different kind of inhabitance. It is a call for action, and a demand for collective politics, as a politics based not on the possibility that we might be reconciled, but on learning to live with the impossibility of reconciliation, or learning that we live with and beside each other, and yet we are not as one.[2]

This acknowledgement of the impossibility of sharing someone else's feeling is, according to Ahmed (in a curious echo of Judith Butler), associated with injury or wounding. Ahmed's point here is slightly different from Butler's, in that she is arguing that pain, not violence, is both a marker of and origin for separation from the other. Pain also, in Ahmed's formulation, represents a 'call' and a 'demand' to the other for a 'collective politics' paradoxically grounded in recognition of irreconcilable difference. Empathy, in this model, is not sharing pain (because this is impossible); it could, however, mean trying to develop alternative relations between self and other that can acknowledge separation and difference whilst attempting to approach someone else's pain. This is not synonymous with sympathy (which, if we return to Suzanne Keen's definition, implies that 'I feel pity for your pain'); instead, it is about critically analyzing both what is at stake in feeling, be it pity or empathy, for someone else's suffering, and indeed, what these emotions might mask or ignore (as we saw in Chapter 3).[3]

Ahmed's use of the phrase 'a different kind of inhabitance' above also evokes the ghostly imagery of possession that I observed in Butler's *Giving an Account of Oneself* (see Chapter 4), as 'inhabitance' implies being haunted or inhabited by another, as well as physically occupying a space. What we are haunted by, in this analogy, would be the recognition of irreconcilable separation from the other coupled with the recognition of our own responsibility towards the other (because, as Ahmed puts it, 'pain surfaces in relation to others, who bear witness to pain, and authenticate its existence'; this 'requires an ethics').[4] For Ahmed, as for Butler, it is difficult to determine what the requisite ethical approach would look like, but it is clearly related to an acknowledgement of responsibility rooted in injury or loss. This is also suggested by the word 'inhabitance' itself, which can mean 'the state of having legal right to claim the privileges of a recognized inhabitant; especially, the right to support in case of poverty, acquired by residence in a town' (Webster's Dictionary). The language here of 'recognition' (which confers the status of inhabitant), 'rights', and 'privileges' reminds us that empathy cannot be located in terms of a straightforward self/other binary according to which both self and other appear to have equal if disparate positions. Instead, empathy must be understood as being negotiated within specific socio-political structures according to which individuals, rights, and privileges are not universally or equally accessible or recognized. This of course raises a question as to how, or indeed whether, one can empathize with someone who lacks rights, privilege, and recognition in social terms (whose life is deemed 'ungrievable', to paraphrase Butler), and also, of course, what the impact of that empathy (or indeed, conversely, of a lack of empathy) might be on the other.

In a discussion of empathy and reading, Megan Boler argues that there are 'modes of empathy that permit the reader's exoneration from privilege and complicities' by assuming the possibility of a universal identification or understanding that does not need to account for or indeed threaten the reader's position of privilege. Her point that 'those "others" whose lives we imagine don't want empathy, they want justice', is perhaps not entirely fair, given that establishing justice is arguably impossible without trying to understand how the other feels — so that empathy may generate a quest for justice — but the inadequacy of empathy, if it is reduced to shared feeling, is evident in her formulation.[5] The notion of a 'reader's exoneration from privilege and complicities' requires interrogation in relation to texts that narrate someone else's pain. In *Feeling Power*, Boler contends that 'recognizing my position as "judge" granted through the reading privilege, I must learn to question the genealogy of any particular emotional response'.[6] The position of the reader as judge suggests that the reader is empowered to make decisions, yet decisions which are partly driven by feelings (hence the reference to 'emotional response'), feelings which, as Boler observes, require interrogation. The concept of 'reading privilege' is particularly suggestive: if we return to Hélène Cixous's *Vivre l'orange*, which I discussed in the Introduction, Cixous's textual emphasis on framing her close reading of Clarice Lispector by her lack of action supporting suffering women in Iran highlights not only the distance between herself and these women, but also her awareness of her privileged position as a reader (who contemplates an orange instead of participating in political activism to support victims of violence). Boler goes on to argue that 'spectating thus signifies a privilege: allowing oneself to inhabit a position of distance and separation, to remain in the anonymous spectating crowd and abdicate any possible responsibility'; being able to keep a safe distance from someone else's pain is itself a privilege.[7] This is exemplified in Cixous's persistent and uncomfortable contemplation of the orange, yet her text also gestures towards the risks inherent in her failure to engage ethically with the suffering women in Iran and acknowledges her own responsibility.

Distance is, on the one hand, then, a privilege; it is also potentially uncomfortable, as we have seen, and being cognisant of the 'discomfort of distance', as Clare Hemmings puts it, is part of the requirement to read with responsibility.[8] Recurring throughout this study have been figures of distance, marking the gap between reader and text, reader and suffering subject. Part of the responsibility of reading is to avoid on the one hand maintaining a fixed distance between self and other, and on the other hand seeking to erase or deny the reality of that gap. Interestingly, the readers inscribed within Delphine de Vigan's *D'après une histoire vraie* and Chloé Delaume's *Une femme avec personne dedans*, analyzed in Chapter 4, are both unable to maintain a stable distance from the text or from its author. In both cases, the reading encounter is subtended by violence, as the reader either seeks to become, or to consume, the other in the form of (a projected image of) the writing subject. Perhaps what is most striking in these texts, however, is less the violence of the reading encounter within the text — the inscribed suicidal/murderous reader either dies or vanishes — than the discomfort that these readers induce, and that is also evident in the other texts examined in this study.

Boler, discussing ways of teaching approaches to other people's suffering that might encourage responses beyond passive empathy, also uses the word 'inhabit' in her contention that 'a pedagogy of discomfort offers an entrée to learn to in-habit different positions and identities that are ambiguous'.[9] She seems to suggest that there is choice about which positions to occupy; more, she proposes occupying multiple positions, which is precisely the mode of reading that I have tried to adopt in this book. If we replace 'pedagogy' with 'reading', a reading of discomfort should not, however, occupy different positions in order to evade responsibility. Instead, it means addressing one's own responsibility and privilege as a reader (as Cixous does, to some extent, in *Vivre l'orange*) but also recognizing the limits that frame the reading encounter (it is clearly not enough to recognize one's own privilege and to continue to contemplate the orange, in Cixous's case). Being uncomfortable, similarly, is not synonymous with suffering; Cixous, uncomfortably reading Lispector, is markedly separate from and in a privileged position respective to the women in Iran whose appeal for help interrupts her reading, but also in relation to

Lispector's text. Part of the discomfort induced by reading *Vivre l'orange* is precisely the recognition of how comfortable reading itself, even when configured as an engagement with alterity as in Cixous's text, inevitably is.

Ahmed writes: 'We don't tend to notice what is comfortable, even when we think we do'; 'To be comfortable is to be so at ease with one's environment that it is hard to distinguish where one's body ends and the world begins'; 'One fits'. Whilst her descriptions of comfort are very physical, the possibility of a body fitting in comfortably is, she argues, socially constructed and shaped ('Normativity is comfortable for those who can inhabit it'). It is only when one is not at ease that 'the "stitches" between bodies' become visible and it becomes apparent that comfort is constructed through social normativity.[10] Rooting her discussion of comfort in an attempt to 'queer' heteronormativity, Ahmed argues that ' "non-fitting" or discomfort opens up possibilities, an opening up which can be difficult and exciting' and which can render normative positions less comfortable as well as offering different ones.[11] Whether or not feeling uncomfortable enables alternative subject positions to be facilitated — without simply seeking to restore the comfortable status quo or to find a way of fitting into the status quo more comfortably, possibly by taking someone else's place/excluding someone — is of course a difficult question, if, potentially, as Ahmed suggests, also 'exciting'. Admittedly ambivalent, though, the notion of 'not fitting' is potentially useful as the basis for an alternative conception of empathy. By this, I do not mean simply reframing empathy as wearing someone else's ill-fitting shoes. Rather, my work focuses on the ways in which empathy is uncomfortable in terms of how our attempts to empathize with another do not 'fit', observing the 'stitches' that connect, and separate, self and other without assuming these to be reparable yet equally without dismissing their impact. Ahmed writes that 'to feel uncomfortable is precisely to be affected by that which persists in the shaping of bodies and lives'; the reference to persistence here highlights that the stitches or fault lines that mark the relation with the other are repeatedly re-sewn, rather than set permanently in place.[12] Similarly, the attempt to empathize with another cannot be seen as a singular act; it is located within a persistent re-inscription of the relation between self and other, wherein discomfort usefully marks the site both of the limits of empathy and for alternative versions of empathy. It is equally crucial, of course, to explore what it means to feel comfortable in empathizing, and, for instance as I argued in Chapter 3, to expose and analyze the seams of an 'I' or indeed an 'us' that seems too easily established in relation to a suffering 'other'.

In terms of how we approach narratives of other people's suffering, focusing on the ways in which they make us uncomfortable does, of course, run the equally uncomfortable risk of privileging our own responses over their suffering, even failing to 'see' their suffering over and beyond the ways in which it impacts upon us. There is no solution to this as to be comfortable with reading other people's suffering to the extent of losing awareness of one's own limits would evidently be troubling in other ways, and possible only through the 'discomfort of distance' or through complacency, and acknowledging it is part of our responsibility as critical readers. Being uncomfortable can become an impetus to change position, either by finding a more comfortable space — which would leave the status quo untouched — or, more productively, by attempting to modify the uncomfortable space itself to make room for those who hitherto did not fit comfortably. Reading narratives of suffering should not just mean seeking a more comfortable position, but recognizing, and taking responsibility for, one's own discomfort and disorientation, which may in turn become the basis for alternative models of empathy, rooted in the admission of an inability to know, or understand, other people's pain.

Notes to the Afterword

1. Spelman, *Fruits of Sorrow*, p. 165.
2. Ahmed, *The Cultural Politics of Emotion*, p. 39.
3. Keen, 'A Theory of Narrative Empathy', p. 208.
4. Ahmed, *The Cultural Politics of Emotion*, p. 31.
5. Boler, The Risks of Empathy', p. 253.
6. Megan Boler, *Feeling Power: Emotions and Education* (London & New York: Routledge, 1999), p. 170.
7. Ibid., p. 184.
8. Gunaratnam, 'Interview with Clare Hemmings'.
9. Boler, *Feeling Power*, pp. 198.
10. Ahmed, *The Cultural Politics of Emotion*, pp. 147–48.
11. Ibid., p. 154.
12. Ibid.

BIBLIOGRAPHY

❖

ADAMS, TIM, 'Feel the Pain', <http://www.guardian.co.uk/books/2006/jan/29/biography.
features>

ADLER, LAURE, À ce soir (Paris: Gallimard 2001)

AHMED, SARA, The Cultural Politics of Emotion (New York: Routledge, 2012)

ALDER, CHRISTINE M., and JUNE BAKER, 'Maternal Filicide: More Than One Story to Be
Told', Women and Criminal Justice, 9.2 (1997), 15–39

ALTES, LIESBETH KORTHALS, Ethos and Narrative Interpretation: The Negotiation of Values in
Fiction (Lincoln: University of Nebraska Press, 2014)

ANGOT, CHRISTINE, Quitter la ville (Paris: Stock, 2000)

—— Un amour impossible (Paris: Flammarion, 2015)

ANSPACH, MARK, 'Why Did Isabelle Caro Die?' (24 March 2011), <https://journaldumauss.
net/spip.php?page=imprimer&id_article=790>

ARROJO, ROSEMARY, 'Interpretation as Possessive Love: Hélène Cixous, Clarice Lispector,
and the Ambivalence of Fidelity', in Postcolonial Translation: Theory and Practice, ed. by
Susan Bassnett and Harish Trivedi (London: Routledge, 1999), pp. 141–61

AYRES, SUSAN, 'Who is to Shame? Narratives of Neonaticide', William and Mary Journal of
Women and the Law, 14.1 (2007), 55–105

AYRES, SUSAN, and PREMA MANJUNATH, 'Denial and Concealment of Unwanted Pregnancy:
A Film Hollywood Dared Not Do', Journal of Civil Rights & Economic Development, 26
(2012), 197–221

BAIROCH, ALICE, Voyage en anorexie (Paris: Presses du Belvédère, 2007)

BAL, P. MATTHIJS, and MARTIJN VELTKAMP, 'How Does Fiction Reading Influence
Empathy? An Experimental Investigation on the Role of Emotional Transportation',
PLos One, 8.1 (January 2013), 1–11

BALINSKA, MARTA ALEKSANDRA, Retour à la vie: quinze ans d'anorexie (Paris: Odile Jacob,
2003)

BARON-COHEN, SIMON, The Essential Difference: Male and Female Brains and the Truth About
Autism (New York: Basic Books, 2003)

—— The Science of Evil: On Empathy and the Origins of Cruelty (New York: Basic Books,
2011)

BAUDELLE, YVES, 'Autofiction et roman autobiographique: incidents de frontière', in Vies en
récit: formes littéraires et médiatiques de la biographie et de l'autobiographie, ed. by Robert Dion
and others (Quebec: Éditions Nota bene, 2007), pp. 43–70

BENNETT, JILL, Empathic Vision: Affect, Trauma and Contemporary Art (Stanford, CA: Stanford
University Press, 2005)

BERLANT, LAUREN, 'Poor Eliza', American Literature, 70.3 (1998), 635–68

—— 'Introduction: Compassion (and Withholding)', in Compassion: The Culture and Politics
of an Emotion (New York & London: Routledge, 2004), 1–13

BERTIN, MARIE, and ROSELYNE BERTIN, Journal sans faim (Paris: Rageot, 2004)

BIDISHA, ' "It Unlocks You from the Inside ": Staging Véronique Olmi's Infanticide Novel',
Guardian, 18 February 2012, 'Guardian Books', <https://www.theguardian.com/books/
2012/feb/18/beside-the-sea-veronique-olmi-monologue>

BLACK, LYNSEY, 'Paper Women: The Representation of Female Offenders in Irish News-papers' (Masters dissertation, Dublin Institute of Technology, 2009)

BLOOM, PAUL, 'Empathy and its Discontents', *Trends in Cognitive Sciences*, 21.1 (2017), 24–31

BOLER, MEGAN, 'The Risks of Empathy: Interrogating Multiculturalism's Gaze', *Cultural Studies*, 11.2 (1997), 253–73

—— , *Feeling Power: Emotions and Education* (London & New York: Routledge, 1999)

BOUDOURESQUE, FRÉDÉRIC, 'Procès Chabot: "J'avais les jambes qui tremblaient"', 3 March 2015, <http://www.leprogres.fr/ain/2015/02/27/suivez-en-direct-le-proces-des-bebes-congeles>

BRAY, ABIGAIL, 'The Anorexic Woman: Reading Disorders', *Cultural Studies*, 10.3 (October 1996), 413–29

—— *Hélène Cixous: Writing and Sexual Difference* (London: Palgrave Macmillan, 2004)

BRISAC, GENEVIÈVE, *Petite* (Paris: Editions de l'Olivier, 1994)

BROWN, LAURA, 'Not Outside the Range: One Feminist Perspective on Psychic Trauma', *American Imago*, 48.1 (1991), 119–33

BRUMBERG, JOAN JACOBS, *Fasting Girls: The History of Anorexia Nervosa* (Cambridge, MA: Harvard University Press, 1988)

BUTLER, JUDITH, *Frames of War: When is Life Grievable?* ((London: Verso, 2009)

—— *Giving An Account of Oneself* (New York: Fordham University Press, 2005)

—— *Precarious Life: The Powers of Mourning and Violence* (New York: Verso, 2004)

—— 'Reply from Judith Butler to Mills and Jenkins', *differences*, 18.2 (2007), 180–95

CAIN, RUTH, '"How to Say Hello to the Sea": Literary Perspectives on Medico-Legal Narratives of Maternal Filicide', in *Motherhood in Literature and Culture: Interdisciplinary Perspectives from Europe*, ed. by Gill Rye and others (London: Routledge, 2017), pp. 223–37

—— 'Véronique Olmi's *Beside the Sea*: Law, Psychiatry and the Moral Dilemmas of Filicide' (podcast), Institute of Modern Languages Research, lecture given 11 May 2012, <https://www.sas.ac.uk/videos-and-podcasts/culture-language-and-literature/veronique-olmi-s-beside-sea-law-psychiatry-and>

CAIRNS, LUCILLE, 'Dissidences charnelles: The Female Body in Revolt', in *The Flesh in the Text*, ed. by James Baldwin, James Fowler, and Shane Weller (Oxford: Peter Lang, 2007), pp. 205–25

—— 'Bodily Dis-ease in Contemporary French Women's Writing: Two Case Studies', *French Studies*, 69.4 (2015), 494–508

CARO, ISABELLE, *La Petite Fille qui ne voulait pas grossir* (Paris: Poche, 2010)

CARUTH, CATHY, *Literature in the Ashes of History* (Baltimore, MD: Johns Hopkins University Press, 2013)

—— *Unclaimed Experience: Trauma, Narrative and History* (Baltimore, MD, & London: Johns Hopkins University Press, 1996)

CHAYET, DELPHINE, 'Ces mères infanticides sont incapables de s'expliquer', *Le Figaro*, 29 July 2010, <http://www.lefigaro.fr/actualite-france/2010/07/29/01016-20100729ARTFIG00580-ces-meres-infanticides-sont-incapables-de-s-expliquer.php>

CHEN, YING, *L'Ingratitude* (Arles: Actes Sud, 1999)

CHOI, SHINE, *Re-Imagining North Korea in International Politics: Problems and Alternatives* (New York: Routledge, 2014)

CIXOUS, HÉLÈNE, *Le Jour où je n'étais pas là* (Paris: Galilée, 2002)

—— *Vivre l'orange/To Live the Orange* (Paris: Des femmes, 1979)

CLERCK, GENEVIÈVE DE, 'Le Dialogue hypermoderne d'Amélie Nothomb ou la poétique d'un sabotage heureux' (PhD thesis, University of Louisiana at Lafayette, 2006)

CLOHESY, ANTHONY M., *The Politics of Empathy: Ethics, Solidarity, Recognition* (London: Routledge, 2014)

CODE, LORRAINE, 'I Know Just How You Feel: Empathy and the Problem of Epistemic Authority', in *Rhetorical Spaces: Essays on Gendered Locations* (London & New York: Routledge, 1995), pp. 120–43

COLONNA, VINCENT, *Autofictions et autres mythomanies littéraires* (Auch: Tristram, 2004)

CONLEY, VERENA ANDERMATT, *Hélène Cixous: Writing the Feminine* (Lincoln & London: University of Nebraska Press, 1984)

CONSTANT, PAULE, *La Bête à chagrin* (Paris: Gallimard, 2007)

COPLAN, AMY, 'Understanding Empathy: Its Features and Effects', in *Empathy: Philosophical and Psychological Perspectives*, ed. by Amy Coplan and Peter Goldie (Oxford: Oxford University Press, 2011), pp. 3–18

—— 'Will the Real Empathy Please Stand Up? A Case for a Narrow Conceptualisation', *Southern Journal of Philosophy*, 49 (2011), 40–65

COURJAULT, JEAN-LOUIS, *Je ne pouvais pas l'abandonner* (Paris: Michel Lafon, 2010)

CRUICKSHANK, RUTH, *Fin de millénaire French Fiction: The Aesthetics of Crisis* (Oxford: Oxford University Press, 2009)

CUMMINGS, LINDSAY B., *Empathy as Dialogue in Theatre and Performance* (London: Palgrave Macmillan, 2016)

CUNY, JUSTINE and MARIE-THÉRÈSE, *Ce matin j'ai décidé d'arrêter de manger* (Paris: Oh!, 2007)

CVETKOVICH, ANN, *An Archive of Feelings: Trauma, Sexuality, and Lesbian Public Cultures* (Durham, NC: Duke University Press, 2003)

DAMLÉ, AMALEENA, 'The Becoming of Anorexia and Text in Amélie Nothomb's *Robert des noms propres* and Delphine de Vigan's *Jours sans faim*', in *Women's Writing in Twenty-first-century France: Life as Literature*, ed. by Amaleena Damlé and Gill Rye (Cardiff: University of Wales Press, 2013), pp. 113–26

DANILEWSKY, LÉA, 'Le Traitement médiatique de l'affaire dite "des bébés congelés": représentations des figures de "femme" et de "mère" à travers le discours médiatique; Véronique Courjault, monstre ou martyre?', <http://doc.sciencespo-lyon.fr/Ressources/ Documents/Etudiants/Memoires/Cyberdocs/MFE2010/danilewsky_l/pdf/ danilewsky_l.pdf>

DARRIEUSSECQ, MARIE, 'L'Autofiction: un genre pas sérieux', *Poétique*, 107 (1996), 369–80

—— *Bref séjour chez les vivants* (Paris: P.O.L., 2001)

—— 'Encore là', in *Naissances: récits*, ed. by Isabelle Lortholary (Paris: Iconoclaste, 2005), pp. 11–29

—— 'Je est unE autre', in *Écrire l'histoire d'une vie*, ed. by Annie Oliver (Rome: Edizioni Spartaco, 2007), pp. 105–21, <http://www.mariedarrieussecq.com/autres_textes>

—— *Rapport de police: accusations de plagiat et autres modes de surveillance de la fiction* (Paris: P.O.L., 2010)

—— *White* (Paris: P.O.L., 2003)

DAULL, SOPHIE, *Camille, mon envolée* (Paris: Philippe Rey, 2015)

DECKER, HANNAH, *Freud, Dora and Vienna 1900* (New York: Free Press, 1991)

DELAUME, CHLOÉ, *Le Cri du sablier* (Paris: Farrago/Léo Scheer, 2001; Folio, 2003)

—— *La Règle du jeu* (Paris: Presses universitaires de France, 2010)

—— *Une femme avec personne dedans* (Paris: Du Seuil, 2012)

DELVIG, LOU, *Jours sans faim* (Paris: Grasset, 2001)

DERRIDA, JACQUES, *Archive Fever: A Freudian Impression*, trans. by Eric Prenowitz (Chicago & London: University of Chicago Press, 1995)

DESALVO, LOUISE, *Writing as a Way of Healing: How Telling Our Stories Transforms our Lives* (London: The Women's Press, 1999)

DETAMBEL, RÉGINE, *Les Livres prennent soin de nous* (Arles: Actes Sud, 2015)

DOUBROVSKY, SERGE, *Fils* (Paris: Galilée, 1977)

DURAND, EMILIE, *Ma folie ordinaire: allers et retours à l'hôpital Sainte-Anne* (Paris: Les Empêcheurs de penser en rond, 2006)

DURAND-SOUFFLAND, STÉPHANE, 'Véronique Courjault: la détresse et la confusion', *Le Figaro*, 11 June 2009, <http://www.lefigaro.fr/actualite-france/2009/06/11/01016–20090611ARTFIG00004-veronique-courjault-la-detresse-et-la-confusion-.php>

DURAS, MARGUERITE, 'Sublime, forcément sublime', in *Marguerite Duras*, ed. by Bernard Alazet and Christiane Blot-Labarrère (Paris: L'Herne, 2005), pp. 69–73

—— 'Sublime, Necessarily Sublime', trans. by Andrew Slade, *Janus Head*, 9.1 (2006), 8–18

DUSAILLAINT-FERNANDES, VALÉRIE, 'Dérouter le lecteur: procédés stylistiques dans *Le Cri du sablier* de Chloé Delaume', in *Aventures et expériences littéraires: écritures des femmes en France au début du vingt-et-unième siècle*, ed. by Amaleena Damlé & Gill Rye (Amsterdam: Rodopi, 2014), pp. 43–54

—— 'Au fil du temps, les masques tombent: mémoire familiale et vérité chez Delphine de Vigan', *French Forum*, 40.2–3 (Spring/Fall 2015), 111–25

EDWARDS, NATALIE, 'Babykillers: Véronique Olmi and Laurence Tardieu on Motherhood', in *Women's Writing in Twenty-first-century France: Life as Literature*, ed. by Amaleena Damlé and Gill Rye (Cardiff: University of Wales Press, 2013), pp. 98–110

—— 'Obliged to Sympathise: Infanticide in *Il y a longtemps que je t'aime* and *A perdre la raison*', *Australian Journal of French Studies*, 52.2 (2015), 174–87

ELLMANN, MAUD, *The Hunger Artists: Starving, Writing and Imprisonment* (Cambridge, MA: Harvard University Press, 1993)

ERNAUX, ANNIE, 'Vers un je transpersonnel', in *Autofiction et cie.*, ed. by Serge Doubrovsky, Jacques Lecarme, and Philippe Lejeune, Cahiers du RITM 6 (Nanterre: Université de Paris X, 1993), pp. 219–21

FELMAN, SHOSHANA, 'Fire in the Archive: The Alignment of Witnesses', *The Future of Testimony: Interdisciplinary Perspectives on Witnessing*, ed. by Antony Rowland and Jane Kilby (New York: Routledge, 2014), pp. 48–68

FELMAN, SHOSHANA, and DORI LAUB, *Testimony: Crises of Witnessing in Literature, Psychoanalysis and History* (New York: Routledge, 1992)

FERREDAY, DEBRA, 'Haunted Bodies', *Borderlands e-Journal* 10.2 (2011), 1–21, <http://www.borderlands.net.au/vol10no2_2011/ferreday_bodies.pdf>

—— 'Anorexia and Abjection: A Review Essay', *Body and Society*, 18.2 (2012), 139–55

FORTIN, JUTTA, *Camille Laurens: le kaléidoscope d'une écriture hantée* (Lille: Presses universitaires du Septentrion, 2017)

FREUD, SIGMUND, *Delusion and Dream: An Interpretation in the Light of Psychoanalysis of 'Gradiva', a Novel by Wilhelm Jensen* (New York: New Republic, 1927)

—— *The Interpretation of Dreams*, trans. by James Strachey, ed. by Angela Richards, The Penguin Freud Library 4 (Harmondsworth: Penguin, 1991)

—— 'Beyond the Pleasure Principle', from *On Metapsychology*, trans. by James Strachey, ed. by Angela Richards, in The Penguin Freud Library 11 (Harmondsworth: Penguin, 1991), 269-339

FÜLÖP, ERICA, 'Amélie's Horse: Writing as Jouissance in Nothomb', in *Cherchez la femme: Women and Values in the Francophone World*, ed. by Erika Fülöp and Adrienne Angelo (Newcastle upon Tyne: Cambridge Scholars Publishing, 2011), pp. 209–24

GARBER, MARJORIE, 'Compassion', in *Compassion: The Culture and Politics of An Emotion*, ed. by Lauren Berlant (New York & London: Routledge, 2004), pp. 15–27

GASPARINI, PHILIPPE, *Est-il je? Roman autobiographique et autofiction* (Paris: Du Seuil, 2004)

GAUTHIER, TIM, *9/11 Fiction, Empathy, and Otherness* (Lanham, MD: Lexington Books, 2015)

GAVIN, HELEN, and THERESA PORTER, 'Infanticide and Neonaticide: A Review of 40 Years of Research Literature on Incidence and Causes', *Trauma Violence Abuse*, 11.3 (July 2010), 99–112

GILMORE, LEIGH, *The Limits of Autobiography: Trauma and Testimony* (London: Cornell University Press, 2001)

GODARD, ANNE, *L'Inconsolable* (Paris: Minuit, 2006)

GOLDIE, PETER, *The Emotions: A Philosophical Exploration* (Oxford: Clarendon Press, 2000)

GRAY, BREDA, 'Empathy, Emotion and Feminist Solidarities', in *Sexed Sentiments: Interdisciplinary Perspectives on Gender and Emotion*, ed. by Willemijn Ruberg and Kristine Steenbergh (Amsterdam: Rodopi, 2011), pp. 207–32

GULL, WILLIAM WITHEY, 'Anorexia Nervosa (Apepsia Hysterica, Anorexia Hysterica)', *Transactions of the Clinical Society of the London*, 7 (1874), 22–28

GUNARATNAM, YASMIN, 'Interview with Clare Hemmings: Why Do Stories Matter?', podcast, <http://www.case-stories.org/clare-hemmingsnew-page/>

HAMMOND, MEGHAN MARIE, *Empathy and the Psychology of Literary Modernism* (Edinburgh: Edinburgh University Press, 2014)

HAMMOND, MEGHAN MARIE, and SUE J. KIM, eds, *Rethinking Empathy Through Literature* (New York & London: Routledge, 2014)

HANNE, ISABELLE, 'Dans l'abîme d'un "parcours meurtrier"', *Libération*, 7 December 2009, <http://www.liberation.fr/medias/2009/12/07/dans-l-abime-d-un-parcours-meurtrier_597795>

HANSEN, ELAINE TUTTLE, *Mother Without Child: Contemporary Fiction and the Crisis of Motherhood* (Berkeley: California University Press, 1997)

HAVERCROFT, BARBARA, 'Le Soi est une fiction', *Fictions de soi*, special issue of *Revue critique de fixxion française contemporaine*, 4 (2012), <http://www.revue-critique-de-fixxion-francaise-contemporaine.org/rcffc/article/view/fx04.12/671>

HEMMINGS, CLARE, 'Affective Solidarity Feminist Reflexivity and Political Transformation', *Feminist Theory*, 13.2 (2012), 147–61

—— *Why Stories Matter: The Political Grammar of Feminist Theory* (Durham, NC: Duke University Press, 2011)

HENKE, SUZETTE, *Shattered Subjects: Trauma and Testimony in Women's Life-writing* (London: Palgrave Macmillan, 2000)

HEPWORTH, JULIE, *The Social Construction of Anorexia Nervosa* (London: Sage, 1999)

HILL, LESLIE, *Marguerite Duras: Apocalyptic Desires* (London: Routledge, 1993)

HINDMARCH, CELIA, *On the Death of a Child*, 3rd edn (Boca Raton, FL: CRC Press, 2009)

HODAPP, CHRISTA, 'Giving an Account of Oneself by Judith Butler (Review)', *The Pluralist*, 8.1 (2013), 115–18

HOCHMANN, JACQUES, *Histoire de l'autisme* (Paris: Odile Jacob, 2009)

—— *Une histoire de l'empathie* (Paris: Odile Jacob, 2012)

HOLMES, DIANA, 'To Write is a Transitive Verb: Nancy Huston and the Ethics of the Novel', *Contemporary French and Francophone Studies*, 14.1 (2010), 85–92

HUGUENY-LÉGER, ELISE, 'Duras ou les contradictions d'une intellectuelle aux prises avec l'espace public', *French Cultural Studies*. 22.4 (2011), 321–31

—— 'Filatures de soi: Detectives, Deception and Deceit in the Crime-fictions of Calle, Laurens and Nothomb', in *Rewriting Wrongs: French Crime Fiction and the Palimpsest,* ed. by Angela Kimyongür and Amy Wigelsworth (Newcastle upon Tyne: Cambridge Scholars Publishing, 2014), pp. 145–61

HUSTON, NANCY, *Instruments des ténèbres* (Arles: Actes Sud, 1996)

—— 'Novels and Navels', *Critical Inquiry*, 21.4 (Summer 1995), 708–21

—— *Dolce agonia* (Arles: Actes Sud, 2002)

IBBETT, KATHERINE, 'Pity, Compassion, Commiseration: Theories of Theatrical Relatedness', *Seventeenth-century French Studies*, 30.2 (2008), 196–208

INCHLEY, MAGGIE, 'Hearing the Unhearable: The Representation of Women Who Kill Children', *Contemporary Theatre Review*, 23.2 (2013), 192–205

JAFFE, AUDREY, *Scenes of Sympathy: Identity and Representation in Victorian Fiction* (Ithaca, NY: Cornell University Press, 2000)

JENKINS, ANGELA, SIMON MILLAR, and JAMES ROBINS, 'Denial of Pregnancy — a Literature Review and Discussion of Ethical and Legal Issues', *Journal of the Royal Society of Medicine*, 104.7 (2011), 286–91

JENSEN, WILHELM, *Gradiva: A Pompeiian Fantasy*, trans. by Helen M. Downey, in Sigmund Freud, *Delusion and Dream: An Interpretation in the Light of Psychoanalysis of 'Gradiva', a Novel by Wilhelm Jensen* (New York: New Republic, 1927)

JORDAN, SHIRLEY, 'Autofiction in the Feminine', *French Studies*, 67.1 (2013), 76–84

—— 'Reconfiguring the Public and the Private: Intimacy, Exposure and Vulnerability in Christine Angot's *Rendez-vous*', *French Cultural Studies*, 18.2 (2007), 201–18

JOUBI, PASCALE, 'La Trace de Médée dans *Le Cimetière des poupées* de Mazarine Pingeot', in *MuseMedusa, 3: 'Medea nunc sum: refigurer le mythe de Médée'*, 2015, <>

KEEN, SUZANNE, 'A Theory of Narrative Empathy', *Narrative*, 14 (2006), 207–36

—— 'Narrative Empathy', in *The Living Handbook of Narratology* (Hamburg: Hamburg University, 2013), <http://www.lhn.uni-hamburg.de/article/narrative-empathy>

KIDD, DAVID COMER, and EMANUELE CASTANO, 'Reading Literary Fiction Improves Theory of Mind', *Science*, 342.6156 (18 October 2013), 377–80

KRISTEVA, JULIA, 'Reliance, or Maternal Eroticism', *Journal of the American Psychoanalytic Association*, 62 (2014), 69–85

LACAN, JACQUES, 'Tuché et Automaton', in *Le Séminaire, livre XI: Les Quatre Concepts fondamentaux de la psychoanalyse* (Paris: Du Seuil, 1973)

LaCAPRA, DOMINICK, *Writing History, Writing Trauma* (Baltimore, MD: Johns Hopkins University Press, 2000)

LAMBETERIE, OLIVIA, 'Le Crime de Mazarine Pingeot', interview with Mazarine Pingeot, *Elle*, 29 August 2007, <http://www.elle.fr/Societe/Interviews/Le-crime-de-Mazarine-Pingeot-147544>

LASÈGUE, ERNEST CHARLES, 'De l'anorexie hystérique', *Archives générales de médicine*, 21 (April 1873), 385–403

LAURENS, CAMILLE, *Cet absent-là* (Paris: Gallimard, 2004)

—— *Dans ces bras-là* (Paris: P.O.L, 2000)

—— *Encore et jamais* (Paris: Gallimard, 2013)

—— 'Marie Darrieussecq ou le syndrome du coucou', *La Revue Littéraire*, 32 (Autumn 2007), 1–14

—— *Philippe* (Paris: P.O.L, 1995)

—— *Romance nerveuse* (Paris: Gallimard, 2010)

LEJEUNE, PHILIPPE, *Le Pacte autobiographique* (Paris: Du Seuil, 1975)

LOBB, ANDREA, 'The Agony and the Empathy: The Ambivalence of Empathy in Feminist Psychology', *Feminism & Psychology*, 23.4 (2013), 426–41

McKEARNEY, MIRANDA, and SARAH MEARS, 'Lost for Words? How Reading Can Teach Children Empathy', *Guardian*, 13 May 2015

MAIRESSE, ANNE, 'Le Roman spectaculaire à l'épreuve du quotidien: l'œuvre de Véronique Olmi', *Contemporary French and Francophone Studies*, 10 (2006), 491–98

MARDER, ELISSA, 'The Sex of Death and the Maternal Crypt', *Parallax*, 15:1 (2009), 5–20

MARINOPOULOS, SOPHIE, *Infanticides et néonaticides* (Paris: Fabert, 2011)

—— *La Vie ordinaire d'une mère meurtrière* (Paris: Fayard, 2008)

MEURET, ISABELLE, *Writing Size Zero: Figuring Anorexia in Contemporary World Literatures* (Brussels: European Interuniversity Press, 2007)

—— 'Writing Size Zero: Figuring Anorexia in Contemporary World Literatures', in *Social*

Studies of Health, Illness and Disease: Perspectives from the Social Sciences and Humanities, ed. by Peter Twohig and Vera Kalitzkus (Amsterdam: Rodopi, 2008)

MILLER, CHRISTIAN, 'Defining Empathy: Thoughts on Coplan's Approach', *The Southern Journal of Philosophy*, 49 (2011), 66–72

MILLER, LAURA J., 'Denial of Pregnancy', in *Infanticide: Psychosocial and Legal Perspectives on Women who Kill*, ed. by Margaret G. Spinelli (Washington, DC: American Psychiatric Association, 2003), 81–104

MILLER, NANCY K., and JASON TOUGAW, 'Introduction: Extremities', in *Extremities: Trauma, Testimony, and Community*, ed. by Nancy K Miller and Jason Tougaw (Urbana: University of Illinois Press, 2002), pp. 1–24

MILLS, CATHERINE, 'Normative Violence, Vulnerability, and Responsibility', *differences*, 18.2 (2007), 133–56

MODLINGER, MARTIN, and PHILIPP SONNTAG, 'Introduction: Other People's Pain — Narratives of Trauma and the Question of Ethics', in *Other People's Pain: Narratives of Trauma and the Question of Ethics*, ed. by Martin Modlinger and Philipp Sonntag (Oxford: Peter Lang, 2011)

MONAGHAN, NICOLA, *Criminal Law Directions*, 4th edn (Oxford: Oxford University Press, 2016)

MONAQUE, MATHILDE, *Trouble-tête: journal intime d'une dépression* (Paris: Les Arènes, 2006)

MORELLO, NATHALIE, 'Anorexia, Anger, Agency: Investigating Quests for Self in Three Contemporary Narratives in French', in *Starvation, Food Obsession and Identity*, ed. by Petra M. Bagley, Francesca Calamita, and Kathryn Robson (Oxford: Peter Lang, 2017), pp. 121–41

——'Écrire le néonaticide maternel dans *Le Cimetière des poupées* de Mazarine Pingeot', *Modern and Contemporary France*, 19.1 (2011), 53–68

MOWITT, JOHN, 'Trauma Envy', *Trauma and its Cultural Aftereffects*, special issue of *Cultural Critique*, 46 (Autumn, 2000), 272–97

NOTHOMB, AMÉLIE, *Biographie de la faim* (Paris: Poche, 2006)

——*Robert des noms propres* (Paris: Albin Michel, 2002)

NUSSBAUM, MARTHA, *Upheavals of Thought: The Intelligence of Emotions* (Cambridge: Cambridge University Press, 2001)

OLINICK, STANLEY, 'A Critique of Empathy and Sympathy', in *Empathy*, ed. by Joseph Lichtenberg, Melvin Bornstein, and Donald Silver (Hilisdale, NJ: Erlbaum, 1984), pp. 137–66

OLMI, VÉRONIQUE, *Bord de mer* (Arles: Actes Sud, 2001)

——*Beside the Sea*, trans. by Adriana Hunter (London: Pereine Press, 2012)

ORBACH, SUSIE, 'Size Matters', *Guardian*, 27 September 2007

PARKER, KATE, 'How Reading Can Boost Empathy', *Times Educational Supplement*, 12 June 2018, <https://www.tes.com/news/how-reading-can-boost-empathy>

PEDWELL, CAROLYN, 'Affect at the Margins: Alternative Empathies in *A Small Place*', *Space and Society*, 8 (2013), 18–26

——*Affective Relations: The Transnational Politics of Empathy* (London: Palgrave Macmillan, 2014)

——'Economies of Empathy: Obama, Neoliberalism, and Social Justice', *Environment and Planning D: Society and Space*, 30.2 (2012), 280–97

PHELAN, PEGGY, 'Converging Glances: A Response to Cathy Caruth's "Parting Words"', *Cultural Values*, 5.1 (January 2001), 27–49

PINGEOT, MAZARINE, *Le Cimetière des poupées* (Paris: Julliard, 2007)

PINKER, STEVEN, *The Better Angels of Our Nature: Why Violence has Declined* (New York: Viking, 2011)

PLUTCHIK, ROBERT, 'Evolutionary Bases of Empathy', in *Empathy and its Development*, ed. by Nancy Eisenberg and Janet Strayer (Cambridge: Cambridge University Press, 1987)

RADSTONE, SUSANNAH, 'Trauma Studies: Contexts, Politics, Ethics', *Paragraph*, 30.1 (2007), 9–29

REVOL, ANNE-MARIE, *Nos étoiles ont filé* (Paris: Stock, 2010)

ROBERT-DIARD, PASCALE, 'Mazarine Pingeot, le roman et le congélateur', *Le Monde*, 25 July 2007, <http://www.lemonde.fr/societe/article/2007/07/25/mazarine-pingeot-le-roman-et-le-congelateur_938976_3224.html#RYtGFjZ1UTP1UWUI.99>

ROBSON, KATHRYN, 'Psychic Plagiarism: The Death of a Child in Marie Darrieussecq's *Tom est mort* and Camille Laurens's *Philippe*', *French Studies*, 69.1 (2015), 46–59

—— 'Reading the Anorexic Body: Eating Disorders in Contemporary French Women's Fiction', in *Starvation, Food Obsession and Identity: Eating Disorders in Contemporary Women's Writing*, ed. by Petra M. Bagley, Francesca Calamita, and Kathryn Robson (Oxford: Peter Lang, 2017), pp. 257–76

—— 'Voicing Abjection: Narratives of Anorexia in Contemporary French Women's (Life-) Writing', *L'Esprit créateur*, 56.2 (Summer 2016), 108–20

—— *Writing Wounds: The Inscription of Trauma in Post-1968 French Women's Life-writing* (Amsterdam: Rodopi, 2004)

ROSENBLATT, PAUL C., *Parent Grief: Narratives of Loss and Relationship* (Philadelphia, PA: Brunner/Mazel, 2000)

ROTHE, ANNE, *Popular Trauma Culture: Selling the Pain of Others in the Mass Media* (New Brunswick, NJ: Rutgers University Press, 2011)

RYE, GILL, 'Family Tragedies: Child Death in Recent French Literature', in *Affaires de famille: The Family in Contemporary French Culture and Theory*, ed. by Marie-Claire Barnet and Edward Welch (Amsterdam & New York: Rodopi, 2007), pp. 267–81

—— *Narratives of Mothering: Women's Writing in Contemporary France* (Newark: University of Delaware Press, 2009)

RYE, GILL, and AMALEENA DAMLÉ, 'Women's Writing in Twenty-first-century France: Introduction', in *Women's Writing in Twenty-first-century France: Life as Literature*, ed. by Amaleena Damlé and Gill Rye (Cardiff: University of Wales Press, 2013), pp. 3–16

RYE, GILL, and MICHAEL WORTON, 'Introduction', in *Women's Writing in Contemporary France: New Writers, New Literatures in the 1990s*, ed. by Gill Rye and Michael Worton (Manchester: Manchester University Press, 2003), pp. 1–26

SAPIRO, GISÈLE, 'The Legal Responsibility of the Writer Between Objectivity and Subjectivity: The French Case (Nineteenth to Twenty-first Century)', in *Literary Trials: Exceptio Artis and Theories of Literature in Court*, ed. by Ralf Grüttemeier (London: Bloomsbury Academic, 2016), pp. 21–47

SCHULMAN, ALINE, *Paloma* (Paris: Du Seuil, 2001)

SENNINGER, FRANK, *L'Anorexie: le miroir intérieur brisé* (Paris: Jouvence, 2004)

SILVERMAN, KAJA, *The Threshold of the Visible World* (London: Routledge, 1996)

SIMMONS, J. AARON, 'Giving an Account of Oneself', *Journal for Cultural and Religious Theory*, 7.2 (Spring 2006), 85–90

SINGER, TANIA, and OLGA M. KLIMECKI, 'Empathy and Compassion', *Current Biology*, 24.18 (22 September 2014), R875–78

SKLAR, HOWARD, *The Art of Sympathy in Fiction: Forms of Ethical and Emotional Persuasion* (Amsterdam: John Benjamins, 2013)

SLADE, ANDREW, 'Differend, Sexual Difference, and the Sublime: Lyotard, Irigaray, Duras', in *Gender After Lyotard*, ed. by Margret Grebowicz (New York: SUNY Press, 2007), 171–83

SLIMANI, LEÏLA, *Chanson douce* (Paris: Gallimard, 2016)

SMITH, JACLYN, 'Infanticide', in *Different Crimes, Different Criminals: Understanding, Treating and Preventing Criminal Behavior*, ed. by Doris Layton MacKenzie and others, 2nd edn (New York: Routledge, 2015), pp. 11–34

SOLLIEC, CORINNE, *Le Petit Corps* (Paris: Gallimard, 2006)

SPELMAN, ELIZABETH V., *Fruits of Sorrow: Framing our Attention to Suffering* (Boston: Beacon Press, 1998)

SPITZACK, CAROLE, 'THE SPECTACLE OF ANOREXIA NERVOSA', *Text and Performance Quarterly* 13.1 (1993), 1–20

STANGLE, HEATHER LEIGH, 'Murderous Madonna: Femininity, Violence, and the Myth of Postpartum Mental Disorder in Cases of Maternal Infanticide and Filicide', *William and Mary Law Review*, 50 (2008), 699–734

TARDIEU, LAURENCE, *Le Jugement de Léa* (Paris: Éditions Arléa, 2004)

—— *Puisque rien ne dure* (Paris: Stock, 2006)

TRIERWEILER, VALERIE, 'Amélie Nothomb: la stupéfiante', *Paris Match*, 12 August, 2012, <http://www.parismatch.com/Culture/Livres/Amelie-Nothomb-La-stupefiante-157133>

TROUT, COLETTE, *Marie Darrieussecq: ou voir le monde à neuf* (Leiden: Brill, 2016)

TURSZ, ANNE, and JON M. COOK, 'A Population-based Survey of Neonaticides Using Judicial Data', *Archives of Disease in Childhood — Fetal and Neonatal Edition*, 96.4 (July 2011), 259–63

VANDENESCH, FLORA, INTERVIEW WITH SOPHIE DAULL, 'Ce livre est un geste poétique, une posture par le haut', 20 August 2015, <https://toutelaculture.com/livres/interview-sophie-daull-ce-livre-est-un-geste-poetique-une-posture-par-le-haut/>

VIGAN, DELPHINE DE, *Jours sans faim* (Paris: J'ai Lu, 2009)

—— *D'après une histoire vraie* (Paris: Jean-Claude Lattès, 2011)

—— *Rien ne s'oppose à la nuit* (Paris: Jean-Claude Lattès, 2011)

—— *Nothing Holds Back the Night*, trans. by George Miller (London: Bloomsbury, 2013)

VIGNEMONT, FRÉDÉRIQUE DE, and TANIA SINGER, 'The Empathic Brain: How, When and Why?', *Trends in Cognitive Science*, 10.10 (2006), 435–41

VIGOUREUX, ELSA, 'Dominique Cottrez tue ses petits', *Le Nouvel Observateur*, 2 July 2015, <http://tempsreel.nouvelobs.com/justice/20150702.OBS1907/dominique-cottrez-tue-ses-petits-l-hiver-je-pensais-a-eux.html>

VILAIN, PHILIPPE, *L'Autofiction en théorie; suivi de deux entretiens avec Philippe Sollers et Philippe Lejeune* (Paris: Éditions de la Transparence, 2009)

VINCENT, CATHÉRINE, 'Sophie Marinopoulos: portrait psychique et romancé d'une mere infanticide', *Le Monde*, 20 March 2008, <https://www.lemonde.fr/livres/article/2008/03/20/sophie-marinopoulos-portrait-psychique-et-romance-d-une-mere-infanticide_1025298_3260.html>

WAAL, FRANS DE, *The Age of Empathy: Lessons for a Kinder Society* (New York: Crown Publishing Group, 2009)

WALLACE, ALISON, *Homicide: The Social Reality* (Sydney: New South Wales Bureau of Statistics and Research, 1986)

WARIN, MEGAN, *Abject Relations: Everyday Worlds of Anorexia*, Cambridge Studies in Medical Anthropology (New Brunswick, NJ: Rutgers University Press, 2010)

WEARE, SIOBHAN, 'Bad, Mad or Sad? Legal Language, Narratives, and Identity Constructions of Women Who Kill their Children in England and Wales', *International Journal for the Semiotics of Law — Revue internationale de sémiotique juridique* (2016), 1–22, <https://link.springer.com/article/10.1007/s11196-016-9480-y>

WHITEHEAD, ANNE, 'Writing with Care: Kazuo Ishiguro's *Never Let Me Go*', *Contemporary Literature*, 52.1 (Spring 2011), 54–83

——*Medicine and Empathy in Contemporary British Fiction: A Critical Intervention in Medical Humanities* (Edinburgh: Edinburgh University Press, 2017)

WILSON, EMMA, *Sexuality and the Reading Encounter: Identity and Desire in Proust, Duras, Tournier, and Cixous* (Oxford: Clarendon Press, 1996)

——*Cinema's Missing Children* (London & New York: Wallflower Press, 2002)

WISPÉ, LAUREN, 'The Distinction Between Sympathy and Empathy: To Call Forth a Concept, A Word Is Needed', *Journal of Personality and Social Psychology*, 50.2 (2008), 314–21

WOODWARD, KATHLEEN, 'Calculating Compassion', in *Compassion: The Culture and Politics of an Emotion*, ed. by Lauren Berlant (New York & London: Routledge, 2004), pp. 59–86

YOUNG-BRUEHL, ELISABETH, *Subject to Biography: Psychoanalysis, Feminism, and Writing Women's Lives* (Cambridge, MA: Harvard University Press, 1998)

INDEX

❖

www.ingramcontent.com/pod-product-compliance
Lightning Source LLC
LaVergne TN
LVHW061327060426
835511LV00012B/1900